Cyber Situational Awareness

T0134637

Advances in Information Security

Sushil Jajodia,
Consulting Editor
Center for Secure Information Systems
George Mason University
Fairfax, VA 22030-4444
email: jajodia@gmu.edu

The goals of the Springer International Series on ADVANCES IN INFORMATION SECU-RITY are, one, to establish the state of the art of, and set the course for future research in information security and, two, to serve as a central reference source for advanced and timely topics in information security research and development. The scope of this series includes all aspects of computer and network security and related areas such as fault tolerance and software assurance.

ADVANCES IN INFORMATION SECURITY aims to publish thorough and cohesive overviews of specific topics in information security, as well as works that are larger in scope or that contain more detailed background information than can be accommodated in shorter survey articles. The series also serves as a forum for topics that may not have reached a level of maturity to warrant a comprehensive textbook treatment.

Researchers, as well as developers, are encouraged to contact Professor Sushil Jajodia with ideas for books under this series.

Additional titles in the series:
SECURITY AND DEPENDABILITY FOR AMBIENT INTELLIGENCE edited by George Spanoudakis, Antonia Mana Gomez and Spyros Kokolakis; ISBN: 978-0-387-88774-6
IDENTIFYING MALICIOUS CODE THROUGH REVERSE ENGINEERING edited by Abhishek Singh; ISBN: 978-0-387-09824-1
SECURE MULTI-PARTY NON-REPUDIATION PROTOCOLS AND APPLICATIONS by José A. Onieva, Javier Lopez, Jianying Zhou; ISBN: 978-0-387-75629-5
GLOBAL INITIATIVES TO SECURE CYBERSPACE: An Emerging Langscape edited by Michael Portnoy and Seymour Goodman; ISBN: 978-0-387-09763-3
SECURE KEY ESTABLISHMENTS by Kim-Kwang Raymond Choo; ISBN: 978-0-387-87968-0
SECURITY FOR TELECOMMUNICATIONS NETWORKS by Patrick Traynor, Patrick McDaniel and Thomas La Porta; ISBN: 978-0-387-72441-6
INSIDER ATTACK AND CYBER SECURITY: Beyond the Hacker edited by Salvatore Stolfo, Steven M. Bellovin, Angelos D. Keromytis, Sara Sinclaire, Sean W. Smith; ISBN: 978-0-387-77321-6

For other titles published in this series, go to www.springer.com/series/5576

Sushil Jajodia · Peng Liu · Vipin Swarup ·
Cliff Wang
Editors

Cyber Situational Awareness

Issues and Research

 Springer

Editors

Sushil Jajodia
George Mason University
Ctr. Secure Information
Systems
Fairfax VA 22030-4444
USA
jajodia@gmu.edu

Peng Liu
Pennsylvania State University
College of Information
Science & Technology
University Park PA 16802-6823
USA
pliu@ist.psu.edu

Vipin Swarup
The MITRE Corporation
7515 Colshire Dr.
McLean VA 22102-7508
USA
swarup@mitre.org

Cliff Wang
US Army Research Office
Computing and Information
Science Div.
P.O.Box 12211
Research Triangle Park NC 27709-2211
USA
cliff.wang@us.army.mil

ISSN 1568-2633
ISBN 978-1-4614-2475-8   e-ISBN 978-1-4419-0140-8
DOI 10.1007/978-1-4419-0140-8
Springer New York Dordrecht Heidelberg London

Springer is part of Springer Science+Business Media (www.springer.com)

Preface

Motivation for the Book

This book seeks to establish the state of the art in the cyber situational awareness area and to set the course for future research. A multidisciplinary group of leading researchers from cyber security, cognitive science, and decision science areas elaborate on the fundamental challenges facing the research community and identify promising solution paths.

Today, when a security incident occurs, the top three questions security administrators would ask are in essence: What has happened? Why did it happen? What should I do? Answers to the first two questions form the core of Cyber Situational Awareness. Whether the last question can be satisfactorily answered is greatly dependent upon the cyber situational awareness capability of an enterprise.

A variety of computer and network security research topics (especially some systems security topics) belong to or touch the scope of Cyber Situational Awareness. However, the Cyber Situational Awareness capability of an enterprise is still very limited for several reasons:

- Inaccurate and incomplete vulnerability analysis, intrusion detection, and forensics.
- Lack of capability to monitor certain microscopic system/attack behavior.
- Limited capability to transform/fuse/distill information into cyber intelligence.
- Limited capability to handle uncertainty.
- Existing system designs are not very "friendly" to Cyber Situational Awareness.

The goal of this book is to explore ways to elevate the Cyber Situational Awareness capability of an enterprise to the next level by measures such as developing holistic Cyber Situational Awareness approaches and evolving existing system designs into new systems that can achieve self-awareness. One major output of this book is a set of scientific research objectives and challenges in the area of Cyber Situational Awareness.

About the Book

Chapters in this book can be roughly divided into the following six areas:
Overview

- Cyber SA: Situational Awareness for Cyber Defense
- Overview of Cyber Situation Awareness

The Reasoning and Decision Making Aspects

- RPD-based Hypothesis Reasoning for Cyber Situation Awareness
- Uncertainty and Risk Management in Cyber Situational Awareness

Macroscopic Cyber Situational Awareness

- Employing Honeynets For Network Situational Awareness
- Assessing Cybercrime Through the Eyes of the WOMBAT

Enterprise Cyber Situational Awareness

- Topological Vulnerability Analysis
- Cross-Layer Damage Assessment for Cyber Situational Awareness

Microscopic Cyber Situational Awareness

- A Declarative Framework for Intrusion Analysis
- Automated Software Vulnerability Analysis

The Machine Learning Aspect

- Machine Learning Methods for High Level Cyber Situation Awareness

Acknowledgements

We are extremely grateful to all those who contributed to this book. It is a pleasure to acknowledge the authors for their contributions. Special thanks go to Susan Lagerstrom-Fife, Senior Publishing Editor for Springer, and Sharon Palleschi, Editorial Assistant at Springer for their support of this project. Special thanks also go to Shengzhi Zhang at Penn State University, who helped transform several chapters from MS Word to LaTex.

Sushil Jajodia
Peng Liu
Vipin Swarup
Cliff Wang

Contents

Part II The Reasoning and Decision Making Aspects

Part III Macroscopic Cyber Situational Awareness

Part V   Microscopic Cyber Situational Awareness

9   A Declarative Framework for Intrusion Analysis 179
Matt Fredrikson, Mihai Christodorescu, Jonathon Giffin,
and Somesh Jha

10   Automated Software Vulnerability Analysis 201
Emre C. Sezer, Chongkyung Kil, and Peng Ning

Part VI The Machine Learning Aspect

Thomas G. Dietterich, Xinlong Bao, Victoria Keiser,
and Jianqiang Shen

Part I
Overview of Cyber Situational Awareness

Chapter 1
Cyber SA: Situational Awareness for Cyber Defense

P. Barford, M. Dacier, T. G. Dietterich, M. Fredrikson, J. Giffin, S. Jajodia, S. Jha,
J. Li, P. Liu, P. Ning, X. Ou, D. Song, L. Strater, V. Swarup, G. Tadda, C. Wang,
and J. Yen

1.1 Scope of the Cyber SA Problem

Situation Awareness (SA) for cyber defense consists of at least seven aspects:

1. Be aware of the current situation. This aspect can also be called *situation perception*. Situation perception includes both *situation recognition* and *identification*. Situation identification can include identifying the type of attack (recognition is only recognizing that an attack is occurring), the source (who, what) of an attack, the target of an attack, etc. Situation perception is beyond intrusion detection. Intrusion detection is a very primitive element of this aspect. An IDS (intrusion detection system) is usually only a sensor, it neither identifies nor recognizes an attack but simply identifies an event that may be part of an attack once that event adds to a recognition or identification activity.

2. Be aware of the impact of the attack. This aspect can also be called *impact assessment*. There are two parts to impact assessment: 1) assessment of current impact (damage assessment) and 2) assessment of future impact (if the attacker continues on this path or more general if the activity of interest continues - what is the impact?). Vulnerability analysis is also largely an aspect of impact assessment (provides knowledge of us and enables projection of future impact). Assessment of future impact also involves threat assessment.

Paul Barford, University of Wisconsin · Marc Dacier, Symantec · Thomas G. Dietterich, Oregon State University · Matt Fredrikson, University of Wisconsin · Jon Giffin, Georgia Institute of Technology · Sushil Jajodia, George Mason University · Somesh Jha, University of Wisconsin · Jason Li, IAI Inc. · Peng Liu, Pennsylvania State University · Peng Ning, North Carolina State University · Xinming Ou, Kansas State University · Dawn Song, University of California, Berkeley · Laura Strater, SA Technologies, Inc. · Vipin Swarup, MITRE · George Tadda, Air Force Research Laboratory Rome NY · Cliff Wang, Army Research Office · John Yen, Pennsylvania State University

S. Jajodia et al., (eds.), *Cyber Situational Awareness*,
Advances in Information Security 46, DOI 10.1007/978-1-4419-0140-8_1,
© Springer Science+Business Media, LLC 2010

3. Be aware of how situations evolve. Situation tracking is a major component of this aspect.

4. Be aware of actor (adversary) behavior. A major component of this aspect is attack trend and intent analysis, which are more oriented towards the behaviors of an adversary or actor(s) within a situation than with the situation itself.

5. Be aware of why and how the current situation is caused. This aspect includes causality analysis (via back-tracking) and forensics.

6. Be aware of the *quality* (and trustworthiness) of the collected situation awareness information items and the knowledge-intelligence-decisions derived from these information items. The quality metrics include *truthfulness* (or soundness), *completeness*, and *freshness*. This aspect can also be viewed as part of situation perception or more specifically recognition.

7. Assess plausible futures of the current situation. This involves a multitude of technologies for projecting future possible actions/activities of an adversary, paths the adversary might take, and then constraining the possible futures into those that are plausible. This constraining requires an understanding of adversary intent, opportunity, and capability (knowledge of them) as well as an understanding of blue vulnerabilities, etc. (knowledge of "us"). Plausible futures can also be a part of identifying threats and could be considered part of the threat assessment.

Without losing generality, cyber situation awareness can be viewed as a three-phase process [5]: situation recognition (including Aspects 1 and 6), situation comprehension (including Aspects 2, 4, and 5), and situation projection (including Aspects 3 and 7).

Situation awareness is gained by a system, which is usually the (cyber-physical) *system* being threatened by random or organized cyber attacks. Although the ultimate "dream" system is one that can gain self-awareness (and do self-protection) without involving any humans in the loop, this vision is still very distant from the current reality, and there still does not exist a tangible roadmap to achieve this vision (in a practical way). In this paper, we view *human decision makers* as an indispensible "component" of the system gaining situation awareness. Practical cyber SA systems include not only hardware sensors (e.g., a network interface card) and "smart" computer programs (e.g., programs that can learn attack signatures), but also mental processes of human beings making advanced decisions [1, 3].

Finally, cyber situation awareness can be gained at multiple *abstraction levels*: (raw) data are collected at the lower levels and at higher levels, as data is converted to more abstract information. Otherwise, data collected at the lowest levels can easily overwhelm the cognitive capacity of human decision makers. Situation awareness based solely on low level data is clearly insufficient.

The following aspects are typically not included in cyber SA, but they and the aforementioned cyber SA aspects complement each other in achieving the overall goal of cyber defense.

- Identification of better response plans and actions. This aspect could be called *planning*. This aspect stays in the boundary between situation awareness and situation response, during which the planned course of action will be taken. Planning often involves estimating the effects of a response plan before the planned actions are taken. Planning, responses, and actions are all command and control functions (decide and act) and are not typically included in SA. However, without SA one can't effectively do response plans and actions.
- Made decisions on the course of action to take. Situation Awareness enables a decision maker's awareness of a situation and their understanding of the situation up to the point the decision is made. Once a decision is reached, planning and execution (of the response actions) occur.

1.2 Background

Regarding the state of the art of cyber situation awareness, our main observations are as follows:

- Cyber SA systems and Physical SA systems have fundamental differences. For instance, Physical SA systems rely on specific hardware sensors and sensor signal processing techniques, but neither the physical sensors nor the specific signal processing techniques play an essential role in Cyber SA systems (although there is research that has looked at applying signal processing techniques to analyze network traffic and trends). (Cyber SA systems rely on cyber sensors such as IDS', log file sensors, anti-virus systems, malware detectors, and firewalls; they all produce events at a higher level of abstraction than raw network packets.) For another instance, the cyber situation evolving speed is usually orders of magnitude quicker than in physical situation evolution. Finally, cyber attacks/situations have unique semantics.

- Existing approaches to gain cyber situation-awareness consist of vulnerability analysis (using attack graphs), intrusion detection and alert correlation, attack trend analysis, causality analysis and forensics (e.g., backtracking intrusions), taint and information flow analysis, damage assessment (using dependency graphs), and intrusion response. These approaches however only work at the lower (abstraction) levels. Higher level situation-awareness analyses are still done *manually* by a human analyst, which makes it labor-intensive, time-consuming, and error-prone.

- Although researchers have recently started to address the cognitive needs of decision makers, there is still a big gap between human analysts' mental model and the capability of existing cyber situation-awareness tools.

- Existing approaches need to handle *uncertainty* better.

– Uncertainty in perceived data could lead to distorted situation awareness. For example, attack graph analysis toolkits are designed to do deterministic attack consequence estimation. In real time cyber situation-awareness, such consequence estimates could be very misleading due to various uncertainties. Alert correlation techniques cannot handle the inherent uncertainties associated with inaccurate interpretations of intrusion detection sensor reports (such inaccurate interpretations lead to false positives/negatives in determining whether an IDS alert corresponds to an attack).

– Lack of data or complete knowledge may raise additional uncertainty management issues. For example, lack of data leads to incomplete knowledge of "us". Such incompleteness may be caused by imperfect information about system configurations, incomplete sensor deployment, etc.

- Existing approaches lack the reasoning and learning capabilities required by gaining full situation-awareness for cyber defense.

- The seven aspects of cyber situation awareness (see Section 1.1) have been treated as separate problems, but full cyber situation awareness requires all these aspects to be integrated into one solution. Such a solution is in general still missing. Furthermore, looking beyond cyber SA and considering how cyber SA solutions complement the other cyber defense technologies, cyber SA activities need to be better integrated with effect achieving or environment influencing activities (e.g., intrusion response activities).

1.3 Research Goals

At a high level, the basic objectives of a comprehensive cyber SA research agenda may be the ones listed below.

- The objective is to develop new algorithms that will (a) greatly enhance machines' intelligence in gaining self-situation-awareness so that one day machines could protect themselves, and (b) automate human decision maker's cognitive situation-awareness processes.

- If successful, the systems being-protected will recognize and learn about evolving situations, generate and reason about situation response plans and actions, and automatically respond to intrusions.

1.4 Research Agenda

1.4.1 Principles and Rationales

The following principles and rationales can help us identify the important research concentration areas and issues.

Rationale 1: Before machines have sufficient artificial intelligence, information systems need to be protected by humans who are able to gain full situation awareness.

Rationale 2: Cyber situation-awareness has at least two purposes: (a) enhance machines' intelligence in gaining situation awareness so that one day machines can gain self-awareness and do self protection; (b) automate human decision maker's cognitive situation-awareness processes.

Principle 1: Full situation-awareness for cyber defense requires a holistic methodology to synthesize perception, understanding and projection.

Principle 2: Information systems with full situation-awareness must manage uncertainty (e.g., through hypotheses and reasoning).

Principle 3: Cyber situation awareness must be gained at multiple abstraction levels.

Principle 4: Cyber situation awareness has two largely orthogonal viewpoints: The *life-cycle view* contains the proper mechanisms for each phase of the cyber SA process, while the *human cognition view* contains the theories and techniques to integrate human analysts into the overall cyber SA framework (or solution). For automation to facilitate human situation awareness, the human has to model or identify activities of interest for which they wish to maintain awareness.

1.4.2 A Collection of Viewpoints on the Research Agenda

One of Cliff Wang's viewpoints on cyber SA is as follows.

> "Over the past two decades, we have witnessed exponential increase in computing power and explosive applications of computing devices. During the same time, information system exploitation and compromises have grown from a novice hobby to the choice of targets by organized crime group and nation/state sponsored adversaries. Unfortunately, our current cyber defense capability is still at an infancy state. Information security practiced daily is art rather than

science. It is quite common for an enterprise to rely its informa-
tion security on a few knowledgeable, but overwhelmed analysts and
a collection of tools that may provide some useful defense against
known or past attacks, but are ineffective against new exploits. It
is hoped that new investment in cyber situation awareness research
will substantially change this picture. New CSA technology will al-
low analysts to obtain a more complete comprehension of what is
going on now, to predicate what might happen next, and to plan and
respond to ongoing and new cyber attacks effectively. Unlike tradi-
tional machine learning applications which may only interact with
physical systems, new CSA technology must deal with sophisticated
adversaries with unpredictable behavior patterns. It is crucial that
CSA research will take a multi-disciplinary approach and incorpo-
rate new advances in areas such as adversarial reasoning, machine
learning, and uncertainty management to establish a new paradigm
in cyber defense."

One of Vipin Swarup's viewpoints on cyber SA is as follows.

"Advanced cyber threats have established a stealthy, persistent pres-
ence on many computer networks and they adapt to evade cyber de-
fenses. We now have ample evidence that despite significant strides
toward building secure, trustworthy systems, advanced cyber adver-
saries are successfully using other means of attack to compromise
our information systems and the missions that rely on those systems.
In this threat environment, cyber SA is a very challenging problem.

We need cyber SA techniques that make use of certain advantages
that cyber defenders have over cyber adversaries. For instance,
defenders have out-of-band intimate knowledge about authorized
users, their organizations and social networks, and the cyber tasks
that they are performing, whereas adversaries need to acquire this
knowledge with various risks. Cyber SA techniques should evolve to
leverage a broad range of such fine-grained contextual information.

Human decision makers (e.g., end-users, mission commanders,
etc.) are often interested primarily in the risks to task/mission suc-
cess that are posed by adverse cyber effects. Hence, we need cyber
SA techniques that can, in a rapidly changing environment, map cy-
ber attributes to their mission analogues, e.g., cyber effects to their
mission consequences, cyber risks to mission risks, etc. "

One of John Yen's viewpoints on cyber SA is as follows.

"The cyber situation awareness overlaps with the situation aware-
ness in the physical battle space. Threats and attacks in the cyber
space could affect missions in many different ways. Hence, it is im-
portant to integrate the cyber SA with the SA in the mission space.

Combining the awareness of the situations in these two spaces enable war fighters to better detect, predict, prevent, and respond to attacks in each space by synthesizing information from both spaces. Rapidly, the cyber space has emerged as the fifth dimension of the battle space, in addition to land, sea, air, and space. A key to integrate the cyberspace SA with the physical SA is to introduce suitable "context" that describes situations across multiple layers. It is also important to allow analyst to maintain situation understanding about the dynamic evolution of multiple situations, so that they can maintain a holistic view in a bigger context, can connect different situations when their relationship emerges, and can predict the evolution of situations, and choose decisions and actions based on their predictive and holistic understanding of both the situation in the cyber space and the mission in the physical space."

One of Peng Ning's viewpoints on cyber SA is as follows.

"Several decades of research on intrusion detection and prevention has demonstrated that dealing with intelligent attackers is by no means an easy task. One particular difficulty comes from the uncertainty of information gathered and used for cyber situational awareness. How to reduce such uncertainty is thus critical to the success of this line of research. A promising direction is to take advantage of the recent advances in trusted computing. For example, we may gain high confidence in the trustworthiness of data gathered for cyber situational awareness by protecting them using a Trusted Platform Module (TPM). Nevertheless, substantial research is necessary to guarantee the successful use of trusted computing technologies to support cyber situational awareness."

One of Jason Li's viewpoints on cyber SA is as follows.

"At current stage cyber SA can be extremely overwhelming for human analysts due to the inherent complexity, scalability, and uncertainty issues. To help ease this difficulty, extensive efforts are needed on transformation: from low-level data to meaningful information, from information to actionable knowledge, and from knowledge to trustworthy intelligence. Such bottom-up transformations can be achieved via enhancing the state-of-the-art alert correlation, vulnerability analysis, damage assessment, and machine learning techniques. These efforts can be very useful to help human analysts understand the current situation and project future situations.

On the other hand, human experts may exhibit unique analysis capabilities that surpass the most advanced security analysis software tools, especially with respect to insights and intuitions. While the knowledge possessed by human experts may vary or even conflict

*with each other, such expertise is extremely valuable and it is neces-
sary to obtain and transfer such expertise into automated cyber SA
software tools. This top-down transformation can be achieved via
knowledge engineering techniques. Therefore, human-in-the-loop
cyber SA means both helping human analysts to better understand
as well as using human experts as the design and analysis guide.
This will entail the design of some kind of novel human-machine interaction framework.*

*Lots of challenging problems need to be solved to meet the goal of
true human-in-the-loop cyber SA. For example, how to connect the
knowledge obtained via the top-down approach (from human) with
that obtained via the bottom-up approach (from raw data and information) is an open problem, although the same term "knowledge"
is used in both approaches. Without such a connection, it is not possible to realize a holistic (or even consistent) cyber SA solution. To
solve this problem, systematic methodologies are needed.*

*One potential methodology is to treat the cyber enterprise as
an organism and design decentralized solutions to handle the challenges related to complexity, scalability, and uncertainty. Essentially,
local software agents can be designed to carry out low-level tasks
such as monitoring, pattern recognition, reporting, and local reaction. Regional managers (another kind of software agents) can work
on a higher-level to coordinate local agents as well as providing a
broader view. Finally, some top-level control center can obtain the
global picture and coordinate overall action planning and responses.
On a nutshell, the overall cyber SA solution using this methodology
can be scalable (local events will be handled locally), effective (views
are broadened as needed), and amenable to implementation (using
distributed computing paradigm which is the nature of cyber enterprise). Uncertainty management can also be naturally incorporated
in this distributed framework using mainstream approaches such as
Bayesian networks. Finally, such a framework can also leverage the
Trusted Computing approach for uncertainty management."*

One of Xinming Ou's viewpoints on cyber SA is as follows.

*"One thing the technical community can benefit from is talking to
security practitioners who have to handle cyber situation awareness
manually due to the lack of automated tools. Even though human
reasoning is not always accurate or effective, human brains work in
a much more flexible manner than what machines can do now and
studying how humans react to uncertain and vague information in
making quick decisions will be an important first step to automate
the process. This can foster a bottom-up theory development process,
where we first simulate what a human does in algorithmic ways, then
extract from the process the mathematical foundation behind them,*

and eventually lead to even more accurate and effective automatic situation awareness technologies.

Another closely related question is quantitative analysis. Can we give a metric on the confidence of assertions coming from an SA system? Can we say that with 80% confidence this machine is compromised? Such quantitative metric is not only useful in deciding upon the optimal countermeasure, but also crucial in risk mitigation before an incident happens. According to an article published by IEEE Security & Privacy, 2003, "most organizations call security a top management priority, and chief executive officers rank security as 7.5 out of 10 in importance, but funding levels don't match the rhetoric. On average, companies spend only 0.047 percent of their revenue on security. Why the disconnect? Simple questions, readily answered in any other business context, are met by information security experts with embarrassed silence. These questions include: Is my security better this year? What am I getting for my security dollars? How do I compare with my peers? Answering such questions requires rigorous security metrics and a risk-management framework in which to compare them." [2]

One of George Tadda's viewpoints on cyber SA is as follows.

"In order for a human to trust automated decision making, the decision process has to be deterministic. Right now, most human decision makers don't trust a machine to decide if they don't know how the decision was reached or if they wouldn't reach the same decision."

One of Somesh Jha and Matt Fredrikson's viewpoints on cyber SA is as follows.

"Previous work in the area of formal methods and automated reasoning can be brought to bear in simplifying and enhancing many tasks in cyber-SA. For instance, we have previously studied the effectiveness of applying data-driven logic programming to the problem of system and network-level intrusion awareness, and found that most of the work involved in producing representative yet manageable views of intrusion scenarios can be automated. However, applying this technique to yield useful results required substantial research effort; it is clear that before further progress towards a more sophisticated reasoning engine can be made, a groundwork must be laid. The entities and principles essential to tasks in cyber-SA need to be established and formalized, and the reasoning techniques themselves must be modified to suit the particular needs of cyber-SA consumers. For example, provenance is of special concern in cyber-SA, as users may need to "dig deeper" past the results of a reasoning engine to learn more or verify conclusions, but this issue has received little attention in the formal methods literature. Once these issues have been

sorted out more, we may benefit from general-purpose reasoning and decision engines for cyber-SA."

One of Sushil Jajodia's viewpoints on cyber SA, especially on the need for vulnerability context in network defense, is as follows.

"Network defense is inherently difficult. Many internet protocols are insecure, software applications are often buggy, and security measures such as firewalls and intrusion detection systems are complex and error prone. There are large volumes of relevant data, such as detected software vulnerabilities, firewall rules, and intrusion alarms. These data are interrelated, but security tools generally lack the ability to provide the context necessary for effective network defense. What is needed is a capability for "connecting the dots" that shows patterns of attack and corresponding paths of network vulnerability. Such a capability would provide a powerful framework for situational awareness in network defense.

Network defense is labor-intensive, requires specialized knowledge, and is error prone because of the complexity and frequent changes in network configurations and threat behaviors. Furthermore, the correct priorities need to be set for concentrating efforts to secure a network. Security concerns in a network are highly interdependent, so that susceptibility to an attack often depends on multiple vulnerabilities across the network. Attackers can combine such vulnerabilities to incrementally penetrate a network and compromise critical systems.

However, traditional security tools are generally only point solutions that provide only a small part of the picture. They give few clues about how attackers might exploit combinations of vulnerabilities to advance a network attack. Even for experienced analysts, it can be difficult to combine results from multiple sources to understand vulnerability against sophisticated multistep attacks. In other words, what is lacking is an understanding of the roles of vulnerabilities within the context of overall network defense."

One of Thomas G. Dietterich's viewpoints on cyber SA is as follows.

"Existing machine learning approaches to intrusion detection and anomaly detection tend to produce many false alarms. The fundamental reason is that the learning systems have a very narrow view (e.g., sequence of system calls; sequence of packets) that is missing key information (e.g., which vulnerabilities have been patched, changes in local network configuration). An important challenge is to develop learning methods that can integrate and fuse a much broader array of contextual information. Traditional statistical methods break down, because the broader the array of information, the

more training examples are required to achieve good performance. We need to develop methods for breaking the learning problem up into modules that can be learned separately and then combined (e.g., [4]).

A second challenge for machine learning in cyber situation awareness is that over time, the relevant features and relationships change as the threats change. Currently, this requires re-engineering the learning system which is costly and requires machine learning expertise. We need machine learning algorithms and user environments that support end users (i.e., system administrators) so that they can diagnose and repair machine learning systems in the field.

A third challenge is to learn from adversarial noise. Machine learning systems typically assume that the input data has random, non-adversarial, measurement noise. An important challenge is to consider cases where malware has the partial ability to delete or modify a subset of the log entries. Can we develop learning methods for learning from adversarial data? One possibility is to first have an abductive "data interpretation" level that maps from the raw logs to the most likely low-level interpretation of events. These, more reliable interpretations then provide a basis for learning."

One of Peng Liu's viewpoints on cyber SA is as follows.

"Some of the main research issues in the area of cyber SA are as follows. (a) Uncertainty and risk mitigation in cyber situation awareness via such techniques as hypothesis-based (probabilistic) reasoning. (b) Situation (knowledge and semantics) representation and modeling: transforming plain (situation-describing) English to machine-readable models; digitizing human (situation-awareness) intelligence. (c) Automating human analysts' cognitive situation-awareness processes. (d) Situation awareness across multiple abstraction levels. (e) Hypotheses and reasoning against incomplete and imperfect situation information. (f) Gaining better cyber situation awareness through machine learning. (g) Integration of situation perception, comprehension, and projection. (h) Identifying cyber SA measures of performance and effectiveness. (i) Information fusion for cyber situation-awareness. (j) Achieving machine self-awareness (k) Attacker behavior and intent analysis."

1.5 Conclusion

The goal of this article is to clarify the cyber situational awareness problem and to propose a tentative research agenda for solving the cyber SA problem. A set of research issues viewed as important by the authors are also briefly discussed.

Acknowledgements

We would like to thank the Army Research Office for sponsoring the workshop on Cyber Situation Awareness held at George Mason University in March 3-4, 2009.

References

[1] H. Gardner, *The Mind's New Science: A History of the Cognitive Revolution*, Basic Books, 1987.

[2] D. Geer Jr., K. S. Hoo, A. Jaquith, "Information security: Why the future belongs to the quants," *IEEE Security & Privacy*, 2003.

[3] P. Johnson-Laird, *How We Reason*, Oxford University Press, 2006.

[4] C. Sutton, A. McCallum, "Piecewise Training for Structured Prediction," *Machine Learning*, To appear.

[5] G. Tadda and et al., "Realizing situation awareness within a cyber environment," In *Multisensor, Multisource Information Fusion: Architectures, Algorithms, and Applications*, B. V. Dasarathy, eds., *Proceedings of SPIE Vol. 624* (SPIE, Bellingham, WA, 2006) 624204, Kissimmee FL, April 2006.

Chapter 2
Overview of Cyber Situation Awareness

George P. Tadda and John S. Salerno

Abstract Improving a decision maker's[1] situational awareness of the cyber domain isn't greatly different than enabling situation awareness in more traditional domains[2]. Situation awareness necessitates working with processes capable of identifying domain specific activities as well as processes capable of identifying activities
that cross domains. These processes depend on the context of the environment, the
domains, and the goals and interests of the decision maker but they can be defined
to support any domain. This chapter will define situation awareness in its broad-
est sense, describe our situation awareness reference and process models, describe
some of the applicable processes, and identify a set of metrics usable for measuring
the performance of a capability supporting situation awareness. These techniques
are independent of domain but this chapter will also describe how they apply to the
cyber domain.

2.1 What is Situation Awareness (SA)?

One of the challenges in working in this area is that there are a multitude of definitions and interpretations concerning the answer to this simple question. A keyword
search (executed on 8 April 2009) of 'situation awareness' on Google yields over
18,000,000 links the first page of which ranged from a Wikipedia page through
the importance of "SA while driving" and ends with a link to a free internet radio
show. Also on this first search page are several links to publications by Dr. Mica
Endsley whose work in SA is arguably providing a standard for SA definitions and

---

George P. Tadda and John S. Salerno, Air Force Research Laboratory Rome NY

[1] Decision maker is used very loosely to describe anyone who uses information to make decisions
within a complex dynamic environment. This is necessary because, as will be discussed, situation awareness is unique and dependant on the environment being considered, the context of the
decision to be made, and the user of the information.

[2] Traditional domains could include land, air, or sea.

S. Jajodia et al., (eds.), *Cyber Situational Awareness*,
Advances in Information Security 46, DOI 10.1007/978-1-4419-0140-8_2,
© Springer Science+Business Media, LLC 2010

techniques particularly for dynamic environments. In [5], Dr. Endsley provides a general definition of SA in dynamic environments:

> *"Situation awareness is the perception of the elements of the environment within a volume of time and space, the comprehension of their meaning, and the projection of their status in the near future."*

Also in [5], Endsley differentiates between situation awareness, *"a state of knowledge"*, and situation assessment, *"process of achieving, acquiring, or maintaining SA."* This distinction becomes exceedingly important when trying to apply computer automation to SA. Since situation awareness is "a state of knowledge", it resides primarily in the minds of humans (cognitive), while situation assessment as a process or set of processes lends itself to automated techniques. Endsley goes on to note that:

> *"SA, decision making, and performance are different stages with different factors influencing them and with wholly different approaches for dealing with each of them; thus it is important to treat these constructs separately."*

The "stages" that Endsley defines have a direct correlation with Boyd's ubiquitous OODA loop with SA relating to Observe and Orient, decision making to Decide, and performance to Act. We'll see these stages as well as Endsley's three "levels" of SA (perception, comprehension, and projection) manifest themselves again throughout this discussion.

As first mentioned, there are several definitions for SA, from the Army Field Manual 1-02 (September 2004), Situational Awareness is:

> *"Knowledge and understanding of the current situation which promotes timely, relevant and accurate assessment of friendly, competitive and other operations within the battlespace in order to facilitate decision making. An informational perspective and skill that fosters an ability to determine quickly the context and relevance of events that are unfolding."*

From [2](pg120):

> *"When the term **situational awareness** is used, it describes the awareness of a situation that exists in part or all of the battlespace at a particular point in time. In some instances, information on the trajectory of events that preceded the current situation may be of interest, as well as insight into how the situation is likely to unfold. The components of a situation include missions and constraints on missions (e.g., ROE), capabilities and intentions of relevant forces, and key attributes of the environment."*

The components of a situation that Alberts identifies are key points of analysis that can be performed as a situation is being recognized or identified. Of particular interest are an analysis of capability, opportunity, and intent when considering friendly or competitive players. [2](pgs 18-19) also provides a definition for awareness as:

> *"Awareness exists in the cognitive domain. Awareness relates to a situation and, as such, is the result of a complex interaction between prior knowledge (and beliefs) and current perceptions of reality. Each individual has a unique awareness of any given military situation."*

And a separate definition for understanding:

> *"Understanding involves having a sufficient level of knowledge to be able to draw inferences about the possible consequences of the situation, as well as sufficient awareness of the situation to predict future patterns."*

Alberts clarifies these three definitions with (note the parallel with Endsley's concepts of perception and projection):

> *"Hence, situation awareness focuses on what is known about past and present situations, while understanding of a military situation focuses on what the situation is becoming (or can become) and how different actions will impact the emerging situation."*

The distinction between Alberts and Endsley is that Alberts separates awareness and understanding while Endsley includes understanding (projection) as a part of awareness. Alberts also seems to imply that analysis of the situation can only be performed as cognitive processes. Finally in [13], the authors don't specifically address SA but they do define situation and impact assessment (recall that Endsley drew a distinction between situation awareness and situation assessment but concluded that situation assessment enables situation awareness):

> *"<u>Level 2 - Situation Assessment</u>: estimation and prediction of relations among entities, to include force structure and cross force relations, communications and perceptual influences, physical context, etc."*

> *"<u>Level 3 - Impact Assessment</u>: estimation and prediction of effects on situations of planned or estimated/predicted actions by participants; to include interactions between action plans of multiple players (e.g. assessing susceptibilities and vulnerabilities to estimated/predicted threat actions given one's own planned actions)"*

There are many other definitions available for situation awareness but the ones described above seem to be or are becoming widely accepted. The JDL Data Fusion Model has been used since the 1990's to describe ideas for sensor fusion and multi-sensor fusion, Dr. Endsley's work over the past 21 years has been used to define several SA supporting applications, and Alberts' work has become the defining work for Network-Centric Operations and Warfare.

Then, What is Situation Awareness? Let's use Endsley's definition with a slight modification as first published in [10]:

> "Situation awareness is the perception of the elements of the environment within a volume of time and space, the comprehension of their meaning, and the projection of their status in the near future to **enable decision superiority**."

This ties together the definitions given above if we allow Alberts'definition to apply to computer automation and to provide additional analysis of the perceived reality. We also need to equate his definition of understanding with Endsley's definition of projection which is a natural association given how they both consider anticipating the future given the current situation. Note that all these definitions include the element of time. Time involves the use of past experience and knowledge to identify, analyze, and understand the current situation and the projection of possible futures. These enable a decision maker to maintain awareness, make decisions, and take action to influence the environment which then requires an update to the situation, causes more decision and actions, and results in a continuous cycle. Reference [3] describes this decision cycle but additional detail is outside the scope of this chapter. The time dimension and continuous nature are also what cause the environment to be dynamic since the situation and elements within the situation will change as time progresses.

The remainder of this chapter will present a model that provides a reference for the above definition of SA, a supporting process model, a breakdown of some of the components and concepts captured by the models, and finally some measures of performance and effectiveness. Most of the ideas described can be applied to any domain and can be considered domain agnostic. Section 4 contains an example for how the domain independent ideas can be specifically applied to the cyber domain.

2.2 Situation Awareness Reference and Process Models

This section extracts from [8], [9], [11], [14] and [15] specific details about the reference model and definitions used for the reference model. The section concludes with a development of a generic process model.

2.2.1 Situation Awareness Reference Model

According to Endsley, SA begins with perception. **Perception** provides information about the status, attributes, and dynamics of relevant elements within the environment. It also includes classifying information into understood representations and provides the basic building blocks for comprehension and projection. Without a basic perception of important environmental elements, the odds of forming an incorrect picture of the situation increase dramatically. **Comprehension** of the situation encompasses how people combine, interpret, store, and retain information. Thus, comprehension includes more than perceiving or attending to information; it includes the integration of multiple pieces of information and a determination of their relevance to an individual's underlying goals and can infer or derive conclusions about the goals. Comprehension yields an organized picture of the current situation by determining the significance of objects and events. Furthermore, as a dynamic process, comprehension must combine new information with already existing knowledge to produce a composite picture of the situation as it evolves. Situation Awareness refers to the knowledge of the status and dynamics of the situational elements and the ability to make predictions based on that knowledge. These predictions represent a *Projection* of the elements of the environment (situation) into the near future.

McGuinness and Foy [6] extended Endsley's Model by adding a fourth level, which they called *Resolution*. This level tries to identify the best path to follow to achieve the desired state change to the current situation. Resolution results from drawing a single course of action from a subset of available actions. McGuinness and Foy believe that for any fusion system to be successful, it must be resilient and dynamic. It must also address the entire process from data acquisition to awareness, prediction and the ability to request elaboration (drill-down) for additional data and finishing with an appropriate action. McGuiness and Foy put Endsley's model and their model into perspective with an excellent analogy. They state that Perception is the attempt to answer the question "What are the current facts?" Comprehension asks, "What is actually going on?" Projection asks, "What is most likely to happen if...?" And Resolution asks, "What exactly shall I do?" The answer to the resolution question isn't to tell a decision maker what specific action to perform or what specific decision to make but instead provides options of end actions and how they affect the environment. Specifics about the actual decision or course-of-action to execute to achieve a chosen effect are carried out by command and control functions.

Another point to be made is that any proposed model should not promote a serial process, but rather a parallel one. Each function (for example in Endsley's model: Perception, Comprehension, Projection with the added Resolution) happens in parallel with continuous updates provided to and from each other. It should also be emphasized that each sub-component (in both models) also continuously interacts with each other and embarks its data/knowledge to the others. Another important note is that throughout any analysis each step should provide a high level of visibility or transparency to the decision maker.

Our SA Reference Model, shown in 2.1, is built by combining the JDL Data Fusion model and Endley's SA Model. In addition to presenting the model, definitions of the various components of the model are provided. In particular, we've refined how one can think of JDL Levels 1 and 2 as well as describe differences between JDL Levels 2/3 and Endsley's idea of projection.

There continues to be a debate as to what JDL Levels 1 and 2 represent. One belief is that JDL Level 1 deals only with the tracking and identification of individual objects while JDL Level 2 is the aggregation of the objects into groups or units through the identification of relationships between the objects. For example, JDL Level 1 objects could be various equipments (tanks, APCs, missiles, etc). At JDL Level 2, equipment along with personnel can be aggregated into a unit or division based on time and space. JDL Level 1 attempts to answer such questions as Existence and Size Analysis (How many?), Identity Analysis (What/Who?), Kinematics Analysis (Where?), and includes a time element (When?). But if we consider this separation between JDL Levels 1 and 2 then several questions arise; how do we

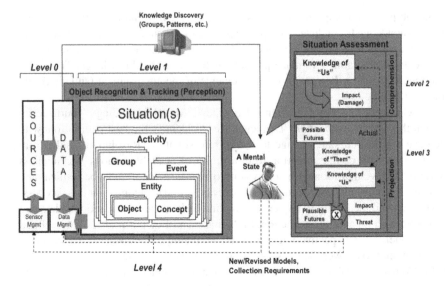

Fig. 2.1 Situation Awareness Reference Model

account for concepts or non-physical objects and can't we track a group or activity like an object? What is a situation? How does the system acquire the necessary a priori knowledge (or relationships) to perform aggregation? What is the difference between models for identifying an object, a group, or an activity?

To begin to answer these questions we first present a number of basic definitions and then use them to refine what we mean by JDL Level 1 and 2. We then will explore the difference between JDL Levels 2 and 3 and what Endsley refers to as Projection.

In [1][3], an **entity** is defined as "something that has a distinct, separate existence, though it need not be a material existence. In particular, abstractions and legal fictions are usually regarded as entities. In general, there is also no presumption that an entity is animate. The word entity is often useful when referring to something that could be a human being, a non-human animal, a non-thinking life-form such as a plant or fungus, a lifeless object, or even a belief." An **object** is "a physical entity; something that is within the grasp of the senses" [1]; "something perceptible by one or more of the senses, especially by vision or touch" (The Free Dictionary). What if the entity is not a physical object? How can we describe it? Generally speaking, an abstract entity still can be associated with a time or existence and an abstract concept (e.g., a phone call, financial transaction, etc.)

A **group** is "a number of things being in some relation to each other". A group can be an interest group (terrorist cell, religious order) or an organizational

---

[3] Clearly we don't want to use Wikipedia® as a definitive reference. However, references to it in this chapter are simply for definitions, e.g., as a dictionary.

group (police, government, Non-Governmental Organization (NGO) or military). An **event** is "something that takes place; an occurrence at an arbitrary point in time; something that happens at a given place and time" [1]. Both entities and groups can be associated with a specific event or events. Snidaro, Belluz and Foresti [12], further decompose an event into 3 classes: Simple, Spatial, and Transitive. They define a Simple event as one which involves only a single entity and with no interaction with other entities; a Spatial event describes events that occur in space and include a location. The third event, Transitive, involves two entities that are connected by some interaction. Spatial events can be a tank (entity) or unit (group) being at a given location at a specified time. If the tank or unit then interacts with another tank or unit then we say we have a Transitive event.

An **activity** is "something done as an action or a movement" [1]. Activities are composed of entities/groups related by one or more events over time and/or space. Thus, by definition an event, group or activity can be considered a complex entity (or in terms of the JDL, an object) and can be tracked and identified similarly to a simple entity. As a side note, the JDL Lexicon, [7], defines an entity as "Any object or object set (or event or event set) which forms the basis of a hypothesis used in data fusion processes" but does not provide a definition for an object or event.

By using the definitions presented above, we argue that activities and the set of these activities at a point in time (which we refer to as the situation) is both a part and a result of JDL Level 1. Models or a priori knowledge is necessary for JDL Level 1 to be capable of identifying the object, group or activity. This a priori knowledge (i.e., the relationships or associations) can be learned through Knowledge Discovery and validated by an operator or provided directly. Here we note that Knowledge Discovery techniques only learn statistically relevant occurrences. As such, new or novel ideas cannot be learned and require knowledge elicitation or conjecture of possible existence by a human. Actually, the conjecture of an activity by an experienced decision maker is a key activity or set of activities of interest that must be considered when providing capabilities for SA. So what are examples of activities? Classical activities can range from force-on-force actions of a conventional war, potential multi-stage or coordinated cyber attacks, potential terrorist attacks (asymmetric) to operations other than war. These activities are composed of a number of interconnected and inter-related events and processes.

We define a **situation** as a *person's world view of a collection of activities that one is aware of at an instance in time.* We also argue that a computer system can identify an activity is occurring based on some a priori knowledge and interconnect a number of objects/events but cannot itself develop or provide Situation Awareness; only a person (the decision maker) can be aware. A computer is a tool that can assist/support a person in developing and maintaining awareness. Thus we argue that there is one situation or world view per person based on their context. **Shared Situation Awareness** is then a consensus view of a number of individual views about a specific activity or set of activities. Likewise, there is a growing community supporting "Shared action plans" to represent group decision making over jointly observed information or data reduction.

The JDL Level 2 definition (given in the first section of this chapter) does not distinguish between time, current or future, while JDL Level 3, Impact/Threat Assessment is specifically associated with the future (estimate of 'predicted' actions). Why can't we have a current threat or impact? How is the current situation different from the projected or forecasted one? Can we have different impacts/threats depending on the timeframe that we are projecting? Our research is leading us to look at JDL Level 2 or Endsley's comprehension level as addressing the current situation (assessment of the current situation tends to be *damage assessment* since the impacts or effects have already occurred) and looking at JDL Level 3 and Endsley's projection level as the projection of the current situation and its analysis (i.e., future impacts and threats). Thus, we split the assessments represented by JDL Levels 2 and 3 based on time rather than functionality.

Additionally, Bosse, Roy and Wark [4] define **Situation Assessment** as, "**a quantitative evaluation of the situation that has to do with the notions of judgment, appraisal, and relevance.**" Two products or components of situation assessment are: Impact and Threat Assessment. Impact assessment is defined as:

> "...*the force of impression of one thing on another; an impelling or compelling effect. There is the notion of influence: one thing influencing another. In that sense, impact assessment estimates the effects on situations of planned or estimated/predicted actions by the participants, including interactions between action plans of multiple players.*"

In [4], they also define threat assessment as "*an expression of intention to inflict evil, injury, or damage. The focus of threat analysis is to assess the likelihood of truly hostile actions and, if they were to occur, projected possible outcomes...*" The only difference we note in their definition of impact/threat assessment is that, like the JDL definition, they are only concerned with the future.

Based on the definitions in [4] we can further define situation assessment as the understanding of the current situation and what it means to 'me' (its damage), the projection of the current situation into the future (which we refer to as the set of plausible futures) and the potential impacts/threats of those plausible futures. In Endsley's Level 2, or comprehension, we need to have an understanding of "us" and what is important to "us" (commonly referred to in the literature as "Blue" but can also include "Grey"). In order to accomplish this we need to know such information as to our resources (capacity and capabilities), what is important to us (salience) and what our vulnerabilities are. Based on this information the identified activities within the current situation can be ranked based on their impact (associated damage) and threat (increased/decreased). Or, the activities could be ranked based on most likely (the greatest impact) and most dangerous (the greatest threat).

Feedback in any control system is very important, especially in an ever changing and dynamic environment. Here we discuss what type of feedback or what JDL calls Process Refinement (Level 4) means for JDL Levels 2/3 and conceptually how it can be implemented. We also present how it is affected by Projection. The basic definition of **Process Refinement** covers two separate but integrated capabilities. For the purpose of our discussion we will divide them into external and internal process.

Externally, we are concerned with providing sensors or collections with positioning information based on forecasted or anticipated movement of objects/entities or groups. The classical example here is the tracking of an object. A common tracking algorithm used in today's system is a Kalman Filter. Kalman Filters provide the ability to forecast where the object could be in one time increment in the future. This position information can then be provided to "better" position the sensor. Theoretically, a similar approach can be done with concepts and groups to include non-physical entities.

Recall that our revised definition of Level 2 is concerned with assessment of the current situation. As one develops their understanding of the current situation, questions may arise and more data could be required to either fill in holes or reduce the uncertainty of given data. These requirements can be considered as additional or revised *collection requirements* and be provided as feedback to the collection requirements process. Level 3 can provide similar data to the collection process, except from a somewhat different perspective. Projected activity or activities are just that and from a single current situation multiple futures can be developed. From each of these futures, the analyst can determine key events that could assist them in determining which one is unfolding. These key events can be used to drive the collection requirements process.

Internal processes also need to be monitored to ensure that the information processing system is performing as designed. At the object level one can suggest, possibly based on environmental inputs, which source is "better" at that time for tracking or identifying the object or sending the same sensor data to multiple algorithms (running in parallel), coming up with possibly different answers and combining the results in some manner. Similar concepts can be used at the activity level. Additionally, a priori knowledge or models could be updated as a part of an internal process refinement function. As new information comes in and new knowledge is developed through the analysis and projection processes, a decision maker (or analyst) may update existing models or add/create new models. It is important to understand that tools can be provided (e.g., data mining, knowledge discovery, etc.) that can assist the user in finding new relationships or patterns but in many cases they also produce meaningless patterns or noise. These tools tend to also be based on past behaviors and activities and may not produce meaningful models to identify new behaviors or activities. In such a case it is important that the human use these tools as input and verify/validate the results. Such tools typically cannot come up with "novel" or never before seen patterns or relationships for which there is little or no data (or in most cases not statistically relevant) to support it. The human is still by far the most capable to develop such models and any technique/interface must take this into account. Figure 2.1 provided a graphical conception of how each of the components defined in this section fit together.

From Observables to Threats (At Time, t)

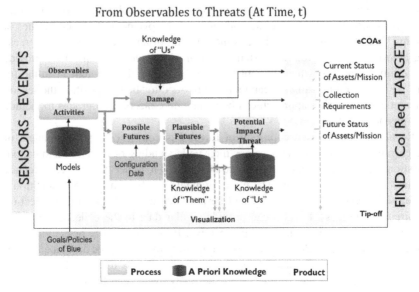

Fig. 2.2 Situation Awareness Process Model

2.2.2 Situation Awareness Process Model

2.2 expands upon the reference model and looks at it as a process in an instance of time. Observables are the input to the process that provides a view of what is going on in the world (primitive elements of the environment). It is assumed that any attributes associated with the observables have been normalized, cleansed, and transformed into a form that can be used by the follow-on processes[4]. The observables we are interested in are cues into the activities that a decision maker needs or is interested in (and thus we refer to these as Activities of Interest, AOI) as a way to gain or maintain awareness. The AOI are based on goals, policies, or in general the "things" of interest. These AOI can be stored and manipulated in such formats as graphs, Bayesian networks, Markov models, or any of the numerous modeling techniques. As observables enter the process, they are categorized and (1) associated with a new stage or step within an existing, ongoing activity; (2) associate with no existing activity and hence become the start of a new activity; or (3) can be a trigger leading to the combination, merging, or removal of existing activities. This process is similar to tracking individual objects (generally referred to as Level 1 fusion) and why we consider this part of the process, even though mostly symbolic, still a Level 1 process or as a form of object ID and tracking. However, in this case our object is an activity, a complex object. The classical tracking problem of association also

---

[4] The specific techniques to perform the operations of normalization, cleansing, or transformation are out of scope of this discussion.

comes in to play when associating an observable to an activity or step of an activity. These activities could also be thought of as hypotheses.

At any given time, say t, we have a set of ongoing activities (defined earlier as the current situation). At this point we are interested in analyzing the meaning of these activities? This is considered to be Situation Assessment (as shown on the right side of the reference model in Figure 2.1). The overall objective of Situation Assessment is to determine if any of the ongoing activities have an impact to 'us'[5] or if they can have (in the future) an impact to 'us'. The first part looks at the current activities and assessing the impact that the activities have had. Since these activities have already happened, we refer to this as "Damage" Assessment, i.e., has any of the identified activities caused an impact and specifically has it caused harm that requires development of a recovery plan to resolve? In order to accomplish this type of assessment, one not only needs the current, known activities, but also what it means to 'us'. The information needed is part of what we call "Knowledge of Us". This data contains knowledge as to the importance of the assets or capabilities to 'us'. Thus, this part of the process identifies to the decision maker whether there is a current impact (damage) to any of our capabilities or assets used to perform a mission as well as any current impacts (damage) to the assets themselves.

Above, we discussed the current situation and assessing the situation including its impact to the mission, but a decision maker may also be interested in a view of what the adversary (or competitor) is doing or may possibly do. This has generally been described as "getting inside the adversary's OODA loop". The sooner we understand what the adversary can/might do the more options become available to the decision maker. The second part of 2.2 addresses this. The first step of the process is to take each of the activities of interest and project them forward based on the a priori knowledge provided as part of the model. Here we don't discuss time itself, i.e., we are not projecting the activities based on time, but rather the next step. In some cases it could take milliseconds to go from one stage to another and in other cases it could be days, or longer. The number of stages that we look forward is defined under "Configuration Data". So based solely on the models themselves, we have projected each current activity one step forward; however, these projected or possible futures do not take into account whether they are plausible. In order to determine plausibility, we need to consider additional knowledge. We need both the "Knowledge of Them" and "Knowledge of Us". Specifically, we need to know whether the adversary has the capability, capacity, and intent/goal and have they possibly exhibited similar behavior in the past. We also need to know whether they have the opportunity to accomplish the intent(s)/goal(s). This opportunity is based in many cases on the vulnerabilities of us (provided as part of the Knowledge of Us). Thus, starting with the list of possible futures, we use the "Knowledge of Them" and "Knowledge of Us" to constrain the possible into the plausible for each activity of interest.

But again what do these plausible futures mean to me/us? To answer this question we again use part of the "Knowledge of Us" (importance of the assets/capabilities)

---

[5] 'Us' is considered to be friendly assets or the friendly environment. In a military sense, 'us' is what we're interested in defending. In a philosophical sense, 'us' can be equated to self and the preservation of self. Or, it can be thought of as the defensive environment of the decision maker.

to identify potential impacts and threats to meeting our objective(s). From this portion of the process we get not only future potential impacts/threats but we can also use this knowledge to determine our future collection requirements. Based on each of the futures, we can identify the key differentiating events that will assist us in determining which of the futures are actually unfolding. The key differentiating events can then determine the collection requirements needed to increase the certainty in identifying whether a plausible future is occurring.

One of the dangers in a reference model such as the one in 2.1 is that it can be perceived as a sequential flow of data or information rather than a descriptive model of components and ideas. To help circumvent this danger, 2.2 attempts to define a process flow and end products that is based on the concepts of the reference model as its framework. A primary feature of the process model is that it defines components that can be implemented as automated computer applications or shared human/computer systems that can then be tied together within system architectures. It also describes the flow of information and when key data sources come into play.

This section has described two models and defined their components. The SA Reference Model provides a set of definitions that can serve as a reference for describing systems that aid with SA while the Process Model captures a process flow at a single instance of time. Together, the two models provide a common set of definitions for situation awareness. One component of both models not yet addressed is Visualization. This will be the topic of the next section.

2.3 Visualization

Visualization is a component across all aspects of both models. Almost any part of the process is open to visualization but comes with its own set of challenges. Depending on what aids the decision maker and in what context they need awareness, activities of interest can be visualized, as well as results of various assessments to include current and future impacts. However, quickly and completely conveying the situation (set of AOIs) to a decision maker, especially in light of large amounts of information, is a very challenging issue.

There are three primary challenges to visualization for this research area. The challenges come about when dealing with abstract or conceptual elements as opposed to strictly geo-spatial or physical elements and result in challenges in visualizing the situation, high-volume data domains, and rapidly conveying the situation and corresponding analysis to a decision maker.

First is the challenge of visualizing a situation without necessarily depending on geo-spatial displays or displays that depend on physical objects. There are a multitude of techniques that are used to visualize raw or roughly correlated data but conveying situations has proven to be a challenge. What is the best way to present both the current and future situation so that sufficient decisions can be reached? There is also the added complexity of visualizing the situation over time so that changes, trends, and projections to the situation can be conveyed. In some contexts, a simple geo-spatial display may be sufficient but when addressing abstract concepts as opposed to physical entities, a geo-spatial display is only a part of the information that needs to be presented to a decision maker. Situation visualization remains a significant research challenge.

In any type of visualization, the ability to reach back into the raw data and to be able to follow the processing path is very important. For a user to be comfortable with the analysis a system performs, a certain level of trust in the conclusions need to be established. This trust can develop through transparency throughout any automated processes and through allowing the user to explore the data themselves to decide if they'd reach the same conclusions.

2.4 Application to the Cyber Domain

The ideas described in the previous sections are not dependent on any particular domain and can be directly applied to the cyber domain as well as many other domains or areas. There are however many challenges in actually implementing them as a way to enable situation awareness for a decision maker. Key to this approach is the identification and modeling of the relevant activities of interest. These activities are the principle driver for what a fusion engine would look for in the observables presented to it. The activities become the basis for the analysis and assessments done to determine current impacts of assets and missions and to derive plausible futures and their future impacts or effects on assets and missions.

What activities of interest might be useful in the cyber domain? To date, this work has focused primarily on defining a model of complex multi-stage network attacks. As a matter of fact, work on the detection and evaluation of this activity has driven a large portion of the research in this area but the work has so far been limited to the single activity of attacks. In exploring other potential AOIs, a network administrator might be interested in policy change detection, firewall configuration problems, network attack, etc. Cyber activities of interest for a company manager might include misuse of company equipment, effect of attacks on business units, etc. There also may be a need for awareness of cross domain activities as we move from operational to more a more strategic level of decision maker. An Air Operations Center commander may be interested in how an effect in the cyber domain influences the ability to execute a flying mission; a dispatcher may be interested in how a network attack influences the routing of city taxis, etc. The point of this is that by using a model of an activity of interest there is tremendous flexibility in how the activity is defined for the area that a decision maker needs awareness and they aren't limited to a single domain at a time. But the challenge is in defining that activity of interest and the observables that can be used to detect or identify that activity.

Specifically for the cyber domain, we've defined a single model to address the AOI of a complex multi-stage cyber attack. The observables are based on common Intrusion Detection Systems as well as application and firewall logs. The current situation is based on the set of "attack tracks" identified at the current time. We're

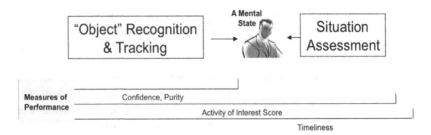

Fig. 2.3 Metrics Mapped to SA Reference Model

currently working on technologies to identify the impact of each attack track on the network assets affected by the attack. In the case of cyber, the environment is the network topology and the collection of data associated with that topology. This environmental information becomes the "knowledge of us" which can be used in performing impact assessment of the current situation. As our research progresses, we're researching the construction and interaction of each of the components within Figure 2.

2.5 Measures of Performance and Effectiveness

This section extracts from [8], [14], and [15]. [8] describes metrics in a generic sense while [14] and [15] are specific to the cyber domain. For the cyber domain, the metrics are specialized by substituting 'attack track' (an attack track is defined as a hypothesis of a complex multi-stage cyber attack that contains all the evidence of an attack) for 'activity of interest'. The current set of generic measures of performance have four dimensions; confidence, purity, cost utility, and timeliness. The metrics that will be described using the definitions for the models described in Section 2. Those definitions describe the various sections of the model with input streams representing "sources"; the output from network sensors and other evidence representing "data"; and attack tracks corresponding to activities and situations. 2.3 shows, at a high level, how each of the metrics that will be discussed map onto the reference model.

The metrics currently measure a system's ability to correctly fuse evidence, produce attack tracks, and prioritize the attack tracks into a meaningful order for a user. One of the metrics, *attack score*, has applicability to systems capable of assessing impact/threat and should improve in value (get closer to 1.0) as a system can more completely analyze the attack track in the context of a network or in importance to effects on a mission. Attack score is in the process of being updated to measure more information than just attacks. The updated measure is being called an "activity of interest score". One last comment on metrics before getting into the bulk of the discussion concerns data reduction. Early work on measures, spoke at length about a Data-Information Ratio (DIR) as shown in equation 2.1. The DIR was intended to measure the overall reduction in the amount of "stuff" that was presented to a user. When data is presented, a user tends to be: 1) overwhelmed by volume and lack of context; 2) has to rely on individual expertise for understanding; and, 3) has to mentally process (fuse, assess, and infer) the data.

$$DIR = \frac{Number\, of\, Complex\, Entities}{Number\, of\, Observations} \tag{2.1}$$

The initial thought was that by automatically aggregating and organizing data into more useful information the user would have less to deal with and could more productively and more effectively maintain awareness of the environment. The DIR has proven to be very informative but at a fairly high level. It tends to indicate the capability of a class of work rather than the capability of individual systems. For instance, in the cyber domain, we've observed an on average data reduction of two orders of magnitude when processing "alerts" (observations or events) into attack tracks (complex entities or activities). The advantage to the user then is that instead of tens of thousands of individual pieces of data to consider they now only have to consider a few hundred possible attack tracks. An attack track only reduces the information initially presented while maintaining the ability to "drill down" into the more detailed data that makes up the track. When combined with a mechanism to prioritize importance of the possible attacks, the power of this general class of analysis begins to become apparent. However, beyond the general data reduction, the DIR doesn't provide a lot of insight into the performance of particular technologies or implementations.

The rest of this section will discuss each of the metrics in more detail. The metrics, or measures of performance, are discussed according to the four dimensions; confidence, purity, cost utility, and timeliness. As shown by the mapping in 2.3, the confidence and purity measures address object recognition and tracking, cost utility includes situation and impact assessment and timeliness covers the entire model.

2.5.1 Confidence

For the cyber domain and assuming our activity of interest is a cyber attack on a network, **confidence** is a measure of how well the system detects the true attack tracks (e.g., the hypothesis of an attack). The confidence dimension consists of four metrics; (1) recall, (2) precision, (3) fragmentation, and (4) mis-association. Consider the diagram shown in 2.4 it represents the space of attack tracks identifiable by a capability supporting Cyber SA. The attack tracks can be classified into three categories; (1) known tracks, (2) detected tracks, and (3) correctly detected tracks. *Known tracks* are the attack tracks given by ground truth and contain all the evidence for a particular attack. *Detected Tracks* are the attack tracks hypothesized by a Cyber SA system under evaluation and contain all the fused evidence. Finally, *Correctly Detected Tracks* are known attack tracks detected by the Cyber SA system. Known

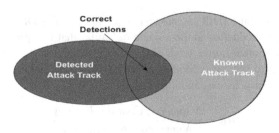

Fig. 2.4 Space of Attack Tracks

tracks not detected would be false negatives and detected tracks not known would
be false positives.

Given this description, the confidence metrics are as described by the equations
below:

$$Recall = \frac{Correct\,Detections}{Known\,Attack\,Tracks} \qquad (2.2)$$

$$Precision = \frac{Correct\,Detections}{Detected\,Attack\,Tracks} \qquad (2.3)$$

$$Fragmentation = \frac{Number\,of\,Fragments}{Detected\,Attack\,Tracks} \qquad (2.4)$$

$$Misassociation =$$
$$\frac{Number\,of\,Detections\,that\,are\,neither\,correct\,detections\,nor\,fragments}{Detected\,Attack\,Tracks}$$
$$(2.5)$$

Two additional definitions are needed to complete the discussion of confidence
metrics. A *fragment* is said to be an attack track that should have been included
within another track (equation 2.4). For example, in an island-hopping attack, a
targeted computer is compromised and then used to originate attacks on other computers. To correctly detect this attack, any time a target becomes an attacker, all the
evidence of this attack should be included in same track as that from the original
attacker through the island all the way to the subsequent targets. Often a fusion engine will not correctly associate the subsequent evidence with the original attack
reporting them as two or more attack tracks. In other words, a single attack is reported as two or more attacks only one of which would be counted as the correctly
detected track. A fragment can give the appearance of a false positive when, in reality, it usually indicates a portion of a more complex attack. *Mis-association* is a
little simpler and captures all "other" detected tracks. A mis-associated track is one
which is neither a fragment nor correctly detected. Summed together, the values for
precision, fragmentation, and mis-association should sum to 1 or cover 100% of the

attack tracks produced by the Cyber SA system. Assessing Cyber SA systems under research and development showed the confidence metrics to be the most useful when determining the overall capability of a system thus far. The traditional tension between recall and precision was observed in that high recall usually meant low precision-detected lots of attacks but couldn't clearly identify them. While, in contrast, high precision (knew the exact attack type and details) would often result in low recall or missed attacks. The fragmentation metric was interesting from the perspective of complex attacks and the level of data reduction. High fragmentation led to more attack tracks being presented which lowered data reduction but still typically maintained the two orders of magnitude reduction. The greatest value in the fragmentation metric was in indentifying that it would be better to keep more complex attacks in a single attack track and also in generating discussion concerning attribution of an attack. For example, if there was evidence of two attack tracks from different original attackers attacking the same target, A. Then, there was subsequent evidence that A was attacking B. Which of the original two attackers would be attributed to the follow-on attack on B? How would the attribution be made? Could you be sure that one of those attackers continued on and that it wasn't a new attack originating with A? These questions remain open areas of research.

2.5.2 Purity

Purity characterizes the quality of the correctly detected tracks (again assuming our activity of interest is a cyber attack on a network). Purity metrics also "look into" a track at the evidence and provide indications as to how well the evidence is being correlated and aggregated into an attack track. There are two metrics used to measure purity; (1) Mis-assignment rate, and (2) Evidence Recall. The equations for these metrics are given below:

$$Mis-AssignmentRate = $$
$$\frac{Total\,No.\,Alerts\,in\,Results - Total\,No.\,Correct\,Alerts\,for\,Assigned\,Results}{Total\,No.\,Alerts\,in\,Results}$$

$$(2.6)$$

$$EvidenceRecall = \frac{Total\,No.\,Correct\,Alerts\,for\,Assigned\,Results}{Total\,No.\,Alerts\,in\,Ground\,Truth\,Identified} \qquad (2.7)$$

By looking at the quality of the correctly detected tracks, the thought was that the metric could indicate how well the Cyber SA system was using the available evidence. Mis-assignment rate could answer the question about whether the system was assigning evidence to a track that wasn't relevant or if it only considered directly useful evidence. While evidence recall was intended to tell us how much of the evidence available was truly being used. When applying the purity metrics to the cyber domain, neither proved to be particularly useful. Mis-assignment rate was probably the stronger of the two in that when the rate was very high it would indicate an incorrect correlation or association of the underlying data. This would essentially indicate a "bug" or flaw in the system's fusion engine. However, it rarely indicated anything about the quality of the detected attacks. Extraneous evidence didn't necessarily have any correlation to lower or higher detection rates. Evidence Recall was even less useful. The thought was that as more evidence was used, the attack detection would be more accurate (higher recall and precision). However, empirically we found almost no relationship between the amount of evidence used and the quality of the detections. In fact, it almost appeared that the less evidence used the better the detections. This almost indicates that there are only a few truly relevant network events that indicate attacks. An open area of research or question is whether there's a minimally complete set of data or events that could indicate the presence of an attack.

2.5.3 Cost Utility

Cost utility is defined as the ability of a system to identify the "important or key" attack tracks with respect to the concept of cost. In [15], two cost utility metrics were described. Since that paper was written, the *weighted cost* metric as applied to the cyber domain is no longer in use. The intent of the metric was to capture or gauge the usefulness of the system by considering the types of attacks detected with a positive weight and penalizing the system for false positives with a negative weight. Different weights were also assigned to different categories of attacks. Weighted Cost is then a simple sum of the values assigned to the types of attacks detected including false positives divided by the sum of the values of the attack tracks in ground truth. Observations when using the weighted cost showed that it didn't add any value in measuring the performance of a Cyber SA system. The metric that appears to have great value in measuring the performance of a Cyber SA system is the attack score. The attack score is an earlier version of the "activities of interest (AOI) score" described in [8]. Attack score is calculated as shown in equation 2.8.

$$AttackScore =$$
$$\frac{\#of\,attacks\,in\,GT \,*\,\#of\,tracks\,in\,GT - sum\,of\,positions\,of\,detected\,attacks}{\#of\,attacks\,in\,GT \,*\,\#of\,tracks\,in\,GT - sum\,of\,\#attacks\,in\,GT}$$

$$(2.8)$$

Attack score tries to measure the presentation of a prioritized list of hypothesized attacks by counting how many actual attacks occur and how close their priority is to the top of the list. In effect, the attack score measures the ability of a system to perform situation assessment as defined in 2.3. The attack score is considered a cost utility measure because the lower in a prioritized list that the actual attack appears implies that more work is performed before the actual attack would be considered or could be acted on. For example, if the actual attack was at the top of the prioritized list, a user's attention would be drawn to it first and action taken. If the actual attack appeared at position 25, then the user would have to consider or "look into" 24 other attack tracks before getting to the actual attack track that was important or required action. Analyzing the 25 tracks indicate a cost in time before being able to take an appropriate action. Thus, an ideal attack score, with all actual attacks (true positives) at the top of the list, would be 1.0. Anything less than an attack score of 1.0 means that some level of effort is expended considering incomplete tracks or false positives. Another way of looking at the attack score is that it measures a system's capability to assess the situation. How the attacks are listed (prioritized) is determined algorithmically and could be influenced by the desire of the user to include; most critical, most damaging, most likely, greatest mission impact, etc. The different prioritization algorithms could influence the ordering of the list which in turn affects the attack score which could also provide differing assessments of the situation. How well this measure can assess the situation and what other metrics may be needed is a potential area of future research. The attack score has tremendous opportunity to be an indicator of improved analysis as more sensor types are considered, as better models are used in the fusion process, or as we improve our capability to add additional methods for situation analysis as described in [8]. With improving analysis, the attack score would approach the ideal of 1.0.

2.5.4 Timeliness

The final dimension, timeliness is the ability of the system to respond within the time requirements of a particular domain. More specifically, timeliness would need to measure the time elapsed before a decision could be made or action taken. Because we're interested in awareness, it's not simply the time it takes to present or detect an attack or activity but also includes the time it takes to enable awareness of the activity so that a user could make a decision. Timeliness touches the border between a measure of performance and a measure of effectiveness. So far, timeliness is an area of future research. To conclude this section on measures of performance, it's important to note that a single metric is probably inadequate to characterize the performance of a system. Rather, a set of metrics measuring the various dimensions of the problem are needed to fully characterize and provide insight into the performance of the systems.

2.5.5 Measures of Effectiveness

By measures of effectiveness (MoE), we mean measures that consider how effective a system is in enabling a decision maker's situation awareness of the environment of interest. Have the tools or techniques developed to support SA improved or hindered the decision making process? Are alternatives that may not be immediately apparent considered? Can a novice decision maker more quickly become an expert or at least make expert-like decisions? To date, minimal research has gone in to measures of effectiveness but we expect to begin researching MoE both in general and specifically for the cyber domain very soon.

2.6 Conclusion

This chapter has described a generalized approach to enabling situation awareness and how that approach can be applied to the cyber domain. This application then enables Cyber Situation Awareness and ultimately Universal Situation Awareness. The challenging key to this approach is in identifying the activities individual decision makers are interested in and need to maintain awareness of over time. Then once the activity of interests are identified and modeled, the observations necessary to identify the activity need to be defined. Evaluating the effectiveness of the capabilities supporting SA depends on cognitive processes and determining if the technique has improved decision making. Measuring effectiveness for this approach is an open area of research.

Acknowledgements The authors thank Mr. Mike Hinman, AFRL/RIEA; Dr. Moises Sudit and Dr. Adam Stotz, University of Buffalo; Dr. Shanchieh 'Jay' Yang, Rochester Institute of Technology; Mr. Jared Holsopple, Rochester Institute of Technology; and countless others for their valuable insights and contributions to this research. This chapter is approved for public release, case number 88ABW-2009-1866.

References

1. http://www.wikipedia.org.
2. D. S. Alberts, J. J. Garstka, R. E. Hayes, and D. A. Signori. Understanding information age warfare. In *DoD Command and Control Research Program Publication Series*, 2001.
3. J. Antonik. Decision management. In *Military Communications Conference 2007 (MILCOM '07)*, pages 1–5, Orlando, FL, USA, October 2007. IEEE.
4. E. Bosse, J. Roy, and S. Wark. Concepts, models, and tools for information fusion. In *ISIF*, page 43. Artech House, Inc, 2007.
5. M. Endsley. Toward a theory of situation awareness in dynamic systems. In *Human Factors Journal*, volume 37(1), pages 32–64, March 1995.
6. B. McGuinness and J. L. Foy. A subjective measure of SA: The crew awareness rating scal (cars). In *Proceedings of the first human performance, situation awareness, and automation conference*, Savannah, Georgia, USA, October 2000.
7. U.S. Department of Defense, Data Fusion Subpanel for the Joint Directors of Laboratories, and Technical Panel for C3. Data fusion lexicon. 1991.
8. J. Salerno. Measuring situation assessment performance through the activities of interest score. In *Proceedings of the 11th International Conference on Information Fusion*, Cologne GE, June 30 - July 3 2008.

9. J. Salerno, M. Hinman, and D. Boulware. Evaluating algorithmic techniques in supporting situation awareness. In *Proceedings of the Defense and Security Conference*, Orlando, FL, USA, March 2005.
10. J. Salerno, M. Hinman, and D. Boulware. A situation awareness model applied to multiple domains. In *Proceedings of the Defense and Security Conference*, Orlando, FL, USA, March 2005.
11. J. Salerno, G. Tadda, D. Boulware, M. Hinman, and S. Gorton. Achieving situation awareness in a cyber environment. In *Proc of the Situation Management Workshop of MILCOM 2005*, Atlantic City, NJ, USA, October 2005.
12. L. Snidaro, M. Belluz, and G. Foresti. Domain knowledge for security applications. In *ISIF*, 2007.
13. A. Steinberg, C. Bowman, and F. White. Revisions to the JDL data fusion model. In *Joint NATO/IRIS Conference*, Quebec, Canada, October 1998.
14. G. Tadda. Measuring performance of cyber situation awareness systems. In *Proceedings of the 11th International Conference on Information Fusion*, Cologne GE, June 30 - July 3 2008.
15. G. Tadda and et al. Realizing situation awareness within a cyber environment. In *Multisensor, Multisource Information Fusion: Architectures, Algorithms, and Applications 2006*. edited by Belur V. Dasarathy, Proceedings of SPIE Vol. 624 (SPIE, Bellingham, WA, 2006) 624204, Kissimmee FL, April 2006.

Part II
The Reasoning and Decision Making Aspects

Chapter 3
RPD-based Hypothesis Reasoning for Cyber Situation Awareness

John Yen, Michael McNeese, Tracy Mullen, David Hall, Xiaocong Fan, and Peng Liu

Abstract Intelligence workers such as analysts, commanders, and soldiers often need a hypothesis reasoning framework to gain improved situation awareness of the highly dynamic cyber space. The development of such a framework requires the integration of interdisciplinary techniques, including supports for distributed cognition (human-in-the-loop hypothesis generation), supports for team collaboration (identification of information for hypothesis evaluation), and supports for resource-constrained information collection (hypotheses competing for information collection resources). We here describe a cognitively-inspired framework that is built upon Klein's recognition-primed decision model and integrates the three components of Endsley's situation awareness model. The framework naturally connects the logic world of tools for cyber situation awareness with the mental world of human analysts, enabling the perception, comprehension, and prediction of cyber situations for better prevention, survival, and response to cyber attacks by adapting missions at the operational, tactical, and strategic levels.

3.1 Introduction

There are many challenges associated with the understanding of global situations in the dynamic cyber space. First, the situation awareness (SA) of the cyber space involves multiple levels (e.g., instruction level, operating system level, application level, network level, to mission level). Events and hypotheses at different levels are often related for generating, refining, and reasoning. Second, there is a large amount of dynamic data that needs to be monitored at real-time. Third, the rapid tempo of the evolution of situations in the cyberspace requires a cyber SA framework not only to quickly detect cyber threats, but also to predict and anticipate potential future threats. Fourth, the information and knowledge regarding the pattern of cyber attacks is often uncertain and incomplete. Finally, there is a need to close the gap between the "logic world" of the tool and the "mental world" of the analysts.

To address these challenges, this chapter describes a cognitively-inspired hypothesis generation and reasoning framework that aims to help analysts, commanders, and soldiers to gain improved cyber situation awareness in highly dynamic and uncertain cyber space, through a holistic framework that integrates three elements of situation awareness: (1) sensing, (2) comprehension, and (3) projection. To deal with the challenge of the large amount of dynamic data that needs to be

John Yen, Michael McNeese, Tracy Mullen, David Hall, Xiaocong Fan, and Peng Liu, College of Information Sciences and Technology, The Pennsylvania State University

S. Jajodia et al., (eds.), *Cyber Situational Awareness*,
Advances in Information Security 46, DOI 10.1007/978-1-4419-0140-8_3,

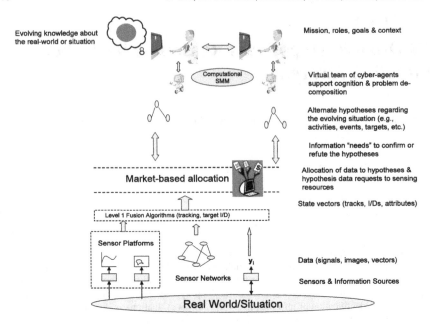

Fig. 3.1 Hypothesis Reasoning in Information Fusion Architecture

monitored, sensing is achieved through hypothesis-driven information gathering. This enables the framework to find a balance regarding the trade-off among exploring alternative, competing, and emerging new hypotheses, and gaining deeper understanding about existing hypotheses. Comprehension is achieved by generating and refining hypotheses through recognition of known patterns as well as a synthesis process (story building). Based on hypotheses, future states can be predicted through simulations as well as anticipated through expectations. Together, these features form a holistic framework for hypothesis generation and reasoning in cyber situation awareness. The framework is based on a naturalistic decision making model: recognition-primed decisions (RPD). Anchoring in such a cognitive model enables the framework to bridge the gap between the mental model of the analysts and the logic model of the tool.

Development of the framework requires the integration of cognitive support for problem decomposition and hypothesis generation, identification of information required to confirm or deny hypotheses, and an information collection system that can allocate sensing resources across competing hypotheses. All of these require the ability to deal with uncertainty and mission-specific constraints such as time and stealth. In data-driven approaches, collected data is mapped to available hypotheses. In our approach, which is shown in Figure 3.1, hypotheses explicitly compete with each other for scarce information collection resources using a market-based approach.

3.2 Naturalistic Decision Making as a Holistic Model for Cyber SA

3.2.1 Decision and Hypotheses

Decisions and hypotheses are often used in contexts such as situation awareness. Before we discuss the role of naturalistic decision making as a framework for cyber situation awareness, we first discuss the relationships between decisions and hypotheses, and the relationship between information seeking (for decisions) and evidence gathering (for hypothesis reasoning).

A piece of evidence is a piece of information that is relevant to some hypotheses. In other words, evidence is implicitly "*contextualized*" whereas information is broader and may not have a clear context. A piece of evidence is first contextualized within a process of investigation, forensics, or diagnosis. Even if a piece of evidence turns out to be irrelevant, it was gathered with an intention to determine its relevance to the context. On the other hand, information does not always have a clear context. In another word, a piece of information is context-free, which means that it can be associated with a wide range of possible contexts; whereas a piece of evidence is often context-specific.

The distinction between context-free and context-specific is not always black-and-white. For instance, when a person reads a newspaper, he/she has a general goal to know about major events, such as the outcomes of sporting events, updates of financial markets, tips to improve the quality of life, etc. While these goals do not necessarily link to decisions, many of them can be viewed as hypotheses. For instance, a person may have hypotheses such as "the real estate market has started its recovery", "the Nittany Lions will win the Big 10 Championship this year", and "the global climate change is highly affected by CO_2 emission". These hypotheses could in turn affect the person's choice about which sections to read, how much time to spend on a story, and, even, how the story is interpreted. These hypotheses can lead to decisions by the newspaper reader. For instance, increasing likelihood of a hypothesis regarding real estate market could lead to a decision to buy or to sell real estate properties.

In this chapter, the term "hypothesis" is used to refer to future states, interests, and statements to be explored. Hence, hypotheses and decisions are often related. Confirmation or rejection of hypotheses are "decisions" themselves. From this perspective, "hypotheses" are the precursor of decisions. However, this is not the only relationship between the two. A decision about a course of action generates a sequence of future states, which can also be viewed as hypotheses. Hence, hypotheses can be generated by decisions. Both of these relationships between hypotheses and decisions are well represented in a naturalistic decision-making model called the Recognition-Primed Decision (RPD) model.

3.2.2 The Recognition-Primed Decision (RPD) Model

The RPD model ([3]) captures how domain experts make decisions based on the recognition of similarities between the current situation and past experiences. The RPD process has two phases: recognition and evaluation. In the recognition phase, a decision maker needs to develop situation awareness and recognize what courses of action (COA) worked before in a similar situation. In the evaluation phase, a decision maker needs to evaluate each COA by imaging how it will evolve. If a COA does not work for the current situation, the decision maker can either adjust it, or find and examine other COAs until a workable solution is obtained.

The RPD model states that "feature-matching" and "story-building" are two typical strategies used by experts to develop situation awareness. In feature-matching, a decision maker tries to find whether he/she has ever experienced situations similar to the current one by matching the set of observed cues (synthesized from information describing the current situation) with the pattern of cues considered in past experiences. In case feature-matching cannot produce an adequate account for the current situation due to lack of experience, story-building will be used to construct an explanation, by coherently linking the observed information. A story gives an explanation of how the current situation might have been emerging. When building a story, a decision maker needs to explore potential hypotheses and evaluate how well each of them may fit what have been observed. Recognition results in four products: (1) relevant cues (what to pay attention to), (2) plausible goals (which goals make sense), (3) expectancies (what will happen next), and (4) course of actions (what actions worked in this type of situation). An expectancy serves as a gate-condition for continuing working on the current recognition. Due to the dynamic and uncertain nature of the environment, it is important to monitor the status of expectancies because a decision maker may have misinterpreted the current situation but he/she cannot recognize it until some expectancy is invalidated as the situation further evolves. In such cases, the decision maker needs to further diagnose the current situation (e.g., to gather more information).

The RPD model provides a holistic framework (including perception, comprehension, projection, as conform to Endsley's Situation Awareness model ([4])) for hypothesis generation and reasoning in cyber situation awareness. From the perspective of *perception*, RPD enables the gathering of relevant information based on the context of hypothesis reasoning. For instance, it gathers missing cues for matching the current situation with experience; it monitors expectancy to detect anomalies. The *comprehension* in the RPD model is realized through the feature-matching process and the story building process. *Projection* in the RPD model is realized through mental simulation, which is driven by hypotheses, as well as the anticipation of expectancy.

3.3 RPD-based Hypothesis Generation and Reasoning for Cyber SA

Analysts for cyber SA need to detect events in cyber space, identify their relationships, hypothesize course-of-action of the enemy, assess/predict damages to assets and impacts to missions. Virtual analyst teams involving human analysts and cyber-agents demand a computational shared mental model (SMM) that allows them to collaborate with each other. Such a SMM, covering entities across a hypothesis space and an evidence space, allows team members to generate and explore alternative hypotheses. Since multiple hypothesis may each explain the existing observations (evidence), the selection among rival and possibly incompatible hypothesis can be improved by collecting additional corroborating (or contradicting) evidence. Hence, multiple hypotheses can be constructed, evaluated and used to guide sensor tasking, data acquisition and fusion processing, so as to support, refine, generate or eliminate hypothesis in the current set of hypothesis. Many hypotheses will require more data to be collected to either support or refute their hypothesis. Limited sensor information collection resources mean that only some of the information "needs" can be satisfied. Hence, section 5 describes a market-based approach for allocating sensor resources.

A key issue in a hypothesis generation and reasoning framework is linking the creation and the refinement of hypotheses (i.e., the logic world of the tool) to situation assessment of the analysts (i.e., the mental world of the humans). We address this issue using RPD agents (i.e., R-CAST) with a shared mental model about the decision making of the human-agent team ([12]; [9]; [10]).

In particular, the R-CAST cognitive agent architecture, shown in Figure 3.2, leverages two features in RPD for hypothesis creation: expectancy monitoring and story building. Expectancy monitoring generates hypotheses that indicate "anomalies" or the success/failure of executing a course-of-action (COA). Story building creates and refines hypotheses from the evidence collected. Hence, the hypothesis space and the evidence space can be co-refined by RPD-enabled agents through (i) generating hypotheses, (ii) sharing information across contexts, (iii) selecting

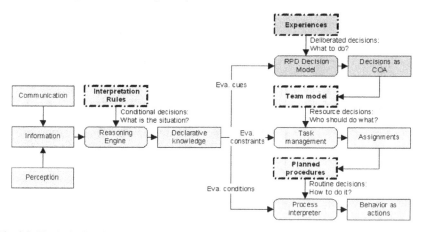

Fig. 3.2 The R-CAST Cognitive Agent Architecture

hypothesis to be explored, and (iv) executing a course of action for gathering information related to chosen hypotheses using sensors.

In this framework, this issue is addressed using agents with a shared mental model about the decision making process. This shared mental model is based on Recognition-Primed Decision (RPD). In particular, architecture leverages three features in RPD for hypothesis creation: (1) recognition-based hypothesis generation, and (2) hypothesis-based story building, and (3) collaborative RPD-based hypothesis generation and reasoning.

3.3.1 Recognition-based Hypothesis Generation

The "feature-matching" process in RPD matches the current situation with previous experiences. The outcome of the recognition enables the creation of hypotheses. Within R-CAST, two schemes are used for this hypothesis creation: (1) generate the first hypothesis that matches the current situation to a satisfactory degree based on the information currently known, and (2) generates all hypotheses that match the current situation to a degree. The first scheme is based on the "satisficing" principle in the RPD model, whereas the second scheme can be viewed as a bounded rationality model. The choice between these two schemes is made when an agent is configured at run time.

The feature-matching process also generates hypotheses about "expected future states" (i.e., called "expectancy" in the RPD model). These hypotheses are used to detect "anomalies" or the success/failure of executing a course-of-action (COA).

3.3.2 Hypothesis-driven Story Building

In the RPD framework, story building is the process of interpreting a situation by making hypotheses using partial information through an iterative and dynamic process. The story building process by a human analyst can draw on a wide range of techniques including, but not limited to, synthesis,

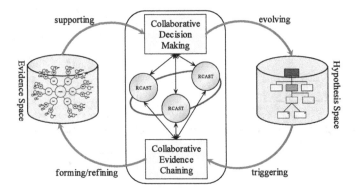

Fig. 3.3 RPD-enabled Collaborative Hypothesis Reasoning

reasoning by analogy, and creative problem solving. To support the story building of the analysts, a cyber SA tool can assist the analyst in several ways. For instance, it can alert the analyst about a new piece of information that results in changing the ranking of hypotheses. It can also assist the analyst in deciding how to allocate information gathering resources based on expected utility of the information. An application of this hypothesis-driven story building is realized in the context of emergency medical decision-making teams ([5]).

3.3.3 Collaborative RPD-based Hypothesis Generation and Reasoning

Cyber agents provide an agent-assisted collaborative evidence chaining approach as depicted in Figure 3.3. Each R-CAST agent assists a human analyst. Hence, a group of human experts can collaborate across their respective organization boundaries through R-CAST agents. Hypothesis Space and Evidence Space can be co-refined by R-CAST agents through collaborative decision making and collaborative evidence chaining. Depending on the active decision space (composed of structured experiences), R-CAST agent can (i) generate hypotheses, (ii) share information (evidence, knowledge), (iii) select hypothesis to be explored, and (iv) execute a course of action for information gathering. An adapted context can be used by a cyber agent to evolve the hypothesis space such that the agent's attention can be restricted only to those hypotheses that are relevant to the updated context. The highlighted hypotheses can be transformed into "entity-relation" patterns (same to the structure of evidence chains but lacking instantiated evidence), which are posted to the shared space as information requirements. Guided by these information needs in the shared space, R-CAST agents gather and share relevant information to form new evidence chains for hypothesis reasoning.

An agent in such a human-agent team has a specific role and responsibility. For example, an RPD agent can be responsible for generating and reasoning about a predetermined set of hypotheses. Organizing agents this way reduces the size of the knowledge required by each agent, and improves their computational efficiency. A team of RPD agents has a shared understanding about the structure of the entire team. This shared understanding about the team structure enables them to assist each other in sharing information relevant to the hypotheses of the teammates.

Multiple agents often need a mechanism to orchestrate their collaboration process. In R-CAST, this is realized by the process manger in a "Process Agent". A process agent orchestrates and coordinates the collaboration process of a team of hypothesis agent, each of which can either describe a sub-process or a hypothesis. The communication among agents is realized in Service-Oriented Architecture (SOA) based on the semantics of proactive information exchanges among agents ([11]).

3.4 Hypergraph-based Hypothesis Reasoning

One of the challenges of cyber situation awareness (SA) is to identify, monitor, and predict the relationships between events and hypotheses in different layers (e.g., impacts of cyber attacks on military missions). Large-scale analysis of multi-dimensional multi-layered heterogeneous networks (which we call *relational networks*) demands a mathematical model that meets the following requirements:

- *Representativeness*: the mathematical model must be able to "capture" all the essential information, knowledge, and hypotheses "contained in" the corresponding multi-dimensional multi-layered relational networks.
- *Simplicity and intuitiveness*: the mathematical model should "look" simple so that the analyst can leverage the "simple look" to *intuitively* "visualize" the semantics of a very complicated relational network in his or her mind. In other words, the mathematical model should have the "ability" to represent complicated relationships regarding hypotheses in simple, intuitive forms.
- *Transforming manually done relational network analysis jobs to mathematical problem definitions and mathematical solutions*. Although not all network analysis jobs can be transformed to mathematics, some important network analysis jobs can be transformed to mathematical problem definitions and solutions, and such a mathematical approach may greatly enhance the efficiency and correctness of network analysis and reduce the workload on human analysts.
- *Computation friendliness*: large-scale analysis cannot completely rely on human analysts. Instead, computer information systems should be fully leveraged to assist analysts in doing such complicated analysis. To build such computer information systems, multi-dimensional relational networks must be represented by the data structures that computer programs can handle. As the intermediate (knowledge) representation between relational networks and computer data structures, the mathematical model and the associated mathematical solutions must be friendly to computer algorithms.

Hypergraphs ([1]; [2]) provide a mathematical foundation to represent multi-layer multi-dimensional relational networks for cyber SA. In mathematics, a hypergraph is a generalization of a graph, where edges can connect any number of vertices. Formally, a hypergraph H is a pair H = (X,E) where X is a set of elements, called nodes or vertices, and E is a set of non-empty subsets of X called hyperedges or links.

Relational networks cannot be elegantly represented by traditional graphs, since edges in a traditional graph can connect only two vertices. As a result, when a relationship involves three or more entities in relational networks, a traditional graph will have to add a new type of "relationship" nodes. In addition, to represent multi-dimensional relationships in relational networks, a single type of relationship nodes is no longer sufficient, and multiple different types of relationship nodes must be defined. All these relationship nodes not only make the graph look very "messy", but also make the analyses much harder.

In contrast, hypergraphs can represent relational networks in a way that meets the above requirements. The ideas and rationale behind hypergraph-based representation are explained below.

3.4.1 Modeling Events as Network Entities

Cyber attacks can be seen as a process, which refers to a sequence of events, involving steps or operations that are usually ordered and/or usually interdependent. Hence, social entities are no longer the primary entities in cyber SA relational networks. Instead, events should be the primary entities, and relational networks should be used to capture the relationships between event entities.

- Since relationships between events are fundamentally "bounded" with the attributes of events, attributes play a central role in hypergraph-based representation of networks. In our model, (a) a hypergraph representing a network is composed of a set of nodes (or vertices) and hyperedges, and each node represents an event entity. (b) Each event node has a unique event ID and a specific set of attributes. We allow an event node to have arbitrary number and types of attributes; and some representative attributes usually are (*action takers, action, action's attributes, location, time*).
- Once attributes are properly modeled, the relationships between entities (i.e., events) in our relational networks can be simply modeled as hyperedges. In our model, each hyperedge has a unique ID and is defined by a specific attribute or a specific group of attributes. For one example, we could use the *location* attribute to define the subset of events that happen at the same node as a hyperedge.
- A unique advantage of hypergraphs is that multi-dimensional relationships can be uniformly modeled. In our model, multi-dimensional relationships can be directly represented by attribute semantics. For example, the location and the time attributes represent two basic dimensions in understanding the relationships between events in weapons of mass destruction (WMD)-proliferating activities. Because a hyperedge can be defined by a *combonation* of attributes, our model allows a meaningful multi-dimensional relationship "subspace" to be easily defined. Moreover, cross-dimension relationships are not difficult to define either, since our model allows a hyperedge to be defined by an arbitrary *function* (value) of a group of attributes, and these attributes may represent different dimensions of the relational network.

Hyperedges provide a very expressive yet intuitive way to model the complicated relationships "contained in" relational networks for hypothesis reasoning in cyber SA.

3.4.2 Hypergraph-based Network Analysis Techniques

Hypergraph-based reasoning about hypotheses within a layer and between different layers of cyber SA taxonomy leverages a wide range of network analysis techniques, which could be transformed to hypergraph-based mathematical problems. We list some of these techniques below:

- Hypergraph *partitioning* is an important problem and has extensive application to many areas ([2]). The problem is to partition the vertices of a hypergraph in k roughly equal parts, such that the number of hyperedges connecting vertices in different parts is minimized
- If two hypergraphs are *isomorphic* to each other, then the two corresponding relational networks could be viewed as having identical cyber attack pattern.
- *Vertex-transitive* and *edge-transitive* hypergraphs could be used to connect individual events into chains for hypothesis reasoning.
- *Q-analysis* can be directly applied to hypergraph-based analysis about structural characteristics based on linkage between layers, and to solve some important network analysis problems with applications to hypothesis reasoning in cyber SA.

These hypergraph-based techniques are important foundations for developing tools to analyze complex relationships between a large amount of events over a large number of nodes and assets in the cyber space to prevent, predict, mitigate, and respond to cyber attacks from the perspective of

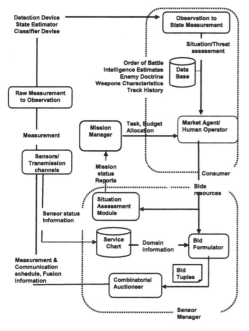

Mission Manager: Assesses mission level decisions (e.g., task priority to mission goal), allocates tasks and budget to agents

Sensor Manager: acts as competitive market for buyers and sellers of sensor resources.

– Sensors and transmission channels are modeled as sellers. Sensors sell their sensor schedule (i.e., their "attention") and transmission channels sell raw bandwidth.

– Consumers of the sensor network (hypotheses) are interested in higher-end products such as target tracks, environmental searches, and target identification.

To address these commensurability issues, the Sensor Manager provides a means to bundle raw resources into products that consumers want using *Service chart database* and *Bid formulator.*

Fig. 3.4 Market-based Sensor Management

assets, platforms, to missions at the tactical, operational, and strategic levels. To fully unitize limited resources for gathering real-time information related to hypotheses, the next section describes a market-based approach for allocating sensor resources.

3.5 Market-based Evidence Gathering

Identifying and making tradeoffs involved in information production, whether by hypothesis generation or any means, is a difficult problem that market-based systems "solve" by allowing values of hypotheses, or utilities, to drive the selection process. Essentially this transforms the traditional "data driven" approach (in which multiple sensors and information sources are used, with a focus on how to process the collected data) to a hypothesis-centered approach in which one or more hypotheses treat the information collection and distribution system as a market and vie to acquire goods and services (e.g., information collection, processing resources to support or refute a hypotheses) ([7]).

The sensor manager acts as a competitive market for buyers and sellers of sensor resources, as shown in Figure 3.4. Sensors are modeled as sellers. Sensors sell their sensor schedule (i.e., their "attention"). Hypotheses are modeled as buyers, and are interested in higher-end products estimated enemy plans, intent, and impacts to missions. To address these commensurability issues, the sensor manager provides a means to bundle raw resources into products that consumers want using a service chart database and a specialized bid formulator module.

The service chart specifies detailed domain information, such as characteristics of various sensors. The SM accepts consumer bids, which it then hands off to the bid formulator. As part of this process, the bid formulator needs to evaluate the value of a particular allocation to the overall consumer task. For example, a consumer-hypothesis may be willing to pay more to buy a specific sensor with "excellent" applicability to a perceived threat, than to get another type of sensor with just "good" applicability. The bid formulator must also consider synergistic constraints, such as sensor A working in conjunction with sensor B may be able to provide more accurate tracking for hypothesis X than the more powerful sensor C working alone.

Once the bids are formulated, the sensor manager conducts an auction to set prices and allocate the available sensors as needed. Auctions that sell bundles of goods are called combinatorial auctions. Buyers can express their preferences over a combination of goods, thus efficiently represent synergies (or lack of) between goods. Solving the auction winner determination problem finds an allocation of resources that maximizes revenue (thus implicitly importance or utility) given the constraint that each resource can be sold to no more than one bidder ([6]). We have implemented several winner determination algorithms, and developed a new anytime one, that can be used in real-time situations to allocate resources efficiently [8].

3.6 Summary

In this book chapter, we have described an RPD-based framework to connect the logic world of cyber situation awareness (SA) tool with the mental world of human analysts, with an emphasis on hypothesis generation and reasoning. The framework is based on a holistic decision-making model (i.e., recognition-primed decision) that integrates key components of Endsley's Situation Awareness model: perception, comprehension, and projection. From the perspective of hypothesis reasoning, the framework supports the generation of hypotheses through a recognition process and a story building process. Gathering of evidence (i.e., perception) is fully integrated with hypothesis reasoning so that the value of evidence is determined by the context of hypothesis reasoning. To deal with reasoning about multi-dimensional relationships between hypotheses in different layers related to cyber situation awareness (e.g., events, threats, damages, and their impacts to missions), hypergraph-based techniques enable the creation and the reasoning of hypotheses involving complex multi-dimensional relationships in relational networks. These analyses can be realized by collaborative agent teams, which can be organized into a hierarchical structure. Finally, market-based techniques are employed to make effective utilization of soft sensors for cyber situation awareness. Together, this framework offers a holistic framework for the perception, the comprehension, and the prediction of cyber situations for better prevention, survival, and response to cyber attacks by adapting missions at the operational, tactical, and strategic levels.

Acknowledgements The research described in the chapter is the synthesis of several research projects conducted at Penn State's College of Information Sciences and Technology. In particular, the research regarding using RPD-enabled agents (i.e., RCAST) as teammates and decision aids has been supported by Army Research Lab under Advanced Decision Architecture Collaborative Technology Alliance (ADA CTA). The research regarding developing flexible hierarchical decision framework using RCAST has been supported by Office of Naval Research. The research regarding RCAST-MED is partially supported by an internal grant from the Pennsylvania State University, and is conducted in collaboration with Shizhou Zhu, Dr. Madhu Reddy, and Dr. Christopher De-Flitch from Hershey Medical Center at Penn State University. The research on hypergraph-based hypothesis reasoning benefited from initial suggestions and many insightful discussions with Dr. Henry C. Foley and Dr. Lee Giles.

References

1. Berge C. and Ray-Chaudhuri D. Hypergraph seminar, ohio state university. In *Lecture Notes in Mathematics 411 Springer-Verlag*, 1972.
2. Karypis G., Aggarwal R., Kumar V., and Shekhar S. Multilevel hypergraph partitioning: applications in vlsi domain. In *IEEE Transactions on Very Large Scale Integration (VLSI) Systems*, volume 7(1), pages 69–79, 1999.
3. Klein G. A recognition-primed decision making model of rapid decision making. In *G. Klien, J. Orasanu, R. Calderwood and C., Zsambok Eds., Decision Making In Action: Models and Methods*, pages 138–147, 1993.
4. Endsley M. R. Toward a theory of situation awareness in dynamic systems. In *Human Factors*, volume 37(1), pages 32–64, 1995.
5. Zhu S., Abraham J., Paul S. A., Reddy M., Yen J., Pfaff M., and et al. R-cast-med: Applying intelligent agents to support emergency medical decision-making teams. In *Proceedings of the 11th Conf. on Artificial Intelligence in Medicine (AIME 07)*, Amsterdam, The Netherlands, 2007.
6. Mullen T., Avasarala V., and Hall D. Customer-driven sensor management. In *IEEE Intelligent Systems*, volume 21, pages 41–49, 2006.
7. Sandholm T., S. Suri S., Gilpin A., and Levine D. Cabob: A fast optimal algorithm for winner determination in combinatorial auctions. In *Management Science, Special issue on Electronic Markets*, volume 51(3), pages 374–390, 2005.
8. Avasarala V., Polavarapu H., and Mullen T. An approximate algorithm for resource allocation using combinatorial auctions. In *Proceedings of IEEE/WIC/ACM international Conference on Intelligent Agent Technology*, page 571, Washington, DC, USA, 2006.
9. Fan X., Sun B., Sun S., McNeese M., Yen J., Jones R., Hanratty T., and Allender L. Rpd-enabled agents teaming with humans for multi-context decision making. In *AAMAS'06*, pages 34–41, Japan, 2006.
10. Fan X. and Yen J. R-cast: Integrating team intelligence for human-centered teamwork. In *Proceedings of Twenty-Second AAAI Conference on Artificial Intelligence*, pages 1535–1541, 2007.
11. Fan X., Yen J., and Volz R. A theoretical framework on proactive information exchange in agent teamwork. In *AI Journal*, volume 169(1), pages 23–97, 2005.
12. Fan X., Sun S., McNeese M., and Yen J. xtending recognition-primed decision model for human-agent collaboration. In *AAMAS'05*, pages 945–952, The Netherlands, 2005.

Chapter 4
Uncertainty and Risk Management in Cyber Situational Awareness

Jason Li, Xinming Ou, and Raj Rajagopalan

Abstract Handling cyber threats unavoidably needs to deal with both uncertain and imprecise information. What we can observe as potential malicious activities can seldom give us 100% confidence on important questions we care about, *e.g.* what machines are compromised and what damage has been incurred. In security planning, we need information on how likely a vulnerability can lead to a successful compromise to better balance security and functionality, performance, and ease of use. These information are at best qualitative and are often vague and imprecise. In cyber situational awareness, we have to rely on such imperfect information to detect real attacks and to prevent an attack from happening through appropriate risk management. This chapter surveys existing technologies in handling uncertainty and risk management in cyber situational awareness.

4.1 Reasoning about Uncertainty is a Necessity

In the physical world it is commonplace that one must deal with uncertainty when security is concerned. For example, law enforcement agencies do not (and cannot) know every aspect of every individual citizen's life. But when a crime is committed there are effective investigative methods to capture the perpetrators. As a result we are not living in havoc where crimes are committed everywhere. Like the law enforcement agencies, cyber defenders also have to deal with a great deal of uncertainty, the degree of which is compounded by the nature of computing. For example, it is impossible for a system administrator to know what is going on within every computer inside an enterprise network. Even when every activity on every device can be logged, there is currently no effective way to process the logs due to their vagueness as attack indicators as well as the sheer volume of them. For example, a log showing SSH log in from an external IP address could be from a legitimate user, or from an adversary who has stolen a valid user credential. An HTTP packet overflowing a buffer in the web service could be due to an application error or an attempt to gain privilege on the server. Cyber defenders do not know who the attackers are nor where they are. Even with the help of intrusion detection systems (IDS), the large number of false positives brings significant uncertainty to the true interpretation of IDS alerts. And there are still false negatives where some attacks will not be reported by any IDS sensor. There are plenty of zero-day

Jason Li, Intelligent Automation, Inc. · Xinming Ou, Kansas State University · Raj Rajagopalan, HP Labs

S. Jajodia et al., (eds.), *Cyber Situational Awareness*,
Advances in Information Security 46, DOI 10.1007/978-1-4419-0140-8_4,

vulnerabilities[1] in application software and there is no way to know for sure which software can be exploited by an attacker. With the large number of personal computers, laptops connected from home, and various emerging digital devices becoming part of enterprise networks, system administrators can no longer have a static picture of the network topology nor the precise configuration of every device in the network. The bottom line is, it is not possible for cyber defenders to be completely "certain" or "accurate" about all security-relevant information, yet they need to make decisions in the security management process, which is largely manual and ad-hoc these days. Unlike crimes in the physical world, automation has enabled cyber crimes to be conducted at a much higher speed and volume; without significant automation on the defense side we would not be able to effectively stem the threats.

The uncertainty challenge exists in all three phases of cyber situation awareness: prior security risk management, real-time intrusion detection, and posterior forensics analysis. The nature of uncertainty in these three aspects are slightly different. In risk management what we are uncertain about is the likelihood that a vulnerability exists in a piece of software, the chances that a vulnerability can be exploited successfully, the possibility that a user may succumb to social engineering, and so on. This type of uncertainty is in some sense "static" and reflects various kinds of risks inherent in a system. We call it the *static uncertainty*. The uncertainty in real-time situation awareness mostly arises from the invisibility of attackers in cyber space — it is hard to know where the attackers are and what choices he(she) has made in carrying out the attack. As a result all the IDS sensors can only capture the symptomatic phenomena caused by attacks but cannot positively ascertain whether an attack has happened and succeeded. The same problem exists for forensics analysis, with added difficulty caused by the gigantic amount of data but also more processing time available compared with the intrusion detection problem. We use the term "intrusion analysis" to encompass both the problem of intrusion detection and forensics analysis. We call the type of uncertainty found in intrusion analysis the *dynamic uncertainty*, since they are mostly related to dynamic events. We will focus our discussion on the dynamic uncertainty but will also briefly address the static uncertainty.

4.2 Two Approaches to Handling Dynamic Uncertainty

The challenge in handling dynamic uncertainty is how to start from imprecise and limited knowledge about attack possibilities, and quickly sift through large amounts of log information to identify a small set of data that altogether makes the picture of attacks clear. In doing so, the uncertainty about the system's security will be drastically reduced. For example, in many network intrusions, a small number of system logs are often sufficient to show that an attack has certainly happened, as well as how it progressed. The difficulty is how to start from uncertain views of the potential problem (*e.g., IDS alerts*) and quickly search for a few log entries from Terabytes of them so that the attacker's trace is clearly shown. System administrators are highly time-constrained. An automatic tool that can sift through the ocean of uncertainty to quickly and accurately locate the problem areas will be highly valuable in practice.

4.2.1 The logical approach

It has long been recognized that logical relations in computer attack conditions are important to consider in security analysis [5, 12, 52]. Modeling of such relations have yielded various ap-

---

[1] A zero-day vulnerability is one that has not been reported publicly but known by the underground hackers.

proaches to vulnerability analysis [3, 7, 10, 13, 18, 19, 25, 27, 36, 38, 39, 44, 45, 50, 51, 53] and IDS alert correlation [7, 9, 33, 35, 37, 54]. They have all adopted a somewhat deterministic logic in modeling: if the pre-condition of an attack is true, the post-condition is true. While these types of logical relations are important, they cannot account for the uncertainty in cyber security analysis. For example, an abnormal high network traffic is often an alert to system administrators on potential security problems. How can we model this in a deterministic logic? Does the observation reflect an attack activity? What is its pre- and post-conditions? It is hard to give definite answers to these questions because many events (both attack and non-attack activities) could cause a high network traffic. Another example is zero-day vulnerabilities, which have enabled a large number of intrusions into enterprise networks. One cannot make a deterministic judgment on whether a piece of software contains a zero-day vulnerability, but has to consider this possibility in security defense.

4.2.2 The statistical approach

A natural approach to handling uncertainty is to use statistical models, and there have been numerous attempts of this in the past [4, 11, 17]. However, there is a fundamental limitation in solving the uncertainty problems in cybersecurity using statistical models *alone*. Attackers do not play by rules. They adapt and do not typically follow a statistical pattern, as demonstrated by various forms of evading techniques [14, 15]. Thus, it is unlikely that statistical models alone can provide high-confidence conclusion on observed security events. Nevertheless, many such events have a statistical nature. A high network traffic deviating from the statistical norm gives a valuable hint on potential problems, and the confidence level on the true causes of such alerts can be statistically described as false positives and false negatives. It is important to account for the statistical differences in various assertions' confidence level. For example, compared with the anomalous high network traffic, a netflow filter that shows communication with known BotNet controllers is a more confident assertion on attacker activity. A simple and effective model for such statistical differences on assertion confidence will help in tackling the uncertainty problem.

To summarize, both deterministic logics and statistical models are valuable tools in cyber defense, but neither alone is sufficient to tackle the uncertainty challenge. Combining the two, however, will likely yield a reasoning method much more powerful than their sum. A reasoning framework that accounts for *both* logical relations *and* confidence differences among the various assertions will be the key in handling uncertainty in cybersecurity. How to design such a framework and apply it in security analysis is still an open problem. In the next two sections we will illustrate two recent attempts at achieving this "marriage" between logical causality and uncertainty. Section 4.3 describes an approach through statistical graphical model (Bayesian Network) derived from attack graphs [24]; Section 4.4 describes a variant of modal logic empirically developed from studying real intrusion incidents [40, 41].

4.3 From Attack Graphs to Bayesian Networks

To carry out enterprise security analysis, attack graphs have become the main-stream approach [3, 18–20, 26, 38, 50, 51, 53]. An attack graph illustrates all possible multi-stage attacks in an enterprise network, typically by presenting the logical causality relations among multiple privileges and configuration settings. Such logical relations are *deterministic*: the bad things will certainly happen in their worst forms as long as all the prerequisites are satisfied, and no bad things will happen if such conditions do not hold. While it is important to understand such logical relations, the deterministic nature has limited their use in practical network defense, especially when uncertainty has to been dealt with such as in intrusion detection and response.

4.3.1 A case study

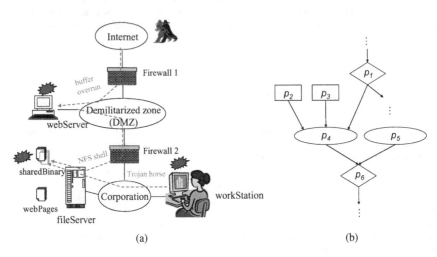

(a)   (b)

Fig. 4.1 An example attack scenario and attack graph.

Let us look at an example as shown in Figure 4.1, which is based on a real intrusion [38]. Suppose the following potential attack paths are discovered after analyzing the configuration. An attacker first compromises `webServer` by remotely exploiting vulnerability `CVE-2002-0392` to get local access on the server. Since `webServer` is allowed to access `fileServer` through the NFS protocol, he can then try to modify data on the file server. There are two ways to achieve this. If there are vulnerabilities in the NFS service daemons, he can try to exploit them and get local access on the machine; or if the NFS export table is not set up appropriately, he can modify files on the server through the NFS protocol by using programs like NFS Shell[2]. Once he can modify files on the file server, the attacker can install a Trojan-horse program in the executable binaries on `fileServer` that is mounted by machine `workStation`. The attacker can now wait for an innocent user on `workStation` to execute it and obtain control on the machine. Portion of the attack graph corresponding to the above scenario is shown in Figure 4.1 (b).

The node p_4 and its parents p_1, p_2, p_3 express the causality relation in the NFS Shell attack: if an attacker compromises the web server (p_1), the web server can access the file server through the NFS protocol (p_2), and the file server exports a partition to the web server (p_3), then the attacker will be able to launch an NFS Shell attack to access files on the file server (p_4). Suppose we want to use this piece of information in real-time security analysis. When we suspect the web server has been compromised, with how much confidence can we say that the files on the file server have been compromised? The answer is far less certain than the deterministic logic of the attack graph. How can we know whether the attacker has chosen to launch this attack? Even if he did so, how can we

---

[2]   A   program   that   provides   user-level   access   to   an   NFS   server (ftp://ftp.cs.vu.nl/pub/leendert/nfsshell.tar.gz)

know the attack has succeeded? Moreover, how can we account for the real-time observations that may be relevant to the question. For example, a file system integrity checker such as Tripwire [22] may report that certain files have been modified during the period. How shall we update our belief about possible attacks given this observation?

The problem of intrusion analysis is a far more imprecise process than deterministic reasoning. We do not know the attacker's choices thus there is the uncertainty from unknown attacker motivation and behaviors. Cyber attacks are not always 100% guaranteed to succeed thus there is the uncertainty from the imperfect nature of exploits. The defender's observations on potential attack activities are limited and as a result we have the uncertainty from false positives and false negatives of IDS sensors. Nevertheless, the logical causality encoded in a deterministic attack graph is invaluable to understand real-time security events, and will be useful for building practical network defense tools if we can *appropriately* account for the uncertainty inherent in the reasoning process.

4.3.2 Desired properties of Bayesian Networks in Intrusion Analysis

Recent years have seen a number of attempts at using Bayesian Networks to model such uncertainty in security analysis [2, 24, 32, 58]. Bayesian Network (BN) [43] marries the logical structure represented as a directed acyclic graph (DAG) and the uncertain nature of reasoning encoded as the conditional probability table (CPT) associated with every node in the graph. Using a BN model, one can query for questions like "*how likely a machine has been compromised given the current evidence*", "*based on the current observation, what is likely to happen next and what shall I do to prevent it from happening*", and "*which sensors shall be further investigated to confirm/rule out attacks*". This could yield powerful tools for real-time security analysis **if a BN model can be built that reflects reality**. Two key parts in building a BN are: 1) the graph structure and 2) the CPT parameters. Since attack graphs already provide a graphical model that reflects logical causality, it is natural to base the BN structure on the attack graph. How to obtain the CPT parameters has remained a difficult task. We believe the following are desirable properties of a BN model for cyber security analysis:

1. The graphical structure shall modularize and separate various types of uncertainty and avoid mingling different types of uncertainty in the same CPT.
2. The majority of CPT parameters shall be computed automatically from well-defined and realistic data sources.
3. The BN model shall not be too sensitive to perturbation on the CPT parameters.

Cyber security analysis, unlike other more well-behaved problem domains, does not naturally lend itself to statistical analysis. We do not have the ground truths in real traces from which we can learn the large number of CPT parameters, and the attackers are constantly adapting. As a result the CPT parameters need to be produced from often vague and subjective judgments. It is infeasible to ask a human user to assign every CPT parameter for every BN. The vast majority of these numbers need to be computed automatically from various data sources that reflect the various types of uncertainty in cyber security. A BN model that modularizes and separates the various types of uncertainty will make this process easier. Since those numbers are imprecise in nature, the result of BN analysis shall not be too sensitive to CPT parameters.

4.3.3 Building BN's from attack graphs

A Bayesian Network (BN) is a graphical representation of cause-and-effect relationships within a problem domain. More formally, a Bayesian network is a Directed Acyclic Graph (DAG) in which: the nodes represent variables of interest (propositions); the set of directed links represent the causal influence among the variables; the strength of an influence is represented by conditional probability tables (CPT). For example, if we imagine the graph structure in Figure 4.1 (b) is a Bayesian network, the node p_4 could have the following CPT associated with it.

p_1 p_2 p_3	p_4
T T T	0.8
otherwise	0

If all of p_4's parents are true, the probability of p_4 being true is 0.8. In all other cases the probability is 0 (p_4 is false). For any node in the DAG, given its parents, that node is conditionally independent of any other node that is not its descendent. This conditional independence makes a Bayesian network model a compact representation of the joint probability distribution over the interested variables. Bayesian networks can also serve as the inference engine, and can compute efficiently any queries over the variables modeled therein [43].

The semantics of BN's graph structure corresponds to that of an attack graph, especially a type of attack graphs called "logical attack graph" [38, 46] where each vertex is associated with a proposition and the arcs represent the logical causality relations between the vertices. We give the meaning of the propositions in the example of Figure 4.1.

p_1 : execCode(webServer,apache)
p_2 : reachable(webServer,fileServer, nfsProtocol,nfsPort)
p_3 : nfsExportInfo(fileServer,/export, write,webServer)
p_4 : nfsShellAttackAccomplished(fileServer, /export, write)
p_5 : localFileAccessAcomplished(fileServer, /export, write)
p_6 : accessFile(fileServer,write,/export)

The vertices are divided into three types. The square vertices are the ones that do not have any parent (*e.g.* p_2, p_3). They typically represent the input to the attack-graph generator — network reachability, configuration settings, potential vulnerabilities in software applications, security advisories, and so on. The diamond vertices represent privileges an attacker could obtain, such as user apache's privilege on the web server (p_1) and file modification privilege on the file server (p_6). Since there may be more than one way to obtain a privilege, the incoming arcs to a diamond vertex form a logical OR relation. For example, p_6 can be enabled by either p_4 or p_5. Thus, we call those vertices "OR node". The elliptic vertices, on the other hand, represent the logical AND relations and are called "AND node". Many attacks can only be accomplished when multiple preconditions are met, and the AND nodes capture this semantics. In the example, the attack p_4 can be accomplished only when all its three parents are true, and hence it is an AND node. Such OR and AND semantics can be easily encoded in the CPT's of a Bayesian network, which subsumes the deterministic logical relations. Thus there is no need to distinguish the AND/OR node types when we convert the attack graph to a BN.

If we want to construct a Bayesian Network from an attack graph for real-time security analysis, can we simply use the unmodified graph structure and attach CPT's to all the nodes to capture the uncertainty in reasoning? The answer is no. For example, we know that due to the uncertainty from attacker choice, p_4 may not become true after all of p_1, p_2, and p_3 are true simply because the attacker did not choose to launch the attack. To model this uncertainty under this unmodified graph structure, we would have to use the CPT associated with node p_4. However, there may be other reasons why p_4 does not become true after all its parents are true — for example, the attacker may have chosen to launch the attack but the attack failed due to the difficulty nature of the exploit. Such uncertainty arising from the inherent nature of a vulnerability will have to be encoded in the same CPT associated with p_4. Thus the CPT number 0.8 will have a number of contributing factors in it, which makes the generation and maintenance of the CPT parameters a difficult task.

For example, when we see the same attack activity in other parts of the network, we may want to increase the likelihood that an attacker may choose to use this attack. But in the unmodified graph structure there is no easy way to separate this attacker-choice uncertainty from the other factors in the CPT number of 0.8. As a result this type of correlation cannot be conducted elegantly. In this case the BN structure does not modularize various types of uncertainty into separate CPT's, and it violates principal 1 introduced in Section 4.3.2. This is just one example problem we have discovered in the current literature on building BN's from attack graphs for security analysis. We believe a more disciplined BN construction methodology needs to be studied to better capture the uncertainty in cyber security.

In summary, Bayesian Network provides a promising approach to handle uncertainty in cyber situational awareness. But key challenges still remain as to how to build/maintain the BN model efficiently. This is still a rapidly evolving field and interested readers are encouraged to consult the relevant literature cited in this chapter.

4.4 An Empirical Approach to Developing a Logic for Uncertainty in Situation Awareness

While statistical graphical models like Bayesian Network are theoretically rigorous and proven effective in other areas of research, when it comes to intrusion analysis they have an un-addressed gap, namely how to set statistical parameters in terms of hard probability distributions. For security analysis, it is nearly impossible to obtain the ground truth in real traces and it is hard if not impossible to realistically simulate attack scenarios. Similarly, while it would be ideal to characterize intrusion analysis tools in terms of hard metrics such as alarm compression ratio combined with true and false positive ratios (see [54] for definitions and other metrics), it is impossible to calibrate tools without representative data with known ground truth. At the same time, the fact that human system administrators have been using manual analysis and low-level tools to detect attacks in logs and real-time alerts inspires us to formulate a logic, *in an empirical manner*, that approximates human reasoning that works with a qualitative assessment on a few confidence levels that are relatively easy to understand. We acknowledge that this formulation not only hides the lack of knowledge of base probabilities but also reflects the great deal of ambiguity that exists in intrusion analysis of real data. We hope that by creating an option to specify the confidence level explicitly and by providing general practical tools to manipulate these uncertain pieces of knowledge, we can bypass some of these fundamental problems and gain experience that may make some statistical approaches viable in the future.

4.4.1 A case study

We first show a case study we conducted by interviewing a system administrator for a university campus network. He told us about how he identified compromised machines on the campus network during a security incident, which was due to a zero-day vulnerability in the TrendMicro anti-malware service. All the reasoning and correlation was done manually but was very effective. We then identify the rationale behind the decisions he made at various points, and design a logic that captures this reasoning process. The logic is capable of handling uncertainty which is crucial for real-time security analysis, since the observations are often vague and limited, and we do not know where the attacker is and what choices he made in an attack.

4.4.1.1 Scenario description

The scenario is illustrated in Figure 4.2(1), and described below. System Administrator (SA) noticed an abnormal increase in campus-network traffic (*Observation 1*). SA took the netflow dump for that time period and ran a packet capture tool on it to search for known malicious IP addresses, and identified that four Trend Micro servers initiated IRC connection to some known BotNet controllers (*Observation 2*). SA hence determined that the four TrendMicro servers likely had been compromised. He sat down at one of them and dumped the memory, from which he found what appeared to be malicious code (*Observation 3*). He also looked up for all the open TCP socket connections and noticed that the server had been connecting to some other Trend Micro servers on campus through the IRC channel (*Observation 4*). He hence determined that those servers were also compromised. He did the same thing for the other identified servers and found more compromised servers. Altogether he identified 12 compromised machines and took them off line.

We observe that all the alerts above contain some amount of uncertainty regarding their implication. Observation 1 could just mean some users started downloading movies through BitTorrent. Observation 2 has a higher degree of likelihood that the identified servers are compromised, but simply an IRC connection to a known BotNet controller does not necessarily mean the machine has been compromised. For example, it could be that some system admin was probing BotNet controllers for research purposes. (The interviewed system administrator actually does this himself.) Observation 3 is also a strong indication that the machine has been controlled by an attacker. But it is not always easy to determine whether a suspicious module found in the memory dump is indeed malicious, especially with zero-day vulnerabilities as in this case. So this alert also contains some amount of false positive. Observation 4, like observation 2, cannot directly prove that the machines observed are under the control of attackers. However, when we put all the four pieces of evidence together, it becomes clear that an attack has certainly happened and succeeded, and we can tell with almost certainty which machines have been compromised. We observe two key components in human reasoning on uncertain information: 1) from the current beliefs based on the current observation, use logical reasoning to determine what additional observation could help to "strengthen" the beliefs' confidence; 2) from a large number of possibilities, derive a high-confidence belief corroborated by a number of complementary evidences logically linked together. For example, even though the SA was not sure whether the abnormal high traffic really indicated an attack, he knew that this observation is logically linked to network activity, which can also be observed by netflow dump. When from the netflow dump the TrendMicro servers were shown to communicate with malicious IP addresses, and from the memory dump a potentially malicious code module was found, the two pieces of evidence both indicated that the server was likely compromised, thus strengthening the belief's confidence to almost certain.

4.4.2 Encoding the case study in logic

Figure 4.2(2) presents a high-level view of the reasoning framework. The framework consists of two layers: observations and an internal reasoning model, both with uncertainty. The observations are from system monitoring data such as IDS alerts, netflow dumps, syslog, *etc.* They are mapped into the internal reasoning model as conditions representing unobservable security status under interest. For example, `abnormal high traffic` is an observation, and `an attacker is performing some network activity` is an internal condition. Logical relations exist between observations and internal conditions with varying degrees of certainty. For example, we can say `abnormal high traffic indicates the possibility that an attacker is performing some network activity`. Another example: `netflow dump showing a host communicating with known BotNet controllers indicates that an attacker likely has compromised the host`. Likewise, there are logical relations among the various internal conditions and these relations contain

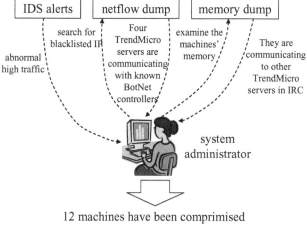

12 machines have been comprimised

(1) Case scenario

Observations with uncertainty

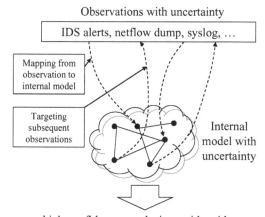

high-confidence conclusions with evidence

(2) Vision of applying a logic with uncertainty to real-time security analysis

Fig. 4.2 Case study and vision for automated situation awareness

varying degrees of certainty as well. For example, one can say after an attacker compromised a machine, he may possibly perform some network activity from the machine, and after an attacker sends an exploit to a machine, he will likely compromise the machine. These statements capture the rationale behind human reasoning when manually detecting intrusions from the logs. The internal model is analogous to a human brain — observations are reflected into a human's thinking as beliefs with varying strengths, and the beliefs are related to one another with varying strengths as well. We design logical rules to capture both aspects and a formalized reasoning process to simulate human's thinking such that 1) we can target observations to a small subset of all possible data through hints provided by the internal reasoning process; 2) we can sift through the uncertain observations and internal conditions to reach high-confidence beliefs for situation awareness.

4.4.2.1 Notations

There are two types of facts in our logic: those for observations and those for internal conditions. We use $obs(F)$ to denote a fact about observations, and $int(F)$ to denote a fact about internal conditions. For example, $obs(netflowBlackListFilter(172.16.9.20, 129.7.10.5))$ is an observation from the netflow blacklist filter that machine 172.16.9.20 is communicating with a known malicious IP address 129.7.10.5, and $int(compromised(172.16.9.20))$ is an internal condition that machine 172.16.9.20 has been compromised. We use three modality operators p, l, c, standing for "possible, likely, certain" to express different confidence levels. p represents low confidence, l represents high confidence, and c is the almost certainty which is the goal of situation awareness. The logic formulation consists of two parts: *observation correspondence* which maps observations to internal conditions, and *internal model* that captures logical relations among internal conditions. The two parts for this example are shown in Figure 4.3 and 4.4 respectively.

$$A_1 : obs(anomalyHighTraffic) \xmapsto{p} int(attackerNetActivity)$$
$$A_2 : obs(netflowBlackListFilter(H, BlackListedIP)) \xmapsto{l} int(attackerNetActivity)$$
$$A_3 : obs(netflowBlackListFilter(H, BlackListedIP)) \xmapsto{l} int(compromised(H))$$
$$A_4 : obs(memoryDumpMaliciousCode(H)) \xmapsto{l} int(compromised(H))$$
$$A_5 : obs(memoryDumpIRCSocket(H_1, H_2)) \xmapsto{p} int(exchangeCtlMessage(H_1, H_2))$$

Fig. 4.3 Observation correspondence

4.4.2.2 Observation correspondence

Observation correspondence gives a "meaning" to an observation, in the form of internal conditions. For example, in A_1 an abnormal high network traffic (*anomalyHighTraffic*) is mapped to $int(attackerNetActivity)$, meaning an attacker is performing some network activity. This is a low-confidence judgment thus the modality operator is p. Intuitively the p mode means there is other equally possible interpretations for the same observation. Rule A_2 and A_3 give the meaning to an alert identified in a netflow analysis. There are a number of filtering tools available that can search for potential malicious patterns in a netflow dump, such as "capture daemon" and "flow-nfilter". This rule deals with one filter that identifies communication with known malicious IP addresses. Since any such activity is a strong indication of attacker activity and the fact that the machine involved has been compromised, the modality of the two rules is l. There are still other possibilities, *e.g.*, the communication could be issued by a legitimate user who wants to find out something about the malicious IP address. But the likelihood of that is significantly lower than what is represented by the righthand side of the two rules. Rule A_4 says if memory dump on machine H identifies malicious code, then H is likely to be compromised. Rule A_5 says that if the memory dump identifies open IRC sockets between machine H_1 and H_2, then it is possible that the IRC channel is used to exchange control messages between BotNet machines.

We present these observation correspondence rules not to expect everyone would agree on them. For example, some reader may think the modality of rule A_4 shall be c. This is completely OK. One advantage of such a logic is that it facilitates discussion and sharing of security knowledge. Empirical experiences from a large community can help tune the modality parameters in those rules. We envision a rule repository model like that for Snort[3], where a community of participants contribute and agree upon a set of rules in an open language. Currently there are only coarse-grained classification and some natural-language explanations for the meanings behind each Snort alert. The logic language can be used by the Snort rule writers to develop a number of internal-model predicates so that the observation correspondence rules provide meanings to the various IDS alerts, which can then be reasoned about automatically.

$$I_1 : int(compromised(H_1)) \xrightarrow{pc} int(sendExploit(H_1,H_2))$$
$$I_2 : int(sendExploit(H_1,H_2)) \xrightarrow{lp} int(compromised(H_2))$$
$$I_3 : int(compromised(H_1)), int(compromised(H_2)) \xrightarrow{pc} int(exchangeCtlMessage(H_1,H_2))$$

Fig. 4.4 Internal model

4.4.2.3 Internal model

The $\xrightarrow{m_1 m_2}$ operator in the internal model represents the "leads to" relationship between internal conditions, and as a result the arrow must be aligned with time: since the righthand side is caused by the lefthand side, it must happen no earlier than the lefthand side. However, the *reasoning* can go along both directions, and hence two modality operators (m_1, m_2) are associated with each rule. For example, rule I_1 says "if an attacker has compromised machine H_1, he can send an exploit from H_1 to another machine H_2." The forward reasoning has a low certainty: the attacker may or may not choose to send an exploit after compromising a machine. Thus the forward reasoning is qualified by the p modality. Reasoning on the reverse direction however has the c modality: if an attacker sends an exploit from one machine to another, he shall have already compromised the first machine. In rule I_2, the fact that an attacker sends an exploit to a machine leads to the compromise of the machine. The forward reasoning is also not certain, since the exploit may fail to execute on the target host. We have used the confidence level l — attackers typically make sure their exploit will likely work before using it in an attack. On the other direction, sending in a remote exploit is just one of many possible ways to compromise a host. Thus the reverse reasoning for I_2 has the p modality. I_3 is the only rule in this model that has two facts on the lefthand side. Like in typical logic-programming languages, the comma represents the AND logical relation. The forward direction has the p modality: if an attacker compromised two machines H_1, H_2, the two machines can possibly exchange BotNet control messages between them to coordinate further attacks. The backward direction has the c modality: if two machines are exchanging BotNet control messages, both of them must have been compromised.

The above logical formulation is encoded in Prolog and a preliminary deduction system is implemented to simulate the "confidence strengthening" process in human reasoning. The key deduction rule for this is shown below.

$$\frac{int(F,l) \Leftarrow Pf_1 \quad int(F,l) \Leftarrow Pf_2 \quad Pf_1 \parallel Pf_2}{int(F,c) \Leftarrow strengthenedPf(Pf_1,Pf_2)}$$

We use $int(F,m) \Leftarrow Pf$ to indicate the internal fact F is true with modality m, and Pf is the proof which shows the derivation steps in the logic arriving at the conclusion. The $\parallel$ relation indicates two proofs are *independent*, which is defined as sharing no common observations and internal

---

[3] A widely used network intrusion detection system: http://www.snort.org/

facts. This deduction rule states that if we have two disjoint reasoning traces to reach a fact with confidence level l, then the fact's confidence level can be boosted to c. The application of this simple reasoning engine has already shown interesting results [41].

This is just the first small step towards achieving the vision presented in Figure 4.2. There are still great challenges ahead and significant research efforts are needed to tackle these challenges. Detailed technical description of the approach can be found in some recent manuscripts [40, 41].

4.4.3 Comparison with previous approaches

There have been numerous approaches to intrusion alerts correlation proposed in the past [7, 9, 33, 35, 37, 54]. They provide important insights into logical causality relations in IDS alerts, but fall short of a systematic solution to the real-time security analysis problem due to: 1) the lack of capabilities for representing varying degrees of uncertainty in assertions derived from system monitoring data and using these uncertain judgments to reach (almost) certain conclusions, and 2) the lack of a unified framework capable of handling *any* security-relevant information — not just IDS alerts.

The confidence level about "true" system conditions derived from an observation varies depending on the nature of the observation. A key challenge in situation awareness is how to sift through the ocean of uncertain observation and reach a conclusion with high confidence. To this end it is necessary to distinguish the different confidence levels in the reasoning process. Zhai *et al.* [58] uses Bayesian networks to correlate complementary intrusion evidence from both IDS alerts and system monitoring logs so that highly confident traces can be distinguished from less confident ones. However, one big question in such statistical models is how to obtain the numerical parameters, such as the conditional probability tables (CPT) associated with every node in a BN which may affect the analysis result. The paper presented a formulation for computing the CPT entries but it is far from clear how the computation can be justified theoretically or validated empirically. In comparison, the approach discussed above represents the various certainty levels qualitatively as modality operators, and the uncertainty levels are directly integrated into the reasoning process. As a result the reasoning system will have more leverage on utilizing the varying degrees of uncertainty to make better decisions.

Another drawback of the previous approaches is that the reasoning models often center around IDS alerts with pre- and postconditions. This will limit the model's capability to reason about a larger variety of system monitoring data. As illustrated in our case study, in some intrusions IDS alerts only play the role of triggering investigation. Sometimes there is no IDS alert at all either because there are no IDS devices deployed or the IDS devices missed the attack completely. Yet the system administrator was still able to trace to the compromised machines. Moreover, in our case study we found it very difficult to come up with a pre- and postcondition model for every possible observation. For example, what shall be the pre- and postconditions for an abnormal high network traffic? There are too many possibilities and a single pre- and postcondition won't be sufficient. Centering the reasoning model around IDS alerts with pre- and postconditions will likely become inflexible when more types of system monitoring information need to be included in the reasoning process. In comparison, the observation correspondence model in our logic gives a meaning to *any* observation (not just IDS alert). This model is more direct: it gives an observation a meaning about itself, instead of a meaning in terms of other conditions that can be logically linked to it. Another general model for incorporating all possible types of data in security analysis is M2D2 [33]. Compared with M2D2, our model is much more simple. For example, we do not classify information into various categories with mathematical notations such as functions and relations. Rather, everything in our model is just a simple "statement" — one that can be easily translated into natural language. Such simplicity in modeling has shown the advantage in incorporating a large variety of security-relevant information. Also M2D2 is not able to represent the varying degrees of uncertainty levels useful for security analysis. Given the complexity of cyber attacks and the large number of system monitoring tools, it is important to have a simple logic that can encode all possible types of security relevant information and capture the uncertain nature of such data's meanings in security analysis.

The limitation of statistical models has been discussed before. Instead of directly applying these existing models, we propose to start from the bottom and design a logic that approximates human reasoning. Unlike quantitative probabilities, the qualitative assessment on confidence levels such as "possible", "likely", and "certain" are relatively easy to be understood and used by human experts. As the first step we design a logic with *modality operators*[4] that capture the various qualitative confidence levels in reasoning about situation awareness. It is possible that this logic derived from empirical study can be refined and re-formalized in some existing statistical models described above, the well-studied theories on modal logic [23], or a combination of both. Another advantage of the logical approach is that the justification for a conclusion can be generated in the form of logical proofs. This makes it clear what conditions are used and what assumptions are made in reaching the conclusion. How to produce such justification is far less obvious in statistical models.

4.5 Static Uncertainty and Risk Management

Another important aspect of uncertainty in cyber situation awareness is the static uncertainty or the inherent risk in a system. Analysis and management of such risks is especially crucial to make sensible decisions in security investment. This has become a critical challenge in security management since enterprise networks have become essential to the operation of companies, laboratories, universities, and government agencies. As they continue to grow both in size and complexity, vulnerabilities are regularly discovered in software applications which are exploited to stage cyber attacks. Currently, management of security risk of an enterprise network is an art and not a science. There is no objective way to measure the security of an enterprise network. As a result it is difficult to answer such questions as "are we more secure than yesterday", or "how should we invest our limited resources to improve security", or "how does this vulnerability impact the overall security of my system". By increasing security spending an organization can decrease the risk associated with security breaches. However, to do this tradeoff analysis there is a need for quantitative models of security instead of the current qualitative models.

The issue of security metrics has long attracted much attention [21, 29, 30], and recent years have seen significant effort on the development of quantitative security metrics [1, 6, 8, 28, 34, 42, 47]. However, we are yet to establish metrics that can objectively quantify security risk. Part of the reason is that the treatment on many aspects of security still stays at the deterministic level. For example, resistance to attacks is often regarded as binary: an attack is either impossible or trivial. This is remote from realistic security management, where one has to admit the varying degrees of exploit difficulty levels to distinguish more imminent threats from less ones.

4.5.1 CVSS metrics

The Common Vulnerability Scoring System (CVSS) [31, 49] provides an open framework for communicating the characteristics and impacts of IT vulnerabilities. CVSS consists of three metric groups: Base, Temporal and Environmental. Each of this group produces a vector of compressed textual representation that reflects various properties of the vulnerability (*metric vector*). A formula takes the vector and produces a numeric score in the range of 0 to 10 indicating the severity of the vulnerability. The most important contribution of CVSS is the metric vector: it provides a wide

---

[4] Similar to the modality operators in modal logic [23].

range of vulnerability properties that are the basis for deriving the numerical scores. We use the term "CVSS metrics" to denote the metric vectors and the term "CVSS scores" to denote the numerical scores. Any CVSS score must be published along with the CVSS metrics. The CVSS metrics convey much richer information than the numerical scores and are closer to measurable properties of a vulnerability.

AC metric	Description
High	Specialized access conditions exist.
Medium	The access conditions are somewhat specialized.
Low	Specialized access conditions or extenuating circumstances do not exist.

(a) The CVSS Access Complexity Metric

E metric	Description
Unproven (U)	No exploit code is available, or an exploit is entirely theoretical.
Proof-of- Concept (POC)	Proof-of-concept exploit code or an attack demonstration that is not practical for most systems is available. The code or technique is not functional in all situations and may require substantial modification by a skilled attacker.
Functional (F)	Functional exploit code is available. The code works in most situations where the vulnerability exists.
High (H)	Either the vulnerability is exploitable by functional mobile autonomous code, or no exploit is required (manual trigger) and details are widely available. The code works in every situation, or is actively being delivered via a mobile autonomous agent (such as a worm or virus).

(b) The CVSS Exploitability Metric

Table 4.1 Example CVSS metrics

The Base group represents the intrinsic and fundamental characteristics of the vulnerability that are constant over time and user environments. The Temporal group represents the characteristics of vulnerability that change over time but not among user environments. The Environmental group represents the characteristics of a vulnerability that are relevant and unique to a particular user environment. Generally, the base and temporal metrics are specified by vulnerability bulletin analysts, security product vendors, or application vendors because they typically have better information about the characteristics of a vulnerability and the most up-to-date exploit technology than do users. The environmental metrics, however, are specified by users because they are best able to assess the potential impact of a vulnerability within their own environments. We observe that how a vulnerability may impact the security of an enterprise network can only be assessed when the security interactions among components of the network are taken into account. Since attack graphs capture security interactions within an enterprise network, it is possible that the Basic and Temporal metrics can be used in combination with attack graphs to compute a cumulative risk metric for an enterprise network.

As some examples, the *Access Complexity (AC)* metric in the Base group and the *Exploitability (E)* metric in the Temporal group are shown in Table 4.1. The AC metric gauges the complexity of exploiting a vulnerability based on whether special conditions, *e.g.* certain race conditions, are necessary to successfully exploit the vulnerability. A "High" AC metric indicates a vulnerability is inherently difficulty to exploit, and thus will likely have a low success likelihood. The E metric measures the current state of exploit techniques or code availability. Public availability of easy-to-use exploit code increases the number of potential attackers by including those who are unskilled, thereby increasing the vulnerability's overall success likelihood.

4.5.2 Combining CVSS and Attack Graphs

The main limitation of CVSS is that it provides scoring of individual vulnerabilities but it does not provide a sound methodology for aggregating the metrics for a set of vulnerabilities in a network to provide an overall network security score. For example, there can be a situation in which the individual vulnerability scores are low but they can be combined to compromise a critical resource. The overall security of a network configuration running multiple services cannot be determined by simply counting the number of vulnerabilities or adding up the CVSS scores. Attack graphs can be used to model causal relationship among vulnerabilities. Recent years have seen a number of attempts at calculating quantitative metrics by combining CVSS metrics on attack graphs [16, 48, 55–57]. We expect that these models can also be used to suggest configuration changes that mitigate the threats to an enterprise.

4.6 Conclusion

Both aspects of uncertainty: static uncertainty and dynamic uncertainty, are important in cyber situational awareness. We discussed two promising approaches to addressing the dynamic uncertainty challenge, and briefly introduced the CVSS metrics which can be used in combination with attack graphs to address the static uncertainty challenge for automated risk management. The research for systematically handling uncertainty and risk in cyber space is still in a preliminary stage. However, without addressing this problem in a scientific manner, it will be difficult to achieve sustainable cyber defense.

References

1. Ehab Al-Shaer, Latif Khan, and M. Salim Ahmed. A comprehensive objective network security metric framework for proactive security configuration. In *ACM Cyber Security and Information Intelligence Research Workshop*, 2008.
2. Magnus Almgren, Ulf Lindqvist, and Erland Jonsson. A multi-sensor model to improve automated attack detection. In *11th International Symposium on Recent Advances in Intrusion Detection (RAID 2008)*. RAID, September 2008.
3. Paul Ammann, Duminda Wijesekera, and Saket Kaushik. Scalable, graph-based network vulnerability analysis. In *Proceedings of 9th ACM Conference on Computer and Communications Security*, Washington, DC, November 2002.
4. Stefan Axelsson. A preliminary attempt to apply detection and estimation theory to intrusion detection. Technical report, Chalmers Univ. of Technology, 2000.
5. R. Baldwin. Rule based analysis of computer security. Technical Report TR-401, MIT LCS Lab, 1988.
6. Davide Balzarotti, Mattia Monga, and Sabrina Sicari. Assessing the risk of using vulnerable components. In *Proceedings of the 2nd ACM workshop on Quality of protection*, 2005.
7. Steven Cheung, Ulf Lindqvist, and Martin W Fong. Modeling multistep cyber attacks for scenario recognition. In *DARPA Information Survivability Conference and Exposition (DISCEX III)*, pages 284–292, Washington, D.C., 2003.
8. Elizabeth Chew, Marianne Swanson, Kevin Stine, Nadya Bartol, Anthony Brown, and Will Robinson. *Performance Measurement Guide for Information Security*. National Institute of Standards and Technology, July 2008. NIST Special Publication 800-55 Revision 1.
9. Frédéric Cuppens and Alexandre Miège. Alert correlation in a cooperative intrusion detection framework. In *IEEE Symposium on Security and Privacy*, 2002.

10. J. Dawkins and J. Hale. A systematic approach to multi-stage network attack analysis. In *Proceedings of Second IEEE International Information Assurance Workshop*, pages 48 – 56, April 2004.
11. Dorothy Denning. An intrusion-detection model. *IEEE Transactions on Software Engineering*, 13(2), 1987.
12. Daniel Farmer and Eugene H. Spafford. The COPS security checker system. Technical Report CSD-TR-993, Purdue University, September 1991.
13. William L. Fithen, Shawn V. Hernan, Paul F. O'Rourke, and David A. Shinberg. Formal modeling of vulnerabilities. *Bell Labs technical journal*, 8(4):173–186, 2004.
14. Prahlad Fogla and Wenke Lee. Evading network anomaly detection systems: Formal reasoning and practical techniques. In *Proceedings of The 13th ACM Conference on Computer and Communications Security (CCS 2006)*, Alexandria, VA, October 2006.
15. Prahlad Fogla, Monirul Sharif, Roberto Perdisci, Oleg Kolesnikov, and Wenke Lee. Polymorphic blending attacks. In *Proceedings of The 15th USENIX Security Symposium*, Vancouver, B.C., Canada, August 2006.
16. Marcel Frigault, Lingyu Wang, Anoop Singhal, and Sushil Jajodia. Measuring network security using dynamic bayesian network. In *Proceedings of the 4th ACM workshop on Quality of protection*, 2008.
17. Paul Helman and Gunar Liepins. Statistical foundations of audit trail analysis for the detection of computer misuse. *IEEE Transactions on Software Engineering*, 19(9), 1993.
18. Kyle Ingols, Richard Lippmann, and Keith Piwowarski. Practical attack graph generation for network defense. In *22nd Annual Computer Security Applications Conference (ACSAC)*, Miami Beach, Florida, December 2006.
19. Sushil Jajodia, Steven Noel, and Brian O'Berry. Topological analysis of network attack vulnerability. In V. Kumar, J. Srivastava, and A. Lazarevic, editors, *Managing Cyber Threats: Issues, Approaches and Challanges*, chapter 5. Kluwer Academic Publisher, 2003.
20. Somesh Jha, Oleg Sheyner, and Jeannette M. Wing. Two formal analyses of attack graphs. In *Proceedings of the 15th IEEE Computer Security Foundations Workshop*, pages 49–63, Nova Scotia, Canada, June 2002.
21. Daniel Geer Jr., Kevin Soo Hoo, and Andrew Jaquith. Information security: Why the future belongs to the quants. *IEEE SECURITY & PRIVACY*, 2003.
22. Gene H. Kim and Eugene H. Spafford. The design and implementation of tripwire: A file system integrity checker. In *Proceedings of the 2nd ACM Conference on Computer and Communications Security (CCS)*, 1994.
23. Kenneth Konyndyk. *Introductory Modal Logic*. University of Notre Dame Press, 1986.
24. Jason Li, Peng Liu, and Xinming Ou. Using Bayesian Networks for cyber security analysis. Manusrcipt, 2008.
25. Wei Li, Rayford B. Vaughn, and Yoginder S. Dandass. An approach to model network exploitations using exploitation graphs. *SIMULATION*, 82(8):523–541, 2006.
26. Richard Lippmann, Kyle Ingols, Chris Scott, Keith Piwowarski, Kendra Kratkiewicz, Mike Artz, and Robert Cunningham. Validating and restoring defense in depth using attack graphs. In *Military Communications Conference (MILCOM)*, Washington, DC, U.S.A., October 2006.
27. Richard Lippmann and Kyle W. Ingols. An annotated review of past papers on attack graphs. Technical report, MIT Lincoln Laboratory, March 2005.
28. Pratyusa Manadhata, Jeannette Wing, Mark Flynn, and Miles McQueen. Measuring the attack surfaces of two FTP daemons. In *Proceedings of the 2nd ACM workshop on Quality of protection*, 2006.
29. John McHugh. Quality of protection: measuring the unmeasurable? In *Proceedings of the 2nd ACM workshop on Quality of protection (QoP)*, Alexandria, Virginia, USA, 2006.
30. John McHugh and James Tippett, editors. *Workshop on Information-Security-System Rating and Ranking (WISSRR)*. Applied Computer Security Associates, May 2001.
31. Peter Mell, Karen Scarfone, and Sasha Romanosky. *A Complete Guide to the Common Vulnerability Scoring System Version 2.0*. Forum of Incident Response and Security Teams (FIRST), June 2007.

32. Gaspar Modelo-Howard, Saurabh Bagchi, and Guy Lebanon. Determining placement of intrusion detectors for a distributed application through bayesian network modeling. In *11th International Symposium on Recent Advances in Intrusion Detection (RAID 2008)*. RAID, September 2008.
33. Benjamin Morin, Hervé, and Mireille Ducassé. M2d2: A formal data model for ids alert correlation. In *5th International Symposium on Recent Advances in Intrusion Detection (RAID 2002)*, pages 115–137, 2002.
34. National Institute of Standards and Technology. *Technology assessment: Methods for measuring the level of computer security*, 1985. NIST Special Publication 500-133.
35. Peng Ning, Yun Cui, Douglas Reeves, and Dingbang Xu. Tools and techniques for analyzing intrusion alerts. *ACM Transactions on Information and System Security*, 7(2):273–318, May 2004.
36. Steven Noel, Sushil Jajodia, Brian O'Berry, and Michael Jacobs. Efficient minimum-cost network hardening via exploit dependency graphs. In *19th Annual Computer Security Applications Conference (ACSAC)*, December 2003.
37. Steven Noel, Eric Robertson, and Sushil Jajodia. Correlating intrusion events and building attack scenarios through attack graph distances. In *20th Annual Computer Security Applications Conference (ACSAC 2004)*, pages 350–359, 2004.
38. Xinming Ou, Wayne F. Boyer, and Miles A. McQueen. A scalable approach to attack graph generation. In *13th ACM Conference on Computer and Communications Security (CCS)*, pages 336–345, 2006.
39. Xinming Ou, Sudhakar Govindavajhala, and Andrew W. Appel. MulVAL: A logic-based network security analyzer. In *14th USENIX Security Symposium*, 2005.
40. Xinming Ou, Raj Rajagopalan, and Sakthiyuvaraja Sakthivelmurugan. A practical approach to modeling uncertainty in intrusion analysis. Technical report, Department of Computing and Information Sciences, Kansas State University, 2008.
41. Xinming Ou, S. Raj Rajagopalan, Abhishek Rakshit, and Sakthiyuvaraja Sakthivelmurugan. An empirical approach to modeling uncertainty in intrusion analysis. Under review, February 2009.
42. Joseph Pamula, Sushil Jajodia, Paul Ammann, and Vipin Swarup. A weakest-adversary security metric for network configuration security analysis. In *Proceedings of the 2nd ACM workshop on Quality of protection*, 2006.
43. Judea Pearl. *Probabilistic Reasoning in Intelligent Systems: Networks of Plausible Inference*. Morgan Kaufman, 1999.
44. Cynthia Phillips and Laura Painton Swiler. A graph-based system for network-vulnerability analysis. In *NSPW '98: Proceedings of the 1998 workshop on New security paradigms*, pages 71–79. ACM Press, 1998.
45. C. R. Ramakrishnan and R. Sekar. Model-based analysis of configuration vulnerabilities. *Journal of Computer Security*, 10(1-2):189–209, 2002.
46. Diptikalyan Saha. Extending logical attack graphs for efficient vulnerability analysis. In *Proceedings of the 15th ACM conference on Computer and Communications Security (CCS)*, 2008.
47. Mohamed Salim, Ehab Al-Shaer, and Latif Khan. A novel quantitative approach for measuring network security. In *INFOCOM 2008 Mini Conference*, 2008.
48. Reginald Sawilla and Xinming Ou. Identifying critical attack assets in dependency attack graphs. In *13th European Symposium on Research in Computer Security (ESORICS)*, Malaga, Spain, October 2008.
49. Mike Schiffman, Gerhard Eschelbeck, David Ahmad, Andrew Wright, and Sasha Romanosky. *CVSS: A Common Vulnerability Scoring System*. National Infrastructure Advisory Council (NIAC), 2004.
50. Oleg Sheyner, Joshua Haines, Somesh Jha, Richard Lippmann, and Jeannette M. Wing. Automated generation and analysis of attack graphs. In *Proceedings of the 2002 IEEE Symposium on Security and Privacy*, pages 254–265, 2002.

51. Laura P. Swiler, Cynthia Phillips, David Ellis, and Stefan Chakerian. Computer-attack graph generation tool. In *DARPA Information Survivability Conference and Exposition (DISCEX II'01)*, volume 2, June 2001.

52. Steven J. Templeton and Karl Levitt. A requires/provides model for computer attacks. In *Proceedings of the 2000 workshop on New security paradigms*, pages 31–38. ACM Press, 2000.

53. T. Tidwell, R. Larson, K. Fitch, and J. Hale. Modeling Internet attacks. In *Proceedings of the 2001 IEEE Workshop on Information Assurance and Security*, West Point, NY, June 2001.

54. Fredrik Valeur, Giovanni Vigna, Christopher Kruegel, and Richard A. Kemmerer. A comprehensive approach to intrusion detection alert correlation. *IEEE Transactions on Dependable and Secure Computing*, 1(3):146–169, 2004.

55. Lingyu Wang, Tania Islam, Tao Long, Anoop Singhal, and Sushil Jajodia. An attack graph-based probabilistic security metric. In *Proceedings of The 22nd Annual IFIP WG 11.3 Working Conference on Data and Applications Security (DBSEC'08)*, 2008.

56. Lingyu Wang, Anoop Singhal, and Sushil Jajodia. Measuring network security using attack graphs. In *Third Workshop on Quality of Protection (QoP)*, 2007.

57. Lingyu Wang, Anoop Singhal, and Sushil Jajodia. Measuring the overall security of network configurations using attack graphs. In *Proceedings of 21th IFIP WG 11.3 Working Conference on Data and Applications Security (DBSEC'07)*, 2007.

58. Yan Zhai, Peng Ning, Purush Iyer, and Douglas S. Reeves. Reasoning about complementary intrusion evidence. In *Proceedings of 20th Annual Computer Security Applications Conference (ACSAC)*, pages 39–48, December 2004.

Part III
Macroscopic Cyber Situational Awareness

Chapter 5
Employing Honeynets For Network Situational Awareness

P. Barford, Y. Chen, A. Goyal, Z. Li, V. Paxson, and V. Yegneswaran

Abstract Effective network security administration depends to a great extent on having accurate, concise, high-quality information about malicious activity in one's network. Honeynets can potentially provide such detailed information, but the volume and diversity of this data can prove overwhelming. We explore ways to integrate honeypot data into daily network security monitoring with a goal of sufficiently classifying and summarizing the data to provide ongoing "situational awareness." We present such a system, built using the Bro network intrusion detection system coupled with statistical analysis of numerous honeynet "events", and discuss experiences drawn from many months of operation. In particular, we develop methodologies by which sites receiving such probes can infer—using purely *local* observation—information about the probing activity: What scanning strategies does the probing employ? Is this an attack that specifically targets the site, or is the site only incidentally probed as part of a larger, indiscriminant attack? One key aspect of this environment is its ability to provide insight into large-scale events. We look at the problem of accurately classifying botnet sweeps and worm outbreaks, which turns out to be difficult to grapple with due to the high dimensionality of such incidents. Using datasets collected during a number of these events, we explore the utility of several analysis methods, finding that when used together they show good potential for contributing towards effective situational awareness. Our analysis draws upon extensive honeynet data to explore the prevalence of different types of scanning, including properties, such as trend, uniformity, coordination, and darknet-avoidance. In addition, we design schemes to extrapolate the global properties of scanning events (e.g., total population and

Paul Barford
University of Wisconsin, e-mail: pb@cs.wisc.edu

Yan Chen
Northwestern University, e-mail: ychen@northwestern.edu

Anup Goyal
Northwestern University, e-mail: ago210@cs.northwestern.edu

Zhichun Li
Northwestern University, e-mail: lizc@cs.northwestern.edu

Vern Paxson
University of California, Berkeley / International Computer Science Institute, e-mail: vern@cs.berkeley.edu

Vinod Yegneswaran
SRI International, e-mail: vinod@csl.sri.com

S. Jajodia et al., (eds.), *Cyber Situational Awareness*,
Advances in Information Security 46, DOI 10.1007/978-1-4419-0140-8_5,
© Springer Science+Business Media, LLC 2010

target scope) as inferred from the limited local view of a honeynet. Cross-validating with data from *DShield* shows that such inferences exhibit promising accuracy.

5.1 Introduction

Effective network security administration depends to a great extent on having accurate, concise, high-quality information about malicious activity in one's network. However, attaining good information has become increasingly difficult because the profile of malicious traffic evolves quickly and varies widely from network to network [8, 27], and because security analysts must discern the presence of new threats potentially hidden in an immense volume of "background radiation".

In addition, much of the information available to security analysts from sources such as intrusion detection systems comes in the form of pinpoint descriptions of low-level activities, such as "source *A* launched attack *CVE-XXX* against destination *B*". Standard best practices rarely include automatically acting on such information due to the prevalence of false and redundant alarms. In addition, the information often lacks sufficient breadth for forensic or root cause analysis.

When a site receives probes from the Internet—whether basic attempts to connect to its services, or apparent attacks directed at those services, or simply peculiar spikes in seemingly benign activity—often what the site's security staff most wants to know is *not* "are we being attacked?" (since the answer to that is almost always "yes, all the time") but rather "what is the *significance* of this activity?" Is the site being deliberately targeted? Or is the site simply receiving one small part of much broader probing activity? Is a new worm propagating? Or does the activity in fact reflect a benign error of some sort, with no malicious underpinnings?

For example, suppose a site with a /16 network receives malicious probes from a botnet. If the site can determine that the botnet probed only their /16, then they can conclude that the attacker may well have a special interest in their enterprise. On the other hand, if the botnet probed a much larger range, e.g., a /8, then very likely the attacker is not specifically targeting the enterprise.

The answers to these questions greatly influence the resources the site will choose to employ in responding to the activity. Obviously, the site will often care more about the probing if the attacker has specifically targeted the site, since such interest may reflect a worrisome level of determination on the part of the attacker. Yet given the incessant level of probing all Internet addresses receive [27], how can a site assess the risk a given event reflects?

The long-term objective of such work is to elevate the quality and timeliness of information provided to network security analysts. In this context, we can appeal to the notion of network *situational awareness* as a means for defining information quality, drawing upon the military term referring to "the degree of consistency between one's perception of their situation and the reality" [24], or to having "an accurate set of information about one's environment scaled to specific level of interest" [25].

We envision Network Situational Awareness (NetSA) as providing to an analyst accurate, terse summaries of attack traffic, organized to highlight the most prominent classes of attacks. NetSA should also supplement these reports with drill-down analysis to facilitate countermeasure deployment and forensic study. For example, a NetSA environment should enable an analyst to quickly assess high-level information such as the cause of an attack (*e.g.,* a new worm, a botnet, or a misconfiguration), whether the attacker specifically targeted the victim network, and if this attacker matches one seen in the past.

We can pursue a NetSA environment by coupling the use of *honeynets* for capturing large-scale malicious activity, unpolluted by benign traffic, with the application-level analysis capabilities of a semantically-rich intrusion detection system such as *Bro* [28]. A honeynet is a set of network addresses serving not actual user machines but honeypots. The ability of honeynets to monitor large amounts of address space [36] makes them an appealing source of timely information on new outbreaks and scanning attacks. However, effectively analyzing the potentially vast quantity of data they provide can prove challenging. To do so, we frame how we might employ a system such as Bro to organize and condense the honeypot data into situational awareness summaries that we can quickly scan for large-scale events. Such a system can highlight classes of such events such as *new* activity (i.e., an application-level abstraction not previously seen) and *spikes* of activity of a type previously seen, but now occurring with an unusually large number of offending sources.

One target for such analysis is to accurately attribute events as due to either (*i*) new worm outbreaks, (*ii*) misconfigurations, or (*iii*) botnet "sweeps". We can pursue this objective by developing a set of statistical analyses that consider source-arrival and scanning patterns to characterize different features of large-scale events. By way of illustration, we discuss experiences from operating a prototype of a NetSA environment for an extended period of time, which encompasses numerous large-scale events including well-known worm outbreaks, botnet sweeps, and misconfigurations. We orient much of our methodology with an assumption that most probing events reflect activity from the coordinated *botnets* that dominate today's Internet attack landscape. Our approach aims to analyze fairly large-scale activity that involves multiple local addresses. As such, our techniques are suitable for use by sites that deploy *darknets* (unused subnets), *honeynets* (subnets for which some addresses are populated by some form of honeypot responder, per our discussion above), or in general any monitored networks with unexpected access, including *graynets* (production subnets with restricted access, for which we can detect the botnet probing events).

We proceed with our examination as follows. First, in § 5.2 we present the overall context and related work in which we ground our discussion. In § 5.3, we look at basic techniques for classifying the activity seen by a honeynet, an discuss experiences with these techniques in § 5.4. We then turn to more powerful techniques for automating such classification (§ 5.6), which we develop in terms of first assessing the scanning patterns manifest in a botnet probing event (§ 5.7), and then extrapolating these patterns into inferences regarding the global properties of an event (§ 5.8), such as (in particular) whether the event targeted our site specifically or the Internet more broadly/indiscriminantly. In § 5.9 we assess the efficacy of these approaches as applied to a 2-year dataset of honeynet activity that we gathered. Finally, we briefly summarize the chapter's themes in § 5.10.

5.2 Background

There is a growing body of work on empirical analysis of anomalous or malicious Internet traffic. Of particular relevance are passive monitoring systems such as *network telescopes* (large blocks of unused but routable address blocks) used to evaluate specific components of unwanted traffic [20], such as characterizing levels of DoS attacks by analyzing "backscatter' [23] and assessing the spread and characteristics of infected hosts during worm outbreaks [22]. Another form of passive analysis appears in [37], which develops global characteristizations of intrusions using data collected from DShield [10]. DShield is the Internet's largest global alert repository. We note that DShield data can be quite noisy due to non-uniform sensor density. In addition, DShield is subject to pollution and avoidance [6].

Honeypots are Internet systems deployed for the sole purpose of being compromised in order to assess adversaries. Networks of honeypots are termed *honeynets* [14] and, like network telescopes, are typically deployed on otherwise unused address space. Systems such as Honeyd, iSink and the Internet Motion Sensor simulate honeynets by using *network-level* active responders [5, 29, 36]. These systems offer the benefit of fine-grained attack analysis without the associated control issues of high-interaction honeypots, *i.e.*, no need to manage real systems and deal with them being actually compromised.

The third class are systems that use dark space traffic as a means to generate automated NIDS signatures from Honeynet data. Such systems include Honeycomb [17] and Nemean [38]. The challenges faced by these systems are similar to those affecting of our system, in particular stem from the need to develop efficient mechanisms to summarize IBR data. Similarly, signature generation systems such as Autograph [16] and EarlyBird [33] automatically try to detect worm outbreaks and construct byte-level signatures. These systems could greatly benefit from the enhanced perspective provided through NetSA.

Also related is our previous study describing the broad characteristics of Internet "background radiation" using data collected from honeynets [27]. Here, we focus on automating the process of honeynet monitoring. One of our goals is to characterize the rapidly emerging phenomenon of large "botnets". See [11] for an experience report of tracking botnet activity using a network of VMware-based honeypots.

While the state of the art in terms of building honeynet systems has advanced considerably, the analysis of large-scale events captured by such systems remains in its early stages. The Honeynet project has developed a set of tools for host-level honeypot analysis [1], and one can also operate general exploit analysis tools [9] on high-interaction honeypot systems. At the network level, Honeysnap [2] analyzes the contents of individual connections, particularly for investigating IRC traffic used for botnet command-and-control. Work by Rajab et al., on the other hand, focuses on analyzing a captured bot's activity in order to form a template that can then drive faux command-and-control activity in order to study the long-term use of the botnet to which the bot would belong [31]. These approaches all either focus on single instances of activity, or on study of particular botnets over time (e.g., [31]).

The literature in addition includes a number of forensic case studies analyzing specific large-scale events, particularly worms [18, 21]. Such case studies have often benefited from *a priori* knowledge of the underlying mechanisms generating the traffic of interest. For our purposes, however, our goal is to infer the mechanisms themselves from a starting point of more limited (local) knowledge.

Gu et al. propose a series botnet detection techniques based on behavior correlation [12, 13]. In contract, we main focus on the forensic inference after such detection.

5.3 Classifying Honeynet Activity

We first explore a framework for classifying activity seen by a honeynet. We frame a network situational awareness system architecture for such classification as including seven components:

• **Active responders** are a collection of service emulators, running in Honeyd or iSink. The responders enable fine-grained attack analysis by engaging sources in packet exchanges for specific services. The system we examine in this chapter ran responders on a number of commonly exploited services, including NetBIOS/SMB (ports 137/139/445), DCE/RPC (135/1025), HTTP (80), Mydoom (3127), Beagle (2745), Dameware (6129), MS-SQL (1433), and a generic "echo-responder" for other ports. (Details on responders are provided in [27].)

• A **tunnel filter** sends traffic from the monitored address space to the active responders using UDP encapsulation. The tunnel employs a simple *one-source → one-destination* filter: we allow each source to talk to only the first destination it contacts. This filtering greatly reduces the amount of traffic seen by responders without a substantial impact on the overall attack profiles. Our analysis here includes both filtered and prefiltered data; see [27] for a discussion of ther filtering strategies.

• **Radiation-analy** is a collection of Bro policy scripts to analyze data from active honeypots. With these we aim to enable accurate high-level classification of attack profiles. This is challenging due to the complexity of the dominant protocols such as NetBIOS and MS-SQL. We must strike a balance between specificity and generality, so as to group together activity that is semantically equivalent from an attack perspective, even if not identical as transmitted. We achieve this through two means: (*i*) considering protocol as well as 'well-known" exploit sementics, and (*ii*) aggregating activity at multiple granularities.

The *Radiation-analy* scripts generate summaries at several granularities: (*i*) per-source scanning profiles, (*ii*) connection-level summaries to distill into aggregate source counts of identical connection profiles, and (*iii*) aggregate summaries of *session* profiles, where a session can be comprised of multiple types of connections. We use the first two in the daily evaluations examined

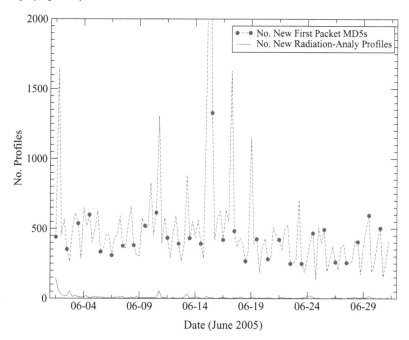

Fig. 5.1 Comparison of first-packet MD5 vs radiation-analy summarization. Figure shows radiation-analy provides significant benefit over simple "first-packet-MD5" classification strategy

here; aggregating session profiles has proven more difficult due to the diversity seen across groups of connections, and so remains as future work.

In Figure 5.1, we compare the effectiveness of radiation-analy summaries with simple first-packet-MD5 classification strategy proposed in [5] for one month. We see that that the radiation-analy summaries enable the system to quickly learn about attack profiles and after the first couple of six hour summaries, we typically see fewer than 10 new profiles per six-hour interval [1]. In contrast the first-packet-MD5 signature caching produces hundreds of new profiles per interval and does not "learn" well .

- **Adaptation**. A key aspect of our framework is that it automatically updates its notions of types of activity over time. Specifically, when activity fails to match an already-known profile, the system inserts a description of the new activity into its database so that in the future it will be identified as something we have previously seen. These descriptions are based on semantic-level "tags" derived from Bro's application-level analysis of the activity. Two examples of such tags are "`445/tcp, binary-upload, CREATE_FILE: "lsarpc"`" and "`RPC bind: afa8bd80-7d8a-11c9-bef4-08002b102989 len=72; RPC request (24 bytes)`".

We can run *Radiation-analy* in a batch mode, and here the output we analyze comes from 6-hour batches. Such runs thus periodically update the Honeynet database and feed *Situational-analy*, each described next.

- **Honeynet database** stores the summarized connection profiles generated by Bro using a database such as MySQL. This enables us to efficiently track temporal changes in the constituents of malicious activity, and allows us to easily query for information such as the complete list of known malicious signatures.

---

[1] This scale is suitable for manual supervision.

• **Situational-analy** is a script that queries the Honeynet database and generates periodic summaries organized to highlight new events (those not previously in the database), large-scale or unusual events, and endemic activity. To identify large-scale and unusual events we compute the deviation of an event's source volume (*i.e.,* the number of distinct source IP addresses) from that seen in the past for that type of event. We compute the deviation as a ratio, denoted β, as follows. Let p_i be the number of sources with connection profile p in time interval i, and m the number of intervals prior to i where we previously observed this profile. Then $\beta_{p_i} = mp_i/\sum_{j=0}^{i-1} p_i$, *i.e.,* the number of sources observed in t_i divided by the mean number of sources observed for this activity, ignoring intervals when it was not observed.

Situational-analy generates situational summaries for high-β events. From experience a threshold of $\beta_{p_i} > 3.0$ for minor escalations and $\beta_{p_i} > 10.0$ for high-β events works satisfactorily, in terms of often yields the events one might reasonably deem "somewhat" and "quite" interesting, respectively. We discuss this further in the next section.

• **Situational In-depth** is a series of statistical analyses we developed to classify large-scale events, described in § 5.5. One can run these as either off-line tools, or for real-time classification.

5.4 Experiences With Activity Classification

In this section we report on experiences from six months' of operation of a NetSA system built along the lines framed in the previous section, running on a 1,280-address honeynet. The six-hour summaries generated by the system alerted us to a host of potential new exploits and botnet incidents over this period. While the details of each incident are not always compelling, the overall insight the NetSA system yields in terms of isolating and summarizing events has been quite clear. The operation, not surprisingly, has required tuning and refinement over time; in particular, we gained experience with examining situational summary reports, we modified the format, β thresholds, and the adaptive rule generator to better provide information at an appropriate level of fidelity for daily use. The situational summaries currently generated have four parts, as follows:

1. **New events:** The report first summarizes *new events*, *i.e.,* those not matching an existing profile as abstracted by the Bro *Radiation-analy* script. This part of the report included the target port, source count, and the newly generated Bro tag for this event, which includes protocol and payload details. In our experience, the number of events in this category is typically less than 5. The target ports can vary widely, while the number of distinct sources identified for these events is usually only 1.
   We have identified many different types of events using this portion of the summary, including a number of misconfigurations and several suspected new virus strains and polymorphisms. *However*, we initially expected that such previously unseen activity would very often prove highly interesting, reflecting significant new forms of malware, once we had operated long enough to fully populate our "known activity" database with the regular background radiation one sees. An important *negative result* is that this has not turned out to be the case. The difficulty is that the low levels of "new" activity we see also often include minor variations of previously seen activity. *The problem of perfectly generalizing activity to avoid flagging variants as "new" has proven quite difficult, and remains a challenge for future work.*

2. **High-β events:** The next section summarizes high-β events ($\beta > 10.0$). This component of the report aims to identify fast-scanning worms and large-scale botnet attacks. The report lists the *Radiation-analy* tag for each event along with hourly and 5-minute breakdowns of the number of unique sources observed, overlap in sources between successive time intervals, number of source /8-s and number of targets scanned. We see on the order of one high beta event per day, though they are sometimes quite bursty, and sometimes a single event spans multiple 6 hr reports. Using the tools presented below, our best assessment is that most of these have been either botnet scans or misconfigurations.

3. **Minor escalations:** The next section summarizes the "minor escalations" in volume ($\beta > 3.0$). The report lists the β value, target port, source count, mean source count in the past, and *Radiation-analy* tag. While we hypothesize that slow-scanning worms exploiting known exploits might initially become visible here, no such worm outbreak took place during our study (nor did any outbreak of a fast-scanning novel worm). Typically this section includes on the order of 10 or fewer events.

4. **Top profiles:** The final section describes the top 10 activity profiles (ranked by distinct source IP count) observed in the 6 hr period. The report includes the target port, source count, and associated *Radiation-analy*. This section provides an ongoing sense of endemic activity. It is most frequently dominated by NetBIOS/SMB and DCE/RPC activity, but we see a significant diversity in terms of other forms of activity.

5.5 Situational Awareness In-depth

Attribute	Misconfig	Botnet	Worm
Source Arrivals:			
Temporal source counts	sharp onset	gradual	sharp onset
Arrival window	narrow	narrow	wide
Interarrival distribution	exponential	exponential *	hyper-exp
Dst/Src Net Coverage:			
Dest-net footprint	hotspots	binomial	binomial
First-dest preference	hotspots	variable	binomial
Source-net dispersion	low-med	low-med	high
Source Macro-analysis:			
Per-source profile	hotspots	variable	variable
Target scope	IPv4	$<= /8$	IPv4
Source lifetimes	short	short	persistent

Table 5.1 Situational Awareness Attributes Summary

In this section we present a set of nine statistical analyses that aim to effectively classify large-scale events. We base each on a hypothesis about the expected behavior of three major classes of large-scale events: worm outbreaks, botnet sweeps, and misconfigurations. Table 5.1 summarizes the expected behavior for each type of event from the perspective of a honeynet. In particular, we focus on source arrivals (a probe from a distinct source IP), individual source characteristics, and network coverage, as discussed in the following sections. While we have yet to identify a single method that works in all cases, taken together these analyses provide a broad perspective on large-scale events.

Two elements of the table merit clarification, both concerning "Interarrival distribution". For this row, "exponential" indicates interarrivals consistent with a Poisson process, *i.e.*, independent arrivals that occur at a constant rate. The "exponential*" entry for Botnets indicates that initially we expected botnet probing to arrive in an *impulse*, rather than as a Poisson process; but, for reasons discussed below, the latter is often instead the case. The "hyper-exp" entry for Worms reflects that while at a given instant in time we might expect arrivals to appear Poisson (assuming the worm is random-scanning with a well-seeded random number generator), we also expect the worm's activity to grow over time as it spreads, so we anticipate seeing a Poisson process whose rate steadily increases until the worm attains saturation.

Incident Name	Type	Date	No. Sources
BitTorrent	NAT misconfig	2005-01-12	25 (1)
eDonkey1	P2P misconfig	2005-02-02	389
eDonkey2	P2P misconfig	2005-02-06	709
eDonkey3	P2P misconfig	2005-02-08	1,034
NB HiddenShare	Botnet	2005-01-31	246
MS-SQL1	Botnet	2005-01-09	104
MS-SQL2	Botnet	2005-02-01	245
MS-SQL3	Botnet	2005-02-03	176
MS-SQL4	Botnet	2005-02-07	1,953
NB Incomplete	Botnet	2005-01-10	6,561
DCERPC_p1025	Botnet	2005-01-10	775
DCERPC_p135	Botnet	2005-04-03	782
DCERPC_p135-2	Botnet	2005-01-29	528
p6101-unknown	Botnet	2005-01-20	30
NB Testfile	Botnet	2005-01-15	96
NB Wkssvc	Botnet	2005-01-11	26,010
CodeRed I	Worm	2001-07-19	154,666
CodeRed I Re-emergence	Worm	2001-08-01	126,311
CodeRed II	Worm	2001-08-04	114,034
Nimda	Worm	2001-08-18	139,351
Witty	Worm	2004-03-20	5,553
Slammer Re-emergence	Worm	2005-03-18	350

Table 5.2 Summary of high-β incidents & worm outbreaks

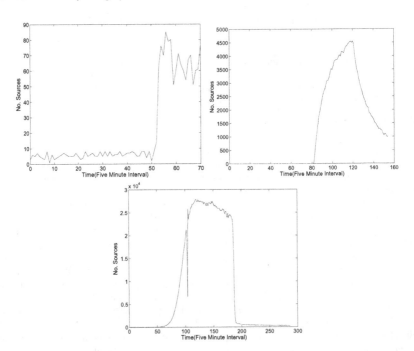

Fig. 5.2 Temporal Source Counts in five minute intervals for (left to right) eDonkey3, Wkssvc Botnet and Code-Red 1

For the analysis presented here, we collected traces for 22 large-scale events, detailed in Table 5.2, to evaluate the utility of each type of analysis. We collected the traces for the misconfiguration and botnet events from our honeynet deployment, while the worm outbreak traces (other than the Slammer resurgence) came from various archival sources. We now turn to a discussion of each type of analysis.

5.5.1 Source Arrivals

• **Temporal source counts:** We hypothesized that a botnet sweep would be characterized by a sharp rise and sharp decay in temporal source counts, as the botnet was first ordered *en masse* to probe, and then completed its probing. In contrast, we expected the growth of worms to reflect the size of the infected population, so the scanning behavior would steadily increase until the worm shut down (*e.g.*, Code Red 1) or was cleaned up.

We evaluate this by considering the scanning activity in terms of the number of distinct sources seen in successive time intervals. Figure 5.2 shows the temporal source counts for three different events: probing of a specific honeynet address that appears due to a misconfiguration in the eDonkey peer-to-peer file sharing system (left); probing for the Windows wkssvc service in an event we believe is most plausibly attributed to a botnet; and historical data from the initial outbreak of Code Red 1 on July 19, 2001. (This last plot exhibits a brief measurement outage at the sharp line towards the left.) While all three events exhibit a relatively sharp onset, that for eDonkey is particularly sharp, Wkssvc is concave down, and Code Red 1 is concave up. These potentially reflect three different types of activity onset: sudden propagation among the sources (eDonkey), propagation that reaches most of the sources quickly but takes time to find all of them (wkssvc), and the logistic growth characteristic of a worm (Code Red 1). In addition, the probable botnet activity is distinguished from the others by its gradual but steady decay.

• **Arrival window:** We next look at the nature by which *new* sources arrive. We initially expected that botnets would exhibit a sharp spike in new arrivals as the master of the botnet pushed out probing commands to each bot. However, this turns out to often not be the case. As we confirmed by analysis of source code from a widely used botnet controller (phatbot), a common way of structuring botnets is not to push commands to them but rather to have the bots *poll and pull*. For the source code we examined, bots wake up every 1000 seconds to check for new commands. Given this behavior, rather than a sharp onset we instead might expect a steady rate of arrival over an interval of 10–20 minutes.

Figure 5.3 shows the arrival rate for three events. The Wkssvc event is clearly more regular than Nimda, but spread out over 10,000 sec. Perhaps this reflects a botnet with a polling interval of 10,000 sec rather than 1000 sec; but, by itself, we cannot really tell, so we find that the arrival window of new sources is insufficient by itself to distinguish worms from botnets.

• **Interarrival distribution:**

If bots indeed poll independently for the instructions, then they will activate with a *uniform distribution* over the polling interval. If in addition the rate at which the bots then reach the honeynet with their probing is independent of when they receive their instructions, then we would expect the arrival of the new sources to also be uniformly distributed over the polling interval; *i.e.*, the arrivals will appear to be form a Poisson process, resulting in exponentially distributed interarrival times. On the other hand, the source interarrival times from worms should exhibit an increasing rate while the worm initially propagates.

To evaluate source interarrival characteristics, we break up events into successive intervals, each with an equal number of sources (*e.g.*, we pick 10 intervals each with 10% of new sources). We then plot the distribution of interarrival times and compare against an exponential reference distribution fitted to the mean. For an evaluation over all the events in our set, we found that botnet and misconfiguration events often show consistency with exponential interarrivals; Worm outbreaks do so, too, but with *different rates for different intervals*.

5.5.2 Destination/Source Net Coverage

• **Destination-net scan footprint:** Another set of salient features for large-scale events concerns which destinations they probe. We would expect misconfigurations to target only a few addresses, while botnets and worms might or might not exhibit localized scanning, which might be structured (more likely for botnets, we might think) or might be randomized (more likely for worms).

We evaluate this behavior by considering the number of scans per source and the number of sources that scanned particular destination IP addresses. Figure 5.4 shows the destination network scan footprint for three different events. The eDonkey misconfiguration event clearly shows hotspots, while the target selection for the worm and botnet scenarios visually appear random and comprehensive.

• **First destination preference** Next, we test for a preference in the first destination chosen by sources. This can reveal trends such as botnet sources that always start sequentially scanning from the top of subnet, or sources of bias in the random number generators used by worms to select targets. To evaluate this behavior, we count the number of times each destination address was chosen by a source as its first target. If the scanning process is entirely random, *i.e.,* there is no bias in the scanning order, then we would expect these counts to have a binomial distribution in terms of n trials (n = # sources) and a probability of success (*i.e.,* a given destination is visited first) $p = 1/1280$.

Figure 5.5 plots the first-destination preference for two events, along with the expected values from the corresponding binomial distribution. The Wkssvc botnet fits the binomial quite well, indicating it chooses its destinations fully at random, while Nimda exhibits a local preference. Not surprisingly, an eDonkey misconfiguration event (not shown) shows a complete lack of fit.

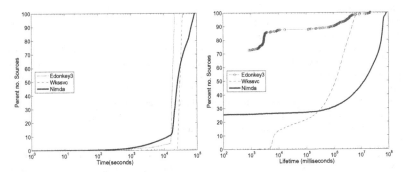

Fig. 5.3 Left: CDF of source arrivals eDonkey3, wkssvc, Nimda; Right: CDF of source lifetimes

• **Source-net dispersion:** Next, we consider the distribution of source hosts across the IPv4 address space. We hypothesize that hosts observed in worm outbreaks will be much more broadly spread across the address space than botnets. Since sources sending traffic to the honeynet interact with an active responder (other than for single-packet UDP probes), we can generally eliminate the possibility of spoofed source IPs. We then compute a histogram of the count of sources seen from each /8 address aggregate. Such plots (not shown) reveal that the source dispersion of known worm outbreaks is much higher than that for likely botnet sweeps or misconfigurations.

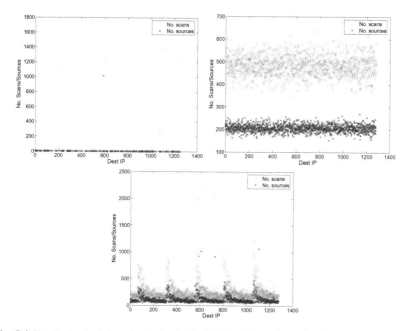

Fig. 5.4 Destination Net Scan Footprint (left) eDonkey Misconfiguration: 2005-02-08 (middle) Wkssvc Botnet Incident: 2005-01-11 (right)Nimda: 2001-09-18

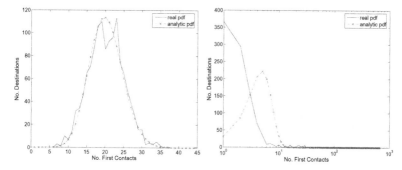

Fig. 5.5 PDF of first destination preference (left) Wkssvc Botnet Incident: 2005-01-11 (right) Nimda: 2001-09-18

5.5.3 Source Macro-analysis

• **Per-source scanning profile:** Next, we investigate the degree to which the scanning profiles of individual sources can provide insight into a large-scale event's aggregate behavior. To do so, we randomly select up to 100 sources and plot the destinations that each visit, sorting on the lowest destination address visited (an alternative might be to sort by arrival time). In addition, we construct phase-space plots of the consecutive honeynet addresses a given source probes. These two plots are complementary: one provides per-source *coverage* information, the other provides per-source *ordering* information. (We find that this analysis is not needed for misconfiguration events due to their restricted scanning profile.)

Figure 5.6 shows examples of scan profiles and associated phase-space plots for an MS-SQL event likely due to a botnet. The left hand plot reveals that there are two types of sources, those covering the entire target space and those scanning a small number of IPs. The phase-space plot on the right suggests that the former set of sources in fact scan the address space sequentially. We also see two parallel lines on either side instead of a single line down the diagonal. This artifact is consistent with a single source using *two independent scanning threads*, each of which traverses the address space separately but at the same rate. We see similar plots for other botnet incidents, suggesting that we need to account for such concurrent scanning when testing for sequential scanners. (Plots for Nimda similarly show the presence of two types of sources—few that cover the entire address space, and the remainder that just target a few IPs. However the phase plot reveals that the sources that scanned the entire address space did not do so sequentially, unlike the MS-SQL scanners. While we explored various ways to extend this analysis, none has proven to be a conclusive indicator of botnet or worm activity.)

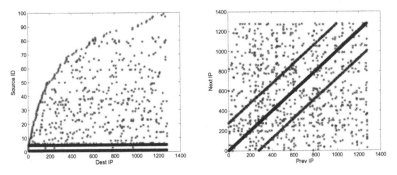

Fig. 5.6 Left: Dest Scanning profiles of 100 random sources ordered by first destination. Right: Phase plot of successive destination IPs scanned in local network the MSSQL Botnet Incident: 2005-02-03

- **Inferring target scope:** A general situational awareness question concerns how broadly a given event was *actually* scoped, as opposed to its prevalence seen within the honeynet. It can matter a great deal whether a given event specifically targeted the monitored network, or only incidentally probed it as part of much broader probing activity.

Roughly, we would expect worms to tend to have global target scope, while botnets and misconfigurations might be considerably more localized. The problem then becomes how to assess global scope given only a single honeynet vantage point. We address this issue in considerable depth later in this chapter. Here, we assess a first, relatively simple attempt to do so by trying to infer and then compare the global scanning rate of each source versus its local (within the honeynet) scanning rate. We base our tool for doing this based on the observation that retransmitted TCP SYN packets will generally be sent within 3 seconds. In general, we can often estimate how many packets a source has sent between two packets we observe by changes in the IPID counter (if the source's OS implements the common policy of incrementing the ID by one for each packet sent). A 3-second interval is sufficiently short it is highly unlikely the IPID field will have completely wrapped (*i.e.*, the source sends > 65,535 packets). Thus, we can use the IPID spacing between retransmitted SYN packets as an estimate of the source's global scan rate. We can extend this

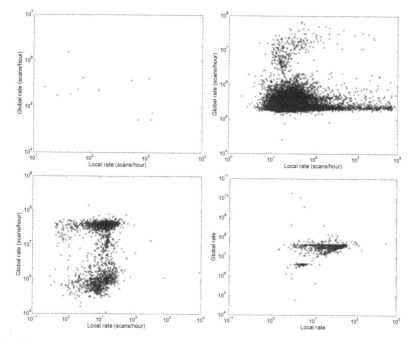

Fig. 5.7 Log-Log plot of global and local scanning rate, ratio provides an estimate of the instantaneous global footprint (left) eDonkey Misconfiguration (2005-02-08) (second) Wkssvc Botnet Incident 2005-01-11 (third) Nimda Worm Outbreak: 2001-09-18 (right) Witty Worm Outbreak [UW Net]: 2004-03-20

trick (which admittedly will often not work for sources that craft their own TCP packets) to UDP sources, too, by considering packets we observed that arrive $\leq$ 3 sec apart.[2]

In addition, we can construct an estimate of the *local scanning rate* for each source by dividing the number of probes from it by its lifetime. We can then estimate the *broader reach* of a source as the ratio of its estimated global rate versus its estimated local rate, multiplied by the size (in addresses) of the honeynet.

Figure 5.7 shows log-log scatter plots of the estimated global and local scanning rates of each source during four different events, confining the plot to sources that contacted at least 5 destinations. For the eDonkey misconfiguration event, we estimate a multiplier between 10^3 and 10^5, so we infer that the misconfiguration does not simply target our honeynet but includes thousands of other targets. The Wkssvc botnet incident yields an estimated multiplier of around 10^4, indicates that the event likely targeted the equivalent of a /8 network. This level of scoping holds for all of the botnet incidents we have analyzed. On the other hand, data from Nimda reveals two clusters of sources.[3] The multiplier here for the higher-cluster is between 10^6 and 10^7 consistent with the entire IPv4 address space. Finally, data from the Witty worm outbreak yields an estimated multiplier of around 10^6. The target network used to collect that data had $\approx$ 8K addresses, so this scales up to a footprint on the order of the entire IPv4 address space, which is the correct scope for Witty.

---

[2] It is also important to keep in mind that UDP sources are more aggressive than TCP, hence their IPID field wraps around sooner. For Witty, the wrap-around time for a typical host was around 10 seconds, compared to TCP where we find it an order of magnitude higher

[3] we attribute this to Nimda's preferential scanning behavior.

• **Source lifetimes:** The final attribute we consider is the lifetime of sources, *i.e.*, for how long do we see them active in the honeynet. We hypothesize that botnet sources will be short lived, since they presumably are told to conduct a specific scan and will stop when they have completed it, while worm sources will be persistent unless they have mechanisms in them to stop scanning after a certain point, which have not been seen to date (other than Code Red 1's die-off on the 20th of each month [34]).

Figure 5.3 plots the CDF of source lifetimes for three events. A lifetime of 0 corresponds to seeing the source very briefly or perhaps only once. We see that our expectation largely holds: botnets and misconfigurations have short lifetimes, while the lifetimes of worm sources are distributed broadly. While this analysis can be a useful discriminator between worms and botnets, its utility is limited by the fact that we need to wait before we can make the determination.

5.6 Towards Automated Classification

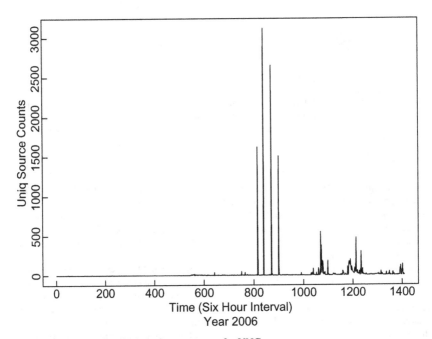

Fig. 5.8 Temporal distribution of source count for VNC.

We now turn to the problem of how to automatically determine the significance of *events* seen by a honeynet. We consider the problem in the context of our experiences with a detection sensor we operated that consisted of ten contiguous /24 subnets within one of the Lawrence Berkeley National Laboratory's /16 networks. Along the lines of the system discussed earlier in this chapter, we deployed Honeyd responders [30] on five of the subnets, in this case we also operated the other five completely "dark". (We use this latter for "liveness" detection.) The Honeyd configuration is similar to that used by Pang et al. in [26]: we simulate the HTTP, NetBIOS, SMB, WINRPC, MSSQL, MYSQL, SMTP, Telnet, DameWare protocols, with echo servers for all other port numbers. We evaluate these analysis techniques using 293 GB of trace data collected over two years (2006 and 2007).

The analysis focuses on inference of the properties of *botnet* probes (rather than worms and misconfigurations, which we included in our scope previously in this chapter). We define a *session* as a set of connections between a pair of hosts with a specific purpose, perhaps involving multiple application protocols. The system extracts events based on the number of unique sources arriving in a window of time. For instance, Figure 5.8 shows source arrival counts for VNC (TCP port 5900) for the year 2006, where each point represents the number of sources within a six-hour interval. Large spikes generally correspond to scanning from worms or botnets, or misconfigurations. We leverage time series analysis to extract such spikes as *events*. Then, we further classify the events into misconfigurations, worms, or botnet probing. (For details on the methodology, see [19].)

For botnet probing, there are numerous scanning strategies that attackers can potentially use. Identifying the particular approach can provide a basis to infer further properties of the events and perhaps of the botnets themselves. We refer to these strategies as *scan patterns*, and undertake to develop a set of scan-pattern checking techniques to understand different dimensions of such strategies: (*i*) monotonic-trend checking, (*ii*) liveness checking, (*iii*) uniformity checking, and (*iv*) dependency checking. Once we identify a probing event's scan pattern, we then use the scan pattern to extrapolate global properties of the event. We focus on two of the most common scan patterns: uniform random scanning, and uniform "live-aware" scanning.

5.7 Assessing Botnet Scanning Patterns

In this section we consider analysis algorithms designed to check a single aspect of the characteristics manifested by a scan. We can then combine the characteristics of an event to construct the full scan pattern in use.

We first classify the scan traffic pattern into monotonic, partially monotonic and non-monotonic trends. For non-monotonic trends, we assess the possible use of a liveness-sensitive or random-uniform scanning (even distribution of scans across the portion of the sensor space). Finally, for random-uniform patterns we test whether we can model the senders as independent.

5.7.1 Monotonic Trend Checking

Question: Do senders follow a monotonic trend in their scanning?

Monotonically scanning the destination IP addresses (e.g., sequentially one after another) is a technique widely used by earlier network scanning tools. In our evaluation, we do find some events that employed the monotonic trend scanning.

For each sender, we test for monotonicity in targeting by applying the Mann-Kendall trend test [15], a non-parametric hypothesis testing approach. We set the significance level to 0.5%, since a higher significance level will introduce more false positives, and for situational awareness we can wind up applying the test to thousands of sources. The intuition behind this test is to assess whether if the data contains a monotonic trend as indicated by the aggregated sign value of the increment (i.e., a value of +1 for a positive increment, 0 for no change, and -1 for a negative increment) of all consecutive value pairs attaining a value that randomness could not plausibly acheive achieve.

We label an entire event as having a *monotonic trend* if more than 80% of senders exhibit a trend. We instead label the event as *non-monotonic* if more than 80% of senders do not exhibit a trend. We label the remainder as *partial monotonic*.

5.7.2 Checking for Liveness-Aware Scanning

Question: Do the bots show sensitivity to "liveness" in their scanning?

By *liveness-aware* scanning, we refer to an event for which the attacker appears to have previously acquired knowledge of which network blocks in the Internet contain active hosts and which appear unused. Liveness-aware scanning can be employed to achieve higher scan efficiency, since time is not wasted on blocks of addresses that will not reap benefit.

We detect the use of a liveness-aware scanning as follows. We operate half of our sensor region in a live fashion, and half "dark" (no responses). If we observe an event only in the live portion, this provides strong evidence that the scan was liveness-aware. However, one consideration is event "pollution"—sources that actually are background noise rather than part of the botnet, but that exhibited similar scanning at the same time, and thus were inadvertently included in the event. Thus, we do not require a *complete* absence of darknet scanning, but instead test for the prevalence of honeynet scans over darknet scans significantly exceeding what we would expect if the event selected indiscriminately between the two.

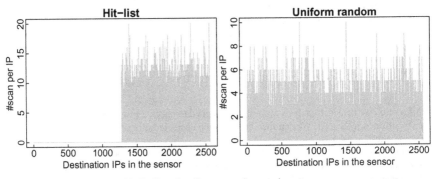

Fig. 5.9 Liveness-aware ("hit-list") and uniform scanning on the sensor.

Figure 5.9 compares a liveness-aware event (WINRPC-070625) versus a random-uniform event (VNC-060729). To distinguish between two such cases, we define the ratio of the number of senders that target the darknet (m_d) over those of the honeynet (m_h) as $\theta = \frac{m_d}{m_h}$. Then we test whether θ crosses a given threshold. Our evaluation suggests the results are not very sensitive to the threshold we choose.

Note that for the events that require application-level analysis to separate the activity from the background traffic (e.g., different types of HTTP probing), sources in the event will necessarily be restricted to the honeynet because application-level dialog requires responses that the darknet cannot provide. In this case we can still perform an approximate test, by testing the volume of traffic seen concurrently in the darknet probing the same port number. Doing so, may miss some liveness-aware events, however, because we tend to overestimate the amount of activity the botnet exhibits in the darknet.

Another issue arises if an attacker chooses a small scan range that happens to include only the live addresses. However, even if this occurs we would also (if it does not reflect previous scanning, i.e., is not liveness-aware) expect it to occur equally often the other way around, i.e., including only darknet addresses—however, in our 2 years of data we do not observe this latter occurrence.

In the 203 events we analyzed, we find 33 (16.3%) reflect liveness-aware events.

5.7.3 Uniformity Checking

Question: Does an event uniformly scan the target range?

A natural scanning technique for bots to employ is uniform random scanning across the target range. We can describe testing for whether scans are evenly distributed in the honeynet sensor as a distribution-checking problem. We employ a simple χ^2 test, which is well-suited for the discrete nature of address blocks. In general, when employing a χ^2 test, key requirement is to ensure that the expected value E_i for any bin should exceed 5 [32], which then drives the selection of how many bins to use. Accordingly, for our particular situation since our events have at least several hundred scans in them, we divide the 2,560 addresses in our Honeynet into 40 bins with 64 addresses per bin. We then use the χ^2 test with a significance level of 0.5%.

5.7.4 Dependency Checking

Question: Do the sources scan independently or are they coordinated?

Sophisticated scanning strategies can introduce correlations between the sources in order to control the work that each contributes more efficiently. To test for such coordination, we use the following hypothesis test: the null hypothesis is that the senders act in a uniform, independent fashion (where we first test for uniformity as discussed above); while the alternative hypothesis is that the senders have some degree of coordination in them, which manifests as a lack of consistency with independence. If an event comprises n scans targeting d destinations in a uniform random manner, we can in principle calculate the distribution of the number of destinations that receive exactly k scans, Z_k. We then reject the null hypothesis if the observed value is too unlikely given this distribution (we again use a 0.5% significance level).

Theorem 5.1. *If n scans target d addresses in a uniform independent manner, the number of addresses Z_0 ($k = 0$) that do not receive any scan follows the probability distribution function:*

$$P(z_0) = \binom{d}{z_0} \times Stirling2(n, d - z_0) \times (d - z_0)! / d^n$$

Stirling2(n, y) denotes the Stirling number of the second kind [35], which is the number of ways to partition n elements to y non-empty sets. For the proof, see [19], which also includes discussion for the more general cases of $k > 0$.

5.8 Extrapolating Global Properties

We now turn to the problem of estimating a botnet event's global scope (target size, participating scanners) based only on local information. This task is challenging because the size of the local sensor may be very small compared to the whole range scanned by a botnet, giving only a very limited view of the scanning event. For our estimation, we considered eight global properties, as shown in Table 5.3.

For both uniform-random and uniform-liveness-aware scanning, the uniformity property enables us to consider the local view as a random sample of the global view. Thus, the operating system (OS), autonomous system (AS), and IP prefix distributions observed in local measurements provide an estimate of the corresponding global distributions (bottom three rows). However, we need to consider that if bots exhibit heterogeneity in their scanning rates, then the probability of observing a bot decreases for slower-scanning ones. Scanning rate heterogeneity introduces a bias

Property name	uniform scanning	uniform liveness-aware	estimation method
Global target scope	Yes	Yes	indirect
Total # of bots	Yes	Yes	indirect
Total # of scans	Yes	Yes	indirect
Average scan speed per bot	Yes	Yes	indirect
Coverage hit ratio	Yes	No	direct
Sender OS distribution	Yes	Yes	direct
Sender AS distribution	Yes	Yes	direct
Sender IP prefix distribution	Yes	Yes	direct

Table 5.3 Global properties inferred from local observations.

towards the faster bots for these distributional properties. By extrapolating the total number of bots, however, we can roughly estimate the prevalence of this effect. It turns out that in all of our analyzed events, we find that more than 70% of the bots appear at the local sensor,[4] allowing us to compare the number of bots seen at the local sensor with the extrapolated global bot population, as shown in Table 5.7. Thus, the bias appears to be relatively small.

The "coverage hit ratio" gives the percentage of target IPs scanned by the botnet. As this metric is more difficult to estimate for liveness-aware probing, we mainly consider uniform scanning, for which certain destinations are not reached due to statistical variations. For uniform scanning, we can directly estimate this metric based on the coverage in our local sensor.

In the remainder of this section we focus on the four remaining properties, each of which requires indirect extrapolation.

5.8.1 Assumptions and Requirements

To proceed with indirect extrapolation, we must make two key assumptions:

First, *the attacker is oblivious to our sensors and thus sends probes to them without discrimination*. This assumption is fundamental to general honeynet-based traffic study, (cf. the probe-response attack developed in [6] and counter-defenses [7]). A general discussion of the problem is beyond the scope of this chapter. However, since we assume such techniques are mainly used by a single enterprise or a set of collaborating enterprises, we need not release sensing information to the public, which counters the basic attack in [6]. With this assumption, we can treat the local view as providing unbiased samples of the global view.

Second, *each sender has the same global scan scope*. This should be true if all the senders are controlled by the same botmaster and each sender scans uniformly using the same set of instructions.

We argue that these two fundamental assumption likely apply to any local-to-global extrapolation scheme. In addition, we check for one general requirement before applying extrapolation, namely consistency with the presumption that *each sender evenly distributes its scans across the global scan scope*. This requirement is valid for both uniform random scanning and random permutation scanning, regardless of whether employing liveness-aware scanning. Therefore, prior to applying the extrapolation approaches, we test for consistency with uniformity (via methodology discussed in Section 5.7), which many of the botnet scan events pass (80.3%).

---

[4] The high percentage of bots appearing at the local sensor arises due to the fact that probing events continue long enough to expose majority of the bots.

Of course there is the usual "arms race" here between attackers and defenders. If techniques such as those we present here become widely used, then attackers will modify their probing traffic to skew the defenders' analysis. We adopt the view common in network security research that there is significant utility in "raising the bar" for attackers even if a technique is ultimately evadable.

Approach	Properties	Affected by botnet dynamics	Require IPID or port # continuity
Both	# of bots	No	No
Approach I	Global target scope	No	Yes
	Total # of scans	No	Yes
	Average scan speed per bot	Yes	Yes
Approach II	Global target scope	Yes	No
	Total # of scans	Yes	No
	Average scan speed per bot	Yes	No

Table 5.4 Additional assumptions and requirements.

There are some additional requirements specific to certain extrapolation approaches, as listed in Table 5.4. Botnet dynamics, such as churn or growth, can influence certain extrapolation approaches. Accordingly these approaches work better for short-lived events. Approach I, as discussed in section 5.8.3, requires continuity of the IP fragment identifier (IPID) or ephemeral port, which holds for botnets dominated by Windows or MacOS machines (in our datasets we found all the events are dominated by Windows machines). We use passive OS fingerprinting to check whether we can assume that this property holds.

5.8.2 Estimating Global Population

Table 5.5 gives the notation for our problem formulation and analysis, marking estimates with "hat"s. For example, $\hat{\rho}$ represents the estimated local over global ratio, i.e., ratio of local sensor size compared to the global target scope of the botnet event; $\hat{G}$ represents the estimated global target scope.

If ρ is small, many senders may not arrive at the sensor at all. In this case, we cannot measure the total bot population directly. Instead, we extrapolate the total number of bots as follows. With the uniform scan assumption discussed above, we have:

$$\frac{m_1}{M} = \frac{m_{12}}{m_2} \tag{5.1}$$

based on the following reasoning. We can split the address range of the sensor into two parts. Since the senders observed in each part are independent samples from the total population M, Equation 5.1 follows from independence. For example, suppose there are total $M = 400$ bots. In the first half sensor, we see $m_1 = 100$ bots, which is $1/4$ of the total bot population. Consider the second half as another independent sensor, so the bots it observes form another random sample from the total population. Then we have a $1/4$ chance to see if there is a bot already seen in the first half. If the second half observes $m_2 = 100$ bots too, the shared bots will be close to $m_{12} = 100/4 = 25$. Since in Equation 5.1 we can directly measure m_1, m_2, and m_{12}, we can solve for M, the total number of bots in the population.

This technique is a simple instance of a general approach used to estimate animal populations known as *Mark and Recapture*. Since the m_1, m_2 and m_{12} are measured at the same time window,[5] the estimated total population M is the number of bots of the botnet in the time window.

T	Event duration observed in the local sensor
d	Size of the local sensor
G	Size of global target scope
ρ	Local over global ratio d/G
M	Total # of senders in the global view in T
m	Total # of senders in the local view in T
m_1	# of senders in the first half of the local view in T
m_2	# of senders in the second half of the local view in T
m_{12}	# of overlapped senders of m_1 and m_2 in T
R	Average scanning speed per bot
R_{G_i}	Global scanning speed of bot i
T_i	Time between first and last scan arrival time from bot i
n_i	Number of local scans observed from bot i in T
Δt_j	Inter-arrival time between the j and $j+1$ scans
Q	Local total # of scans in T

Table 5.5 Table of notations.

5.8.3 Exploiting IPID/Port Continuity

We now turn to estimating the global scan scope. We can consider two basic strategies: first, inferring the number of scans sent by sources in between observations of their probes at the Honeynet (**Approach I**); second, estimating the average bot global scanning speed using the minimal inter-arrival time we observe for each source (**Approach II**, covered in Section 5.8.4).

Approach I is based on measuring changes between a source's probes in the IPID or ephemeral port number. We predicate use of this test on first applying passive OS fingerprinting to identify whether the sender exhibits continuous IPID and/or ephemeral port selection. This property turns out (see below) to hold for modern Windows and Mac systems, as well as Linux systems for ephemeral ports.

IPID continuity. Windows and MacOS systems set the 16-bit IPID field in the IP header from a single, global packet counter, which is incremented by 1 per packet. During scanning, if the machine is mainly idle, and if the 16-bit counter does not overflow, we can use the difference in IPID between two observed probes to measure how many additional (unseen by us) scans the sender sent in an interval. (The algorithm becomes a bit more complex because of the need to identify and correct IPID overflow/wrap, as discussed below. We also need to take into account the endianness of the IPID counter as manifest in the IP header.)

A potential problem that arises with this approach is retransmission of TCP SYN's, which may increment the IPID counter even though they do not reflect new scans. Thus, when estimating global scan speed we divide by the average TCP SYN retransmission rate observed for the sender.

Ephemeral port number continuity. Based on source code inspections, we know that bots often let the operating system allocate the ephemeral source port associated with their scanning probes. These are again usually allocated by sequentially incrementing a single, global, counter. As with IPID, we then use observed gaps in this header field to estimate the number of additional

---

[5] Mark and Recapture requires a "closed system" assumption.

scans we did not see. (In this case, the logic for dealing with overflow/wrapping is slightly more complex, since different OSes confine the range used for ephemeral ports to different ranges. If we know the range from the fingerprinted OS, we use it directly; otherwise, we estimate it using the range observed locally, i.e., the maximum port number observed minus the minimum port number observed.)

For all the botnet events in the two-year Honeynet dataset, OS fingerprinting (via the `p0f` tool) indicates the large majority of bots run Windows 2000/XP/2003/Vista (85%), enabling us to apply both IPID and ephemeral port number based estimation. We also know that the proportion of Windows 95/98/NT4 is very low (0.8%), and only for those cases we need to switch the byte order. (These percentages match install-based statistics [4].)

Global scan speed estimation. As the IPID and ephemeral port number approaches work similarly, here we discuss only the former. We proceed by identifying the top sources originating in at least four sets of scanning. We test whether (after overflow recovery) the IPIDs increase linearly with respect to time, as follows. First, for two consecutive scans, if the IPID of the second is smaller than the first, we adjust it by 64K. We then try to fit the corrected $IPID_i$ and its corresponding arrival time t_i, along with previous points, to a line. If they fit with correlation coefficient $r > 0.99$, this reflects consistency with a near-constant scan speed, and the sender is a single host rather than multiple hosts behind a NAT. When this happens, we estimate the global speed from the slope.

It is possible that multiple overflows might occur, in which case the simple overflow recovery approach will fail. However, in this case the chance that we can still fit the IPIDs to a line is very small, so in general we will discard such cases. This will create a bias when estimating very large global scopes, because they will more often exhibit multiple overflows.

Sources that happen to engage in activity in addition to scanning can lead to overestimation of their global scan speed, since they will consume IPID or possibly ephemeral port numbers more quickly than those that might be simply due to the scanning. To offset this bias, when we have both IPID and ephemeral port estimates, we use the lesser of the two. Furthermore, in our evaluation, for the cases where we can get both estimates, we check the consistency between them, finding that IPID estimates usually produce larger results, but more than 95% of the time within a factor of two of the ephemeral port estimate. (Clearly, IPID can sometimes advance more quickly if the scanner receives a SYN-ACK in response to a probe, and thus returns an ACK to complete the 3-way handshake.)

Global scan scope extrapolation. With the ability to estimate the global scan speed, we finally estimate the global scan scope. Since we know the local scope, the problem is equivalent to estimating the local over global ratio, ρ. Suppose in a botnet event there are m senders seen by the sensor, for which we can estimate the global scan speeds R_{G_i} for a subset of size m'. For sender i, we know T_i (duration during which we observe the sender in the honeynet) and n_i (number of observed scans). We use the linear regression as discussed above to estimate the R_{G_i}, which is also quite accurate. The main estimation error comes from variation of the observed n_i from its expectation. Define $\hat{\rho}_i = \frac{n_i}{R_{G_i} \cdot T_i}$ for each sender. Sender i's global scan speed is R_{G_i}. Globally during T_i, it sends out $R_{G_i} \cdot T_i$ scans. n_i is the number of scans we see if we sample from $R_{G_i} \cdot T_i$ total scans with probability ρ. Therefore, $\hat{\rho}_i$ is an estimator of ρ. If we aggregate over all the m' senders, we get

$$\hat{\rho} = \frac{\sum_i^{m'} n_i}{\sum_i^{m'} R_{G_i} \cdot T_i} \tag{5.2}$$

Average Scan Speed Per Bot. After extrapolating ρ and M, we estimate the average scan speed per bot using:

$$\frac{Q}{R \cdot T \cdot M} = \rho \tag{5.3}$$

Here Q is the number of scans received by the sensor in time T, which should reflect a portion ρ of the total scans. We estimate the total scans by $R \cdot T \cdot M$, where R is the average scan speed per bot. This formulation assumes that each bot participates in the entire duration of the event, which is more likely to hold for short-lived events.

Limitations. Note that the above techniques can fail if attackers either craft raw IP packets or explicitly bind the source port used for TCP probes. Thus, the schemes may lose power in the future. However, crafting raw IP packets and simulating a TCP stack is a somewhat time consuming process, especially given most bots (85+%) we observed run Windows, and in modern Windows systems the raw socket interface has been disabled. Empirically, in our datasets we did not find any case for which the techniques did not apply.

5.8.4 Extrapolating from Interarrival Times

For **Approach II**, we estimate global scanning speed (and hence global scope, via estimating ρ from an estimate of R using Equation 5.3) in a quite different fashion, as follows. Clearly, a sender's global scan speed s provides an upper bound on the local speed we might observe for the sender. Furthermore, if we happen to observe two consecutive scans from that sender, then they should arrive about $\Delta t = 1/s$ apart. Accordingly, the minimum observed Δt gives us a lower bound on s, but with two important considerations: *(i)* the lower bound might be too conservative, if the global scope is large, and we never observe two consecutive scans, and *(ii)* noise perturbing network timing will introduce potentially considerable inaccuracies in the assumption that the observed Δt matches the interarrival spacing present at the source.

We proceed by considering all m senders, other than those that sent only a single scan. We rank these by the estimated global scan rate they imply via $\hat{s} = 1/\hat{\Delta t}$, where $\hat{\Delta t}$ is the minimum observed interarrival time for the sender. Naturally, fast senders should tend to reflect larger estimated speeds, which we verified by comparing $\hat{\Delta t}$ of each sender with how many scans we observed from it. We find that generally the correlation is clear, though with considerable deviations.

Using the fast senders' speeds to form an estimate of the *average* scanning speed may of course overestimate the average speed. On the other hand, our technique aims at estimating a lower bound. Thus, it is crucial to find a balanced point among the possible estimates. We do so by presenting the different sorted estimates from which an analyst can choose the "knee" of the resulting curve, i.e., the point with smallest rank k for which an increase in k yields little change in s. Figure 5.10 shows an example, plotting the top 30 maximum estimated speeds of Event VNC-060729. From the figure we would likely select $k = 6$ as the knee, giving an estimated speed 8.26.

5.9 Evaluation of Automated Classification

We now present an assessment of these techniques using the honeynet traffic described above. The total data spans 24 months and 293 GB of packet traces. Since the extrapolation algorithms have linear computational complexity, for a given event it takes less than a minute to analyze its scan properties and perform extrapolation analysis. We extracted 203 botnet scan events and 504 misconfiguration events. The dataset also includes a few moderate worm outbreaks during the observation period, such as the Allaple worm [3].

We first present characteristics of the botnet scanning events, followed by a look at botnet event correlation. Next we discuss results for the four botnet scan pattern checking techniques and their validation, followed by some findings regarding liveness-aware events. We finish with the presentation of global extrapolation results and their validation using DShield, a world-wide scan repository.

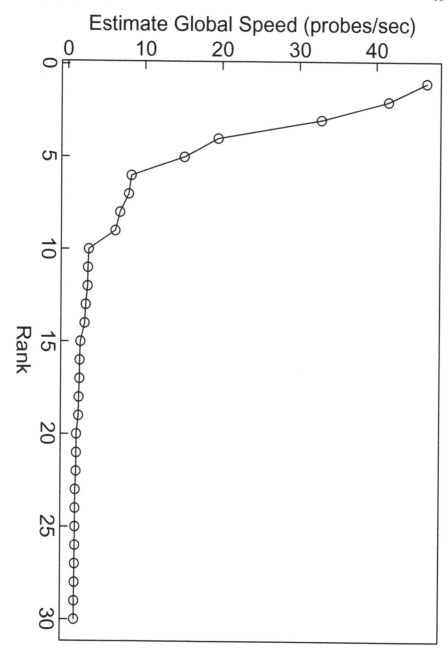

Fig. 5.10 Top 30 estimate speeds of Event VNC-060729.

5.9.1 Basic Characteristics of Botnet Events

Targeted Service	# of kinds of vul./probes	Events
NetBIOS/SMB/RPC	7	81
VNC	1	39
Symantec	1	34
MS SQL	1	14
HTTP	2	13
Telnet	1	12
MySQL	1	6
Others	4	4
total	18	203

Table 5.6 The summary of the events.

Table 5.6 breaks down 203 events according to their targeted services. We see that most of the events targeted popular services with large installed bases. We also see that 30 events reflected pure port reconnaissance without any payloads; another 3 events checked whether the HTTP service was open by requesting the homepage; and the remainder (83.7%) targeted particular vulnerabilities. Therefore, these botnet scans likely reflect attempted exploitations.

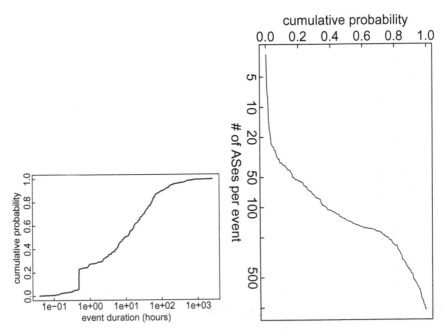

Fig. 5.11 Event Duration.   **Fig. 5.12** # Source ASes.

Figure 5.11 shows the CDF of event duration. A botnet event can last from a few minutes to a few days. We observe 36 events that lasted very close to half an hour, leading to the spike in the cumulative distribution. (We will discuss those events in details in Section 5.9.2.) In Figure 5.12, we show the CDF of unique number of ASes per event. Most of the bots (62.7%) come from more than 100 ASes. Only 3% of events reflect fewer than 20 ASes. This implies that cleaning the botnets from some part of the world (a few ASes) will not make a significant dent in their overall presence, and that blocking based on AS number is very problematic due to large number of ASes involved.

5.9.2 Event Correlation

To assess the temporal and source (bot IP address) correlations of different events, we decide that if two events have more than 20% source addresses in common, we consider them as correlated. We calculate the percentage of sharing as the maximum of the shared addresses over the total addresses of two events. We observe two types of interesting behavior:

Behavior 1: The botmasters ask the same botnet to scan the same vulnerability repeatedly. In our two years of data, we find several event clusters that exhibit this behavior. For example, there is a cluster of 36 events that occur every day, always scanning the same SMB vulnerability. These events form a nearly complete clique, i.e., on average each event shares about 35% of the same source addresses in common with most of the other events. In Figure 5.13, we show a subset of this commonality graph. (The number on an edge labels the percentage of bots sharing.)

Behavior 2: The botmasters appear to ask most of the bots in a botnet to focus on one vulnerability, while choosing a small subset of the bots to test another vulnerability. Apart from these big clusters, we find there are some cases in which two events has very high correlation (more than 80% of source address commonality), and occur very close in time, usually the same day. We find that often the first event is much larger in terms of the number of bots than the second; the second is just a small subset of the bots from the first. This behavior illustrates that the difficulty of fingerprinting botnet activity, if indeed our speculation is correct that botmasters may select a subset of bots to assign to different tasks.

5.9.3 Property-Checking Results

Figure 5.14 shows the breakdown of the events along different scanning dimensions. Six of the 203 events exhibit partial monotonic trends; 16.3% reflect liveness-aware ("hit-list") scanning; 80.3% follow the random-uniform pattern, passing both uniformity and independence tests.

Through manual inspection of the partial-monotonic events, we find that nearly half of the bots scan randomly and another half of bots scan sequentially. All of these bots start to scan at almost the same time, suggesting the activity was indeed of a single origin. Perhaps they reflect two groups of bots controlled by the same botmaster, and the botmaster asking these two groups to use different scan strategies; but in general, this behavior is puzzling.

We in addition test the use of liveness-aware scanning. As mentioned before, we use θ (the ratio of the number of senders in the darknet over to those of the honeynet) to classify the events. Out of the 106 events classified by port number, 33 reflect liveness-aware scanning when using $\theta = 0.5$. In fact, all have empirical values for $\theta < 0.01$, and all of events with $\theta > 0.5$ have $\theta > 0.85$. The 97 other events use popular ports also seen in background radiation, and thus we have to classify them based on application-level behavior. For these, we conservatively assume that all of the senders in the darknet using the same port number are possible members of the event, which tends to overestimate θ. For these 97 events, we did not find any with small θ and most of them

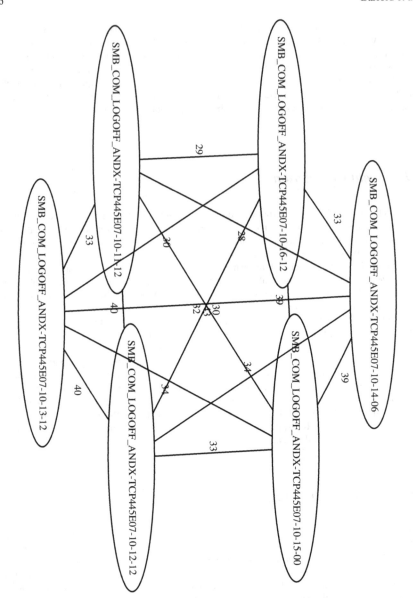

Fig. 5.13 A subset of the cluster of 36 events which all target a same vulnerablity in SMB.

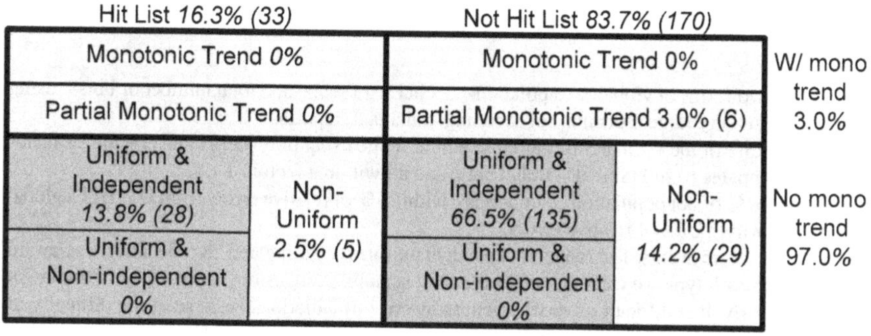

Hit List *16.3% (33)*		Not Hit List *83.7% (170)*		
Monotonic Trend *0%*		Monotonic Trend *0%*		W/ mono trend *3.0%*
Partial Monotonic Trend *0%*		Partial Monotonic Trend *3.0% (6)*		
Uniform & Independent *13.8% (28)*	Non-Uniform *2.5% (5)*	Uniform & Independent *66.5% (135)*	Non-Uniform *14.2% (29)*	No mono trend *97.0%*
Uniform & Non-independent *0%*		Uniform & Non-independent *0%*		

Fig. 5.14 Scan pattern-checking results.

have θ larger than one. We found in all the cases, the results are insensitive to the threshold of θ. In addition, none of the events only target the darknet.

date 2006	desc	ex. scope (I)(/8)	DShield scope (/8)	scope ratio (I)	ex. scope (II)(/8)
08-25	MSSQL	1.48	1	1.48	4.6
11-26	Symantec	0.59	0.75	0.79	0.1
11-27	Symantec	0.76	1	0.76	0.4
11-28	Symantec	0.92	1	0.92	4.0
07-23	VNC	0.63	0.9	0.7	0.9
07-29	VNC	0.63	0.87	0.72	0.9
10-31	VNC	0.80	0.80	1	0.6
08-24	NetBIOS	0.86	1	0.86	3.5
08-25	NetBIOS	1.13	1	1.13	2.5
08-29	NetBIOS	0.89	1	0.89	0.5
09-02	SMB	0.67	0.50	1.34	0.5
07-26	SMB	0.82	1	0.82	4.3

Table 5.7 Global scope extrapolation results and validation.

We find that 34 of the 197 random events fail our test for uniformity. We can visually confirm that all of the remaining 163 events passing the test indeed appear uniform. Three of those that failed appear uniform visually, but have a very large numbers of scans, for which the statistical testing becomes stringent in the presence of a minor amount of noise. In the remaining failed cases, we can see "hot-spot" addresses that clearly attract more activity than others; we do not have an explanation for these.

Finally, we test the 163 uniform cases for coordination, not finding any instances at a 0.5% significance level.

5.9.4 Extrapolation Evaluation & Validation

We validate two forms of global extrapolation—global scan scope and total number of bots—using DShield [10], a very large repository of scanning and attack reports.

Finding: 75% of the estimates of global scanning scope using only local data lie within a factor of 1.35 of estimates from DShield's global data, and all within a factor of 1.5.

Finding: 64% of bot population estimates are within 8% of relative errors from DShield's global data, and all within 27% of relative errors.

For 163 uniform events, 135 reflect independent uniform scanning and 28 reflect liveness-aware scanning. For each type we estimate either the total scanning ranges or the total size of the target lists, respectively. It is difficult to verify liveness-aware extrapolations because of the difficulty of assessing how the limited targeting will align with sources that report to DShield. However, we can validate extrapolations from the first class of events since we find they usually target a large address range. Due to limited data access to DShield, we have only been able to verify 12 cases, as shown in Table 5.7.

5.9.4.1 Global Scope Extrapolation and Validation.

Global scope extrapolation results: In Table 5.7, we show the extrapolated scan scope estimated from the local honeynet compared to an estimation made with the DShield data. Column *ex. scope (I)* shows the honeynet extrapolated scan scope by Approach I. Column *DShield scope* shows the DShield-based estimation. Column *scope ratio* gives the ratio of the extrapolated scan scope by Approach I over the DShield scope. Column *ex. scope (II)* shows the extrapolated scan scope by Approach II. From the results, we see that our findings are consistent with those derived from DShield.

Validation Methodology: We find that most DShield sensors manifest synchronized clocks (i.e., we often find significant temporal overlap between our honeynet events and corresponding DShield reports). For a given extraplation, we take two steps for validation. First, since the extrapolation results all wound up being of /8 size or quite close, we find all the /8 networks (except those with private IP prefixes) with sufficient source overlap with the honeynet events. Secondly, for these /8 networks, we infer the scan scopes and compare them with our results.

Step 1. Let X denote the /8 IP prefix of our sensor. We first calculate the number of shared senders $N(X)$ between our event data and scan logs for X from DShield. We consider additional /8 prefixes Y_i if their numbers of senders shared with the honeynet $N(Y_i)$ are larger than $N(X)/3$, reflecting an assumption that if a botnet uniformly scans multiple /8 prefixes, each should see quite a few sources in common. For X and each Y_i, we select the full width at half maximum (FWHM) of the unique source arrival process as a (conservative) way to delineate the global interval of the event. We then calculate the time range overlap with X for each Y_i; if the overlap of Y_i exceeds 50% of X's interval, we consider that the botnet scanned X and Y_i at the same time.

Step 2. After finding the scanned /8 networks, we estimate the scan scope within each. Alternatively, we compute the ratio of sensors in each network reporting the scans. There are several limitations of DShield data. First, it does not contain complete scan information (only a subset of scans within a prefix are reported). Second, different sensors might use different reporting thresholds and might not see all activity (e.g., due to firewall filtering). Thus all these limitations make calibration of data a challenging task.

To assess the limitations, we check a one-week interval around our events to find which DShield sensors *ever* report a given type of activity. We treat all the reporting sensors in one /24 network as a single unique sensor. For such sensors, we count the number from different /24 networks, denoted by C_{total}. Similarly, we count the number of unique sensors from different /24 networks that reported scans from shared senders of the given event, denoted C_{est}. We reduce the noise from the DShield data by removing sensors that only report a single address within a /24 sensor. We then use C_{est}/C_{total} to estimate the fraction of a /8 networks scanned by the botnet, which gives us a conservative estimate of the event's total range. We add up such fractions if there are multiple related /8 networks discovered in the first step, indicating the results in Column *DShield scope* of Table 5.7.

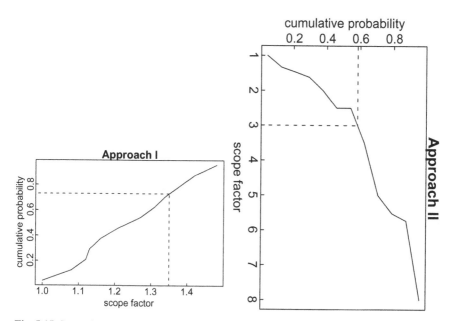

Fig. 5.15 Scope factors of the 12 events validated.

Accuracy Analysis: We define the *scope factor* as $\max(D/H, H/D)$, where the D is the Dshield scope and H is the Honeynet scope. The scope factor indicates the absolute relative error in the log scale. The DShield data shows that such local estimates of global scope exhibit a promising level of accuracy. As shown in Figure 5.15, for Approach I the scope factors of 75% events are less than 1.35, and all of them are less than 1.5. Approach II (column *ex. scope II*) works less well (58% of events are within a factor of three, and 92% within a factor of six), but it may still exhibit enough power to enable sites to differentiate scans that specifically target them versus broader sweeps. In our two-year dataset, we did not find any scan events specifically targeting the site where the sensor resides; this fits with the institute's threat model, which is mainly framed in terms of indiscriminant attacks.

5.9.4.2 Total Population Estimates and Validation

We assume that our honeynet event data and the corresponding DShield data give us two independent samples of the bot population, which presents an opportunity to employ Mark and Recapture. We count the sources observed by DShield sensors of IP prefix X on the same port number in the same time window as the sources of DShield sensors. We term the number of sources in common between our honeynet and DShield as the *shared sources*. Based on the similar idea of Equation 5.1, we know the fraction of the shared sources to the sources of DShield should be equal to the ratio between bots observed in the honeynet and total population. Since DShield sensors will see other scanners (constituting noise) as well, we will likely underestimate the first fraction, and consequently overestimate the bot population. Per the results shown below, we find the estimates very close to those we estimate locally by splitting the sensor into two halves.

Table 5.8 shows the extrapolation and DShield validation results, with column *ex. #bots* giving the bot population extrapolation constructed by splitting the sensor into two halves. Column *#bot DShield* shows the results using DShield's global data. Column *#bots ratio* gives the ratio between the two of these. Note, we only validate the seven port-number-based events (MSSQL, Symantec and VNC). The NetBIOS/SMB events require payload analysis, which we cannot validate through DShield since it does not provide payload information. We find our approach is quite accurate, with 64% of cases within 8% of relative error ($|(our - DShield)|/DShield$).

date 2006	desc	ex. #bots	#bots DShield	#bots ratio
08-25	MSSQL	3100	3139	0.99
11-26	Symantec	228	215	1.06
11-27	Symantec	276	373	0.73
11-28	Symantec	305	331	0.92
07-23	VNC	2752	2712	1.01
07-29	VNC	3628	3696	0.98
10-31	VNC	526	622	0.84

Table 5.8 Extrapolated bot population results and validation.

5.9.4.3 Other Extrapolation Results

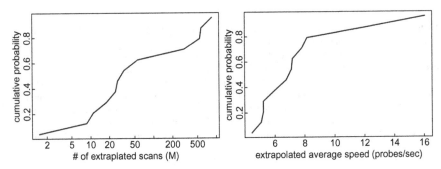

Fig. 5.16 Extrapolated # of scans.   **Fig. 5.17** Extrapolated the average scan speed.

Based on Approach I, we can also infer the total number of scans and extrapolated average scan speed of the bots in each event. In Figure 5.16, we show the extrapolated total number of scans, using a log-scaled X axis. We can see the number of scans sent by the events could differ significantly, given that the duration and the number of bots in each event differ. Figure 5.17 shows the extrapolated average scan speed of the bots.

5.10 Summary

Our quest in this chapter has been to explore methodologies for enriching the set of information at a security analysts's disposal by creating *network situational awareness* (NetSA). We base our study on the premise that honeypot data can provide a source of timely, accurate and concise information for situational awareness—but this data must be organized and condensed to prove useful. To that end, we first examined techniques based on honeynets, analyzers that leverage the Bro NIDS, and a MySQL backend database to facilitate analysis of honeynet data. We then extended the scope of analysis to include approaches for recognizing botnet scanning strategies and inferring the global properties of botnet events.

An evaluation of these tools using extensive honeynet and DShield data demonstrates the promise such approaches hold for contributing to a site's situational awareness—including the crucial question of whether a large probing event detected by the site simply reflects broader, indiscriminate activity, or instead reflects an attacker who has explicitly targeted the site.

References

1. HoneyBow Sensor. http://honeybow.mwcollect.org.
2. Honeysnap. http://www.honeynet.org/tools/honeysnap/index.html.
3. Net-Worm.Win32.Allaple.a. http://www.viruslist.com/en/viruses/encyclopedia?virusid=145521.
4. OS Platform Statistics by W3school. http://www.w3schools.com/browsers/browsers_stats.asp.
5. M. Bailey, E. Cooke, F. Jahanian, J. Nazario, and D. Watson. The Internet Motion Sensor: A Distributed Blackhole Monitoring System. In *Network and Distributed Security Symposium*, San Diego, CA, January 2005.
6. J. Bethencourt et al. Mapping internet sensors with probe response attacks. In *Proc. of the USENIX Security*, 2005.
7. J. Cai et al. Honeynets and honeygames: A game theoretic approach to defending network monitors. Technical Report TR1577, University of Wiscconsin, 2006.
8. E. Cooke, M. Bailey, M. Mao, D. Watson, F. Jahanian, and D. McPherson. Toward understanding distributed blackhole placement. In *Proceedings of CCS Workshop on Rapid Malcode (WORM '04)*, October 2004.
9. J. R. Crandall, Z. Su, and S. F. Wu. On deriving unknown vulnerabilities from zeroday polymorphic and metamorphic worm exploits. In *Proc. of ACM CCS*, 2005.
10. Dshield. http://www.dshield.org.
11. German Honeynet Project. Tracking Botnets. http://www.honeynet.org/papers/bots, 2005.
12. G. Gu et al. Bothunter: Detecting malware infection through ids-driven dialog correlation. In *Proc. of USENIX Security*, 2007.
13. G. Gu et al. Botsniffer: Detecting botnet command and control channels in network traffic. In *Proc. of NDSS*, 2008.
14. The Honeynet Project. http://project.honeynet.org, 2003.
15. M. G. Kendall. *Rank Correlation Methods*. Griffin., 1976.
16. H. Kim and B. Karp. Autograph: Toward automated, distributed worm signature detection. In *13th USENIX Security Symposium*, San Diego, California, August 2004.
17. C. Kreibich and J. Crowcroft. Honeycomb–creating intrusion detection signatures using honeypots. In *2nd Workshop on Hot Topics in Networks (Hotnets-II)*, Cambridge, Massachusetts, November 2003.
18. A. Kumar et al. Exploiting underlying structure for detailed reconstruction of an internet scale event. In *Proc. of ACM IMC*, 2005.

19. Z. Li, A. Goyal, Y. Chen, and V. Paxson. Towards situational awareness of large-scale botnet events using honeynets. Technical Report NWU-EECS-08-08, Northwestern University, 2008.
20. D. Moore. Network telescopes: Observing small or distant security events. Invited Presentation at the 11th USENIX Security Symposium, 2002.
21. D. Moore et al. Inside the slammer worm. *IEEE Security and Privacy*, 2003.
22. D. Moore, C. Shannon, and J. Brown. Code red: A case study on the spread and victims of an internet worm. In *Proceedings of ACM SIGCOMM Internet Measurement Workshop*, November 2002.
23. D. Moore, G. Voelker, and S. Savage. Inferring internet denial of service activity. In *Proceedings of the 2001 USENIX Security Symposium*, Washington D.C., August 2001.
24. Navy Aviation Schools Command. Situational Awareness. https://www.cnet.navy.mil.crm/crm/stand_mat/seven_skills/SA.asp, 2005.
25. Network Centric Operations Industry Consortium. Situational Awareness. http://www.ncoic.org/download/NCOIC_Lexicon_v8.pdf, 2005.
26. R. Pang et al. Characteristics of Internet background radiation. In *Proc. of ACM IMC*, 2004.
27. R. Pang, V. Yegneswaran, P. Barford, V. Paxson, and L. Peterson. Characteristics of Internet Background Radiation. In *Proceedings of the ACM SIGCOMM Internet Measurement Conference*, 2004.
28. V. Paxson. BRO: A system for detecting network intruders in real time. In 7th *USENIX Security Symposium*, San Antonio, Texas, January 1998.
29. N. Provos. A virtual honeypot framework. In *Proceedings of USENIX Security Symposium*, San Diego, CA, August 2004.
30. N. Provos. A virtual honeypot framework. In *Proc. of USENIX Security*, 2004.
31. M. Rajab, J. Zarfoss, F. Monrose, and A. Terzis. A multifaceted approach to understanding the botnet phenomenon. In *Proc. of ACM IMC*, 2006.
32. J. A. Rice. *Mathematical Statistics and Data Analysis*. Duxbury Press, 1994.
33. S. Singh, C. Estan, G. Varghese, and S. Savage. The Earlybird system for real-time detection of unknown worms. In *Operating System Design and Implementation*, 2004.
34. S. Staniford et al. How to Own the Internet in your spare time. In *Proc. of USENIX Security*, 2002.
35. W. E. Weisstein. Stirling Number of the Second Kind. http://mathworld.wolfram.com/StirlingNumberoftheSecondKind.html.
36. V. Yegneswaran, P. Barford, and D. Plonka. On the design and use of internet sinks for network abuse monitoring. In *Proceedings of Recent Advances in Intrusion Detection*, 2004.
37. V. Yegneswaran, P. Barford, and J. Ullrich. Internet intrusions: Global characteristics and prevalence. In *Proceedings of ACM SIGMETRICS*, June 2003.
38. V. Yegneswaran, J. T. Giffin, P. Barford, and S. Jha. An Architecture for Semantic-Aware Signature Generation. In *Proceedings of USENIX Security Symposium*, 2005.

Chapter 6
Assessing Cybercrime Through the Eyes of the WOMBAT

Marc Dacier, Corrado Leita, Olivier Thonnard, Van-Hau Pham, and Engin Kirda

6.1 Foreword

The WOMBAT project is a collaborative European funded research project that aims at providing new means to understand the existing and emerging threats that are targeting the Internet economy and the net citizens. The approach carried out by the partners include a data collection effort as well as some sophisticated analysis techniques. In this chapter, we present one of the threats-related data collection system in use by the project, as well as some of the early results obtained when digging into these data sets.

In [21], the authors offer a thorough presentation of one of the data collection infrastructures used within the WOMBAT project to collect threats-related data. The presentation is very detailed, going as far as explaining the database scheme used to represent the vast amount of information they have access to. In the following pages, we wish to offer to the reader an early synthesis of the various results that have been obtained when analyzing this large amount of information. However, in order for this chapter to be as self-contained as possible, we start the presentation by re-stating the rationales for this work, as well as by providing a summarized introduction to the data collection infrastructure. We invite the reader who is already familiar with the WOMBAT project to skip this part and move directly to the presentation of the results.

Marc Dacier
Symantec, Sophia Antipolis, France, e-mail: marc_dacier@symantec.com

Corrado Leita
Symantec, Sophia Antipolis, France, e-mail: corrado_leita@symantec.com

Olivier Thonnard
Eurecom, Sophia Antipolis, France, e-mail: thonnard@eurecom.fr

Van-Hau Pham
Eurecom, Sophia Antipolis, France, e-mail: pham@eurecom.fr

Engin Kirda
Eurecom, Sophia Antipolis, France, e-mail: kirda@eurecom.fr

S. Jajodia et al., (eds.), *Cyber Situational Awareness*,
Advances in Information Security 46, DOI 10.1007/978-1-4419-0140-8_6,
© Springer Science+Business Media, LLC 2010

6.2 Introduction

Understanding the existing and emerging threats on the Internet should help to effectively protect the Internet economy, our information systems and the Internet users. To reach this goal, it is necessary to collect sound measurements about the ongoing attack processes observed worldwide on the Internet. In the last years, the experimental study of Internet threats has gained much attention and many valuable initiatives now exist for monitoring malicious activities or for capturing malware binaries. Important contributions have been made in the field such as: i) the so-called Darknets and Internet telescopes [23, 30, 35], ii) various projects based on the development of low- or high-interaction honeypots [2, 13, 31, 34, 41], and iii) other initiatives aiming at collecting and sharing firewall and IDS logs [14].

The Leurré.com project was initially launched in 2003 and has since then been integrated and further developed within the WOMBAT project. It is based on a worldwide distributed system of honeypots running in more than 30 different countries covering the five continents. The main objective with this infrastructure is to get a more realistic picture of certain classes of threats happening on the Internet by collecting unbiased quantitative data in a long-term perspective. We have decided to keep in one centralized database very precise information concerning a limited number of nodes under close scrutiny. Concretely speaking, we initially deployed identically configured honeypots based on Honeyd [31] on the premises of several partners around the globe. Within WOMBAT, we have improved the infrastructure in a major way by building and deploying new honeypot sensors based on the ScriptGen technology [17, 18, 20]. These new sensors dramatically improve the interaction with the attackers and, hence, enrich our data collection. We record all packets sent to or from these machines, on all platforms, and we store the whole traffic into a database, enriched with some contextual information and with meta-data describing the observed attack sessions. In the next Sections, we present these two data collection infrastructures and, then, offer a synthesis of some of the results obtained by the WOMBAT partners when analyzing the data at their disposal.

This chapter begins with the presentation of the initial data collection infrastructure that is based on the deployment of low-interaction honeypots, for which we give a series of simple examples that reveal the kind of information that such low level traces can provide. Then, we present how we have extended our infrastructure with the SGNET deployment, which has recently been opened to anybody willing to host one of its sensors. Section 6.5 presents how the identification of so-called *attack events* (representing specific activities over limited period of times) enables us to observe the evolution of what we hypothesize to be *armies of zombies*, some of them remaining visible for more than 700 days. Section 6.6 gets deeper into the analysis of the traces, highlighting the usefulness of applying what we call a *multidimensional analysis* to the honeypot events. Section 6.7 provides some insights into the kind of contextual information that SGNET can offer whenever collecting malware. Concrete examples are given that demonstrate the usefulness of such information in discovering new threats and in better understanding the links between the code injection phase, the shellcode injected and the uploaded malware itself.

6.3 Leurre.com v1.0 Honeyd

6.3.1 Historical background

The Institut Eurécom has started collecting attack traces on the Internet in 2003 by means of honeypot responders. The first platform consisted of three high interaction honeypots built on top of the VMware technology (the interested readers in the platform configuration are invited to read

[12] for more information). As shown in [11, 12], these first experiments allowed us to detect some locality in Internet attacks: activities seen in some networks were not observed in others. To validate this assumption, we decided to deploy multiple honeypots in diverse locations. With diversity, we refer both to the geographical location and to the sensor environment (education, government, private sectors, etc.). However, the VMware-based solution did not seem to be scalable. First, this solution had a high cost in terms of security maintenance. Second, it required significant hardware resources. In fact, to avoid legal issues we would have needed to ensure that these systems could not be compromised and could not be exploited by attackers as stepping stones to attack other hosts. For those reasons, we have chosen a low-interaction honeypot solution, honeyd [31]. This solution allowed us to deploy low-cost platforms, easy to maintain and with low security risk, hosted by partners on a voluntary basis. The low-cost of the solution allowed us to build a distributed honeynet consisting now of more than 50 sensors distributed all over the world, collecting data on network attacks and representing this information under the form of a relational database accessible to all the parters. Information about the identity of the partners and the observed attackers is protected by a Non-Disclosure Agreement signed by each entity participating to the project. We have developed all the required software to automate the various regular maintenance tasks (new installation, reconfiguration, log collection, backups, etc.) to reduce the maintenance overhead related to the management of such a complex system.

6.3.2 Some technical aspects

We describe here some important technical aspects, including the platform architecture, the logs collection mechanism, the DB uploading mechanism, and the data enrichment mechanism.

Platform architecture: As mentioned before, the main objective is to compare unsolicited network traffic in diverse locations. To make sound comparisons, the platform architecture must be the same everywhere. We tried to make our Honeyd-based solution as similar as possible to the initial VMware setup. We configured Honeyd to simulate 3 virtual hosts running on three different (consecutive) IP addresses. We configured Honeyd's personality engine to emulate the presence of two different configurations, namely two identical virtual machines emulating Windows 2000 SP3, and one machine emulating a Linux Kernel 2.4.20. To the first two configurations (resp. the last) correspond a number of open ports: FTP, Telnet, Web server, Netbios name service, Netbios session service, and Service Message Block (resp. FTP server, SSH server, Web server on ports (80), Proxy (port 8080,8081), remote shell (port 514), LPD Printer service (port 515) and portmapper). We require from each partner hosting the platform a fourth IP address used to access the physical host running Honeyd and perform maintenance tasks. We run tcpdump [36] to capture the complete network traces on each platform. As a security measure, a reverse firewall is set up to protect our system. That is, we accept only incoming connections and drop all the connections that could eventually be initiated from our system (in theory, this should never happen). The access to the host machine is very limited: SSH connections are only allowed in a two-hour daily timeframe and only if it is initiated by our maintenance servers.

Data collection mechanism: An automatized mechanism allows us, on a daily basis, to connect to the platforms through an encrypted connection to collect the tcpdump traces. The script downloads not only the last day's log file but also the eventual older ones that could not have been collected in the previous days due to, for example, a connectivity problem. All the log files are stored on a central server.

Data uploading mechanism: Just after the data retrieval, the log files are then uploaded into a large Oracle database by a set of Perl programs. These programs take tcpdump files as input and parse them in order to create different abstraction levels. The lowest one corresponds to the raw tcpdump traffic. The higher level is built on the lower ones and has richer semantics. Due to space constraints, we do not present here all the concepts, but instead we will focus only on the most important notions.

1. **Source**: A source corresponds to an IP address that has sent at least one packet to, at least, one platform. Note that, in our Source model, a given IP address can correspond to several distinct sources. That is, an IP remains associated to a given source as long as there is no more than 25 hours between 2 consecutive packets received from that IP. After such a delay, a new source will be assigned to the IP. By grouping packets by sources instead of by IPs, we minimize the risk of gathering packets sent by distinct physical machines that have been assigned the same IP dynamically after 25 hours.

2. **Large_Session**: it's the set of packets which have been exchanged between one Source and a particular honeypot sensor. A Large_Session is characterized by the duration of the attack, the number of packets sent by the Source, the number of virtual machines targeted by the source on that specific platform, ...

3. **Ports sequence**: A ports sequence is a time ordered sequence of ports (without duplicates) a source has contacted on a given virtual machine. For example, if an attacker sends the following packets: ICMP, 135 TCP, 135 TCP, 139 TCP to a given virtual machine, the associated ports sequence will be represented by the string $I|135T|139T$. Each large session can have, at most, three distinct clusters associated to it.

   This is an important feature that allows us to classify the attacks into different classes. In fact, as mentioned in [12], most attack tools are automatized, it is as likely that the same attack tools will leave the same port sequences on different platforms.

4. **Tiny_Session**: A Tiny_Session groups the packets exchanged between one source and one virtual host. A Large_Session is thus composed of up to three Tiny_Sessions, ordered according to the virtual hosts IP addresses.

5. **(Attack) Cluster**: A Cluster is a set of Sources having exhibited the same network fingerprint on a honeypot sensor. We apply a clustering algorithm on the traffic generated by the sources. The first step of this clustering algorithm consists in grouping large sessions into bags. This grouping aims at differentiating between various classes of activity taking into consideration a set of preliminary discriminators, namely the number of targeted virtual hosts and the unsorted list of port sequences hitting them. In order to further refine the bags, a set of continuous parameters is taken into consideration for each large session, namely: its duration, the total number of packets, the average inter arrival time of packets, and the number of packets per tiny session. These parameters can assume any value in the range $[0, \infty]$, but some ranges of their values may be used to define bag subclasses. This is done through a peak picking algorithm that identifies ranges of values considered discriminating for the bag refinement. Large sessions belonging to a bag and sharing the same matching intervals are grouped together in a cluster.

   A very last refinement step is the payload validation. The algorithm considers the concatenation of all the payloads sent by the attacker within a large session ordered according to the arrival time. If it identifies within a cluster multiple groups of large sessions sharing similar payloads, it further refines the cluster according to these groups. In summary, a cluster is by design a set of large sessions that seem to be originating from a similar attack tool.

6. A **Cluster time series** $\Phi_{T,c}$ is a function defined over a period of time T, T being defined as a time interval (in days). That function returns the amount of sources per day associated to a cluster c.

7. An **Observed cluster time series** $\Phi_{T,c,op}$ is a function defined over a period of time T, T being defined as a time interval (in days). That function returns the amount of sources per day associated to a cluster c that can be seen from a given *observation view point op*. The observation view point can either be a specific platform or a specific country of origin. In the first case, $\Phi_{T,c,platform_X}$ returns, per day, the amount of sources belonging to cluster c that have hit $platform_X$. Similarly, in the second case, $\Phi_{T,c,country_X}$ returns, per day, the amount of sources belonging to cluster c that are geographically located in $country_X$. Clearly, we always have: $\Phi_{T,c} = \sum^{\forall i \in countries} \Phi_{T,c,i} = \sum^{\forall x \in platforms} \Phi_{T,c,x}$

Information enrichment

Finally, to enrich the information about each source, we add to it three other dimensions:

1. **Geographical information**: To obtain geographical location such as: organization, ISP, country of a given IP address, we have initially used Netgeo [25], developed in the context of CAIDA Project. It provided a very surprising result which considered Netherlands and Australia as two of the most attacking countries. As a sanity check, we have used Maxmind [22] and we have detected problems with the Netgeo classification. [29] provides a comparison of these two tools. It comes out from this analysis that Netherlands and Australia were not among the top attacking countries anymore when using different sources of information for the geographical location of attacking IP addresses.
2. **OS fingerprint**: To figure out the OS of attacking hosts, we have used passive OS fingerprinting techniques. We take advantage of disco [1] and pOf [42]. It has been shown that pOf is more accurate than disco. Active fingerprinting techniques such as Nmap, Quezo, or Xprobe have not been considered to minimize the risk of alerting the attacker of our investigations.
3. **Domain name:** We also do the reverse DNS lookup to get the domain name of the attacking machine if it is available.

6.3.3 Generic picture

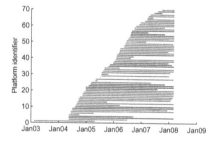 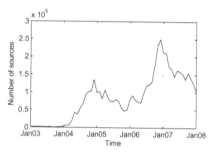

Fig. 6.1 Left: Evolution of platforms, Right: number of sources

Figure 6.1 (left) shows the evolution of platforms. Each curve corresponds to the time life of a platform. As we can see, we started our data collection in January 2003 with one VMware honeypot and we have started to deploy the distributed low interaction honeypots in April 2004. Since then, the number of partners joining us has kept increasing. In total, we have around 50 offical partners and around 20 former partners. These platforms have, in total, covered 37 different /8 networks, locating in 28 different countries in five continents. In total, we have observed 5173624 sources corresponding to 3461745 different IP addresses. Figure 6.1 (right) shows the evolution of the number of sources over time. The variation of the curve is of course influenced by the number of platforms. Note that up to April 2004, the traffic is negligible. After that, the number of sources has increased. It is interesting to observe that the number of sources on the last six months of 2004 is much higher than that of the last six months of 2005 even through, in the second case, we have more platforms. In total, there are 155041 different clusters. Figure 6.2 (left) represents the cumulative distribution function of number of sources per number of cluster. Point (X,Y) on the curve means that Y*100% of the total amount of clusters contain less than X sources. As we can see, most of clusters are very small. There are, in fact, only 15521 clusters containing more than 10 sources each. Interestingly enough, by querying the database one can find that these clusters, ie. around 10% of the total number of clusters, contain in fact 95% of the observed attacks! In other words, the bulk of the attacks is found in a limited number of clusters whereas a very large number of diverse activities originate from a very limited number of sources. In term of attacking machines' OS, according to p0f, almost all attacking machines are Windows ones. This confirms again the results in [11, 12]. Figure 6.3 shows the top ten attacking countries with US in the head, followed by China and Canada. But the surprising thing is that CS (corresponding to former Serbia and Montenegro) is at the fifth position. The reason is that there is one (and only one!) platform which is heavily attacked by this country. In total, it shows up as one of the most attacking countries. Finally, as an example to show the diversity of the attacks over different platforms, Figure 6.2 (right) shows the distribution of the number of different clusters per platform. Each column represents the number of distinct clusters observed on a platform. We have as many columns as number of platforms. As we can see, the attacks are highly diverse. On some platforms, we observe just small number of clusters, but it is not the case for others.

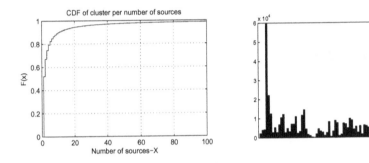

Fig. 6.2 Left:Cumulative distribution function of number of source per cluster; Right:Distribution of number of clusters per platform.

6.3.4 Some illustrative examples

The diversified aspect of real-world datasets, such as honeynet data, makes the task of an analyst rather difficult in selecting and analyzing some appropriate attack characteristics, which may help eventually to make meaningful conclusions about the attack root causes. To illustrate this point, we provide here a series of basic examples of how to analyze various facets of the observed network threats. At this stage, the main ideas we want to convey are: *i)* that several aspects of an attack dataset can potentially deliver meaningful pieces of evidence about attack root causes, and *ii)* that large-scale attack processes manifest themselves through so-called "attack events" on different sensors, which are the basis for the analysis of the underlying root causes.

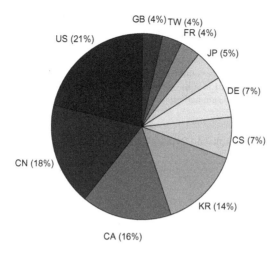

Fig. 6.3 Top ten attacking countries

6.3.4.1 Temporal Evolution of Attack Clusters

Time series analysis can provide valuable information (e.g., trends, abrupt changes, and emerging phenomena) to security practitioners in charge of detecting anomalous behaviors or intrusions in the collected traffic. This first illustration shows a temporal evolution of a given attack cluster, i.e.an aggregated source count of the number of sources belonging to that cluster on a chosen time scale, in this case grouped by day. On Fig 6.4, we can see the evolution of the attack cluster with ID. 17718 in a time period ranging from 1-Dec-06 until 01-Mar-07, either for all platforms together (left plot), or by splitting the time series for each platform separately, so as to analyze the impact of this attack cluster on different platforms.

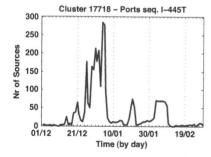
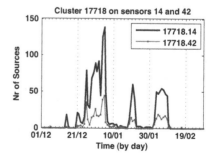

Fig. 6.4 Left: global time evolution of attack cluster 17718, with the sources aggregated by day. Right: time evolution of the same attack cluster for the platforms 14 and 42 separately.

6.3.4.2 Geographical Location of Attackers

Taking back the previous example, we could wonder from which countries the sources belonging to attack cluster 17718 are coming from during the activity period of this attack process. The geographical origins of attackers can be used indeed to identify attack activities having specific patterns in terms of originating countries. Such information can be important to identify, for instance, botnets that are located in a limited number of countries. It is also a way to confirm the existence, or not, of so-called safe harbors for the hackers.

Table 6.1 Geographical distribution for attack cluster 17718 in the time window spanning from 1-Dec-06 until 01-Mar-07.

Country of origin	Nr of Sources	Relative %
CN	1150	35.3
US	378	11.6
CA	255	7.8
FR	236	7.2
unknown	215	6.6
TW	137	4.2
JP	128	3.9
IT	120	3.6
DE	107	3.3
Others	524	16.1

The result of extracting the geographical distribution of cluster 17718 is represented in Table 6.1: the first column indicates the country of origin (represented with its ISO code) and the second column gives the number of sources belonging to that country. The third column indicates the corresponding relative percentage for each country with respect to the total number of sources for this attack process (i.e., 3250 sources in total). With this simple example, we want to show that this kind of aggregated information can in turn be used as input of a correlation process, as it will be demonstrated in Section 6.6.

6.3.4.3 Attackers Subnets Information

The source IP network blocks is a property that nicely complements the geolocation as described before. Instead of giving insight into possible geostrategic decisions made by the attackers, they can typically reveal some strategies in the propagation model of the malware. Indeed, attackers' IP subnets can provide a good indication of the spatial "uncleanliness" of certain networks, i.e., the tendency for compromised hosts to stay clustered within unclean networks, especially for zombie machines belonging to botnets as demonstrated in [8]. Previous studies have also demonstrated that some worms show a clear bias in their propagation scheme, such as a tendency for scanning machines of the same (or nearby) network so as to optimize their propagation [7].

The results of such analysis are presented in Table 6.2[1] in the case of an aggregation of the sources by Class A network blocks, but similar analyses could be performed for other groupings (Class B, C, ...). Again, this kind of feature vector can be used as input for a global correlation process in order to identify attack processes that exhibit similar IP subnets distributions.

---

[1] To preserve the confidentiality related to the IPs of the attackers, the first byte values have been somehow obfuscated in the table. So these are not the real subnet prefixes, but the eventual proximities among them have been preserved.

Table 6.2 Anonymized distribution of Class A-subnets for attack cluster 17718 in the time window spanning from 1-Dec-06 until 01-Mar-07.

Subnet of Origin (Class A)	Nr of Sources
220.x.x.x	451
56.x.x.x	193
80.x.x.x	168
22.x.x.x	160
217.x.x.x	159
86.x.x.x	123
218.x.x.x	113
69.x.x.x	100
66.x.x.x	91
216.x.x.x	90
Others	1602

6.3.4.4 Targeted Platforms or Subnets

Apparently, some recent crimeware toolkits are now able to deliver a specific type of malware to different geographical regions [5]. By using this new feature, cybercriminals can thus set up well targeted campaigns by delivering specialized crimeware in specific regions, being specific countries or its corresponding IP blocks. Therefore, it seems important to look at the relationships that may exist between attack events and the platforms or subnets they have been observed on. Table 6.3 illustrates this kind of information, where the first column gives the Id. of the platform, and each row of the second column indicates the number of sources belonging to attack cluster 17718 that have targeted the corresponding platform. In the last column, the Class A-subnet of each platform is also given. This last illustration gives yet another example of "viewpoint" that could be used in a global correlation process of attack events.

Table 6.3 Distribution of targeted platforms for attack cluster 17718

Targ.Platform	Nr of Sources	Subnet(A)
14	1552	139
76	871	134
42	431	150
57	70	24
71	67	58
53	42	88
55	42	83
Others	175	-

6.4 Leurre.com v2.0: SGNET

6.4.1 Increasing the level of interaction

We have seen in the previous Section how we have been able to generate valuable dataset with quantitative information on the localization and the evolution of Internet unsolicited traffic. We are able to observe interesting behaviors, most of which are very difficult to justify or to attribute to a specific root cause. It is, indeed, very difficult to link a given observation to a class of activities, and our search for answers in this direction had to deal with a limited amount of information about the final intention of the attacker. The low level of interaction of the Leurré.com honeypots is a limiting factor: when a honeypot receives a client request, it is not able to carry on the network conversation with the attacker, nor to "understand" it.

For instance, in our experience within the Leurré.com project, due to the lack of emulation scripts we have been able to observe only the first request of many interesting activities such as the spread of the Blaster worm [6]. But since Blaster sends its exploit in the second request of its dialog on port 135, we have never been able to observe such a payload. Therefore it becomes very difficult to distinguish Blaster's activity from other activities targeting the same port using solely the payload as a discriminating factor.

Fortunately, experience shows that, even such limited amount of information, a large variety of analyses remain applicable and deliver useful results. In order to increase the amount of available information on attackers, we need to increase the level of interaction with the honeypots. However, in order to keep carrying on our deployment of sensors on a voluntary basis, we need to achieve this objective at the lowest possible cost. This led to the development of the ScriptGen approach.

6.4.2 ScriptGen

The ScriptGen technology [19, 20] was created with the purpose of generating honeypots with a high level of interaction having a limited resource consumption. This is possible by *learning* the behavior of a given network protocol when facing deterministic attack tools. The learnt behavior is represented under the form of a Finite State Machine representing the protocol language. The generated FSM can then be used to respond to clients, emulating the behavior of the real service implementation at a very low cost.

The ScriptGen learning phase is completely protocol agnostic: no knowledge is assumed neither about the structure of the protocol, nor on its semantics. ScriptGen is thus able to replay any deterministic run of a protocol as long as its payload is not encrypted. The ScriptGen learning takes as input a set of samples of network interaction between a client and the real implementation of a server. The core of the learning phase is the Region Analysis algorithm introduced in [20]: taking advantage of bioinformatics alignment algorithms [24], the algorithm exploits the statistical variability of the samples to identify portions of the protocol stream likely to carry a strong semantic meaning and discard the others. In order to build reliable representations of the protocol interaction, it is thus necessary to collect a clean set of samples with enough statistical variability to correctly identify semantically important regions. Figure 6.5 shows an example of semantic abstraction for an excerpt of SMTP FSM.

The properties of the ScriptGen approach allow to perform a completely automated incremental learning of the activities as shown in [19]. ScriptGen-based honeypots are able to detect when a client request falls out of the current FSM knowledge (a 0-day attack or, more exactly, a yet unseen attack) by simply detecting the absence of a matching transition. In such case, the honeypot is thus unable to provide a valid answer to the attacker. We showed in [19] how the honeypot can react to this situation relying on a real host (an *oracle*) and acting as a proxy between the attacker and the

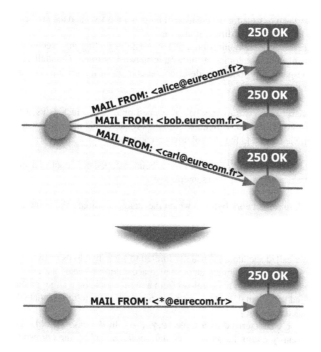

Fig. 6.5 ScriptGen FSM generalization

real host. This allows the honeypot to continue the conversation with the attacker, and to collect a new sample of protocol interaction that can be used to automatically refine the protocol knowledge.

ScriptGen is able to correctly learn and emulate the exploit phase for protocols as complex as NetBIOS [19]. ScriptGen thus allows to build highly interactive honeypots at low cost. The oracles needed to learn new activities can be hosted in a single virtualization farm and contacted by the honeypots through a tunneling system, in a structure similar to Spitzner's *honeyfarm* concept. Differently from classical honeyfarms, access to the real hosts is a rare event resulting from the occurrence of a new kind of attack. As a consequence, systems based on the ScriptGen honeypots potentially have a high degree of scalability.

6.4.3 SGNET: a ScriptGen-based honeypot deployment

We took advantage of this technology to build an experimental honeypot deployment, called SGNET, meant to follow the lines of the Leurré.com deployment but providing a significant improvement in the richness of the collected data.

SGNET and code injections. SGNET is a scalable framework that offers almost the same amount of information than real high interaction systems for a specific class of attacks, namely server-based code injection attacks generated by deterministic scripts. We are aware of the fact that they correspond only to a subset of the possible attack scenarios. However, as of today, they are considered to be responsible for the creation of large botnets [32] and the preferred propagation mechanisms of a large number of different malware.

The final objective of a code injection attack consists in forcing the execution of executable code on a victim machine exploiting a vulnerable network service. Crandall et al. introduced in [10] the epsilon-gamma-pi model, to describe the content of a code-injection attack as being made of three parts.

Exploit (ε). A set of network bytes being mapped onto data which is used for conditional control flow decisions. This consists in the set of client requests that the attacker needs to perform to lead the vulnerable service to the control flow hijacking step.

Bogus control data (γ). A set of network bytes being mapped onto control data which hijacks the control flow trace and redirects it to someplace else.

Payload (π). A set of network bytes to which the attacker redirects the vulnerable application control flow through the usage of ε and γ.

The payload that can be embedded directly in the network conversation with the vulnerable service (commonly called shellcode) is usually limited to some hundreds of bytes, or even less. It is often difficult to code in this limited amount of space complex behaviors. For this reason it is normally used to force the victim to download from a remote location a larger amount of data: the malware. We extend the original epsilon-gamma-pi model in order to differentiate the shellcode π from the downloaded malware μ.

An attack can be characterized as a tuple $(\varepsilon, \gamma, \pi, \mu)$. In the case of, old, classical worms, it is possible to identify a correlation between the observed exploit, the corresponding injected payload and the uploaded malware (the self-replicating worm itself). Thanks to the correlation between the 4 parameters, retrieving information about a subset of them was enough to characterize and uniquely identify the attack. This situation is changing. Taking advantage of the many freely available tools such as Metasploit [33, 37], even unexperienced users can easily generate shellcodes with personalized behavior and reuse existing exploit code. This allows them to generate new combinations along all the four dimensions, weakening the correlation between them. It is thus important to try to retrieve as much information as possible on all the 4 dimensions of the code injection. We designed SGNET in such a way to delegate to different functional components the 4 dimensions, and combine the information retrieved by these components to have an exact picture of the relationships among them.

The ScriptGen approach is suitable for the learning of the exploit network interaction ε, offering the required level of interactivity with the client required to lead the attacker into sending code injection attacks. For the previously stated reasons, in SGNET we extend this capability with the information provided by other tools in order to retrieve information on the other dimensions of the epsilon-gamma-pi-mu (EGPM) model. We take advantage of the control flow hijack detection capabilities of Argos [28] to detect successful code injection attacks, understand the bogus control data γ and retrieve information about the location of the injected payload π. We take advantage of the shellcode emulation and malware download capabilities of Nepenthes [2] to understand the payload π, emulate its behavior and download the malware sample μ.

When facing an attacker, the SGNET activity evolves through different stages, corresponding to the main phases of a network attack. SGNET distributes these phases to three different functional entities: *sensor*, *sample factory* and *shellcode handler*.

The SGNET sensor corresponds to the interface of the SGNET towards the network. The SGNET deployment aims at monitoring small sets of IPs deployed in multiple locations of the IP space, in order to characterize the heterogeneity of the activities along the Internet as observed in [9, 12]. SGNET sensors are thus low-end hosts meant to be deployed at low cost by different partners willing to join the project and bound to a limited number of IPs. The deployment of the sensors follows the same win-win partnership schema explained before. Taking advantage of the

ScriptGen technology, the sensors are able to handle autonomously the exploit phase ε of attacks falling inside the FSM knowledge with minimal resource requirements on the host.

The SGNET sample factory is the *oracle* entity meant to provide samples of network interaction to refine the knowledge of the exploit phase when facing unknown activities. The sample factory takes advantage of a real host running on a virtual machine and monitors the host state through memory tainting. This is implemented taking advantage of *Argos*, presented by Portokalidis et al. in [28]. Keeping track of the memory locations whose content derives from packets coming from the network, Argos is able to detect the moment in which this data is used in an *illegal* way. Argos was modified in order to allow the integration in the SGNET and load on demand a given honeypot profile with a suitable network configuration (same IP address, gateway, DNS servers, ... as of the sensor sending the request). The profile loading and configuration is fast enough to be instantiated on the fly upon request of a sensor.

The Argos-based sample factories provide information about the presence of code injections (γ) and are able to track down the position in the network stream of the first byte being executed by the guest host, corresponding to the byte B_i of the payload π. We have developed a simple heuristic to identify the injected payload π in the network stream starting from the *hint* given by the sample factory [17]. This allows to embed in the ScriptGen learning additional knowledge, namely the a tag identifying the final state of a successful code injection and information within the preceding transitions that allows to extract from the attacker's protocol stream the payload π.

The final steps of the code injection attack trace are delegated to the SGNET shellcode handler. Every payload π identified by the SGNET interaction is submitted to a shellcode handler. The shellcode handler is implemented reusing part of the functionality of the Nepenthes [2] honeypots. We take advantage of Nepenthes shellcode analyzer to "understand" the payload π and emulate its behavior using Nepenthes download modules. In the context of the SGNET, Nepenthes is thus used as an *oracle* for the payload emulation. Differently from the exploit phase, we do not try to learn the Nepenthes behavior in terms of FSM. We consider the payload emulation a too complex interaction to be represented in terms of a FSM.

SGNET Architecture.

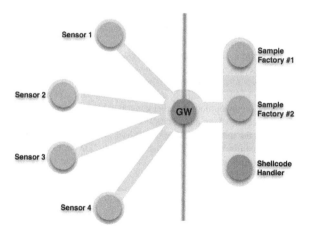

Fig. 6.6 SGNET architecture

The general architecture of the SGNET is presented in Figure 6.6. All the SGNET entities communicate through an ad-hoc HTTP like protocol called Peiros [18]. The Peiros protocol allows communication under the form of a set of service requests, allowing for instance a sensor to require the instantiation of a sample factory. The sensors, distributed over the IP space and hosted by partners of the project, are connected to a central entity called SGNET gateway, that acts as an application-level proxy for the Peiros protocol. The gateway receives service requests from the sensors and dispatches them to a free internal entity, performing a very simple load balancing. The architecture offers a clean separation between the sensors, relatively simple daemons running over inexpensive hosts, and the internal entities, having a higher complexity and higher resource requirement.

We saw how the ScriptGen learning exploits the variability of the samples to produce "good" refinements of the FSM knowledge. The architecture of Figure 6.6 shows how the SGNET gateway offers a unique standpoint to collect interaction samples: all the tunneled conversations between any sensor and any sample factory flow through the gateway. The gateway becomes thus the best candidate to perform ScriptGen refinements to the current FSM knowledge. Once a new refinement is produced, the gateway takes care of updating the knowledge of all the sensors pushing them the FSM updates. This makes sure that all the sensors online at a given moment share exactly the same knowledge of the protocols.

An important aspect related to the ScriptGen learning is the strict relation between the Script-Gen ability to learn exploits and the configuration of the sample factories. If a service is not installed or activated in the configuration of the virtualized host handled by the sample factory, the SGNET architecture will not be able to observe activities targeting it. It is thus important to carefully configure the sample factories in order to maximize the visibility of malicious activities. We chose to address this problem supporting the assignment of different profiles for the IPs of the SGNET sensors, similarly to what was done on the Leurré.com deployment. Each profile is assigned to a different sample factory configuration, with different services and different OS versions to maximize the visibility on network attacks of our deployment.

The description of the SGNET deployment clearly shows a difference with respect to the original Leurré.com deployment. SGNET is a more complex architecture, that succeeds in raising the level of interaction of the honeypots without raising the resource requirements for the partners hosting the sensors. Taking advantage of the ScriptGen learning, the deployment also allows to minimize the usage of expensive resources such as the sample factories, that are needed only to handle those activities that do not fall *yet* in the FSM knowledge. An important concern for the partner taking advantage of this deployment is the security of the solution. SGNET raises the level of interaction of the honeypots; it is thus important to guarantee that the increased interactivity does not impact the safety of hosting a honeypot platform. The network interaction driven by FSM knowledge is virtually as safe as any low-interaction honeypots: the attacker interacts with a simple daemon performing state machine traversals to provide answers to client requests. When a new activity is handled, the sensor acts as a proxy and the attacker is allowed to interact with a real (and thus vulnerable) host. Two measures are in place to ensure the safety of this process. Firstly, the tunneling system ensures that any outbound packet generated by the sample factory is directed only towards the attacking source (blocking any attempt of exploiting the honeypot as a stepping stone to attack others). Secondly, the memory tainting capabilities of Argos allow us to stop execution as soon as the attacker successfully hijacks the host control flow. This does not include for instance successful password brute-forcing attacks, but this class of attacks can be prevented by a careful configuration of the virtualized host.

6.5 Analysis of Attack Events

6.5.1 Identification of Attack Events

6.5.1.1 Attack Event Definition

An attack event is defined as a set of observed cluster time series exhibiting a particular shape during a limited time interval. This time interval typically lasts a couple of days, but it can also be as short as a single day.

The existence of attack events highlights the coordinated activities of several attacking machines. Note that the set can be a singleton. This is typically the case when the set is a peak of activities on a single day. For illustrative purposes, the top plot of Figure 6.7 represents the attack event 225 which consists of cluster 60332 (targeting port 5900 TCP) attacking seven platforms 5,8, 11, ...,31 from day 393 to day 400. Whereas the bottom plot of Figure 6.7 represents the attack event 14 which consists of activities of cluster 0 on day 307 coming almost only from Spain.

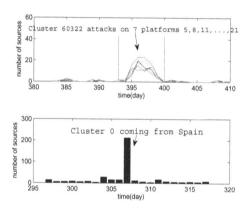

Fig. 6.7 On the top plot, cluster 60232 attacks seven platforms from day 393 to day 400. On the bottom plot, peak of activities of cluster 0 from Spain on day 307.

6.5.1.2 Dataset Description

In order to have a clean dataset for our experiments, we have selected the traces observed on 40 platforms out of the 50 that we had at our disposal. All these 40 platforms have been running for more than 800 days. During this period, note of the platforms has been down for more than 10 times. Furthermore, each one has been up continuously for at least 100 days. All platforms have been up for a minimum of 400 days over that period.

The total amount of sources observed, day by day, on all these 40 platforms can be denoted by the initial time series TS over a period of 800 days.

We can split that time series per country[2] of origin of the sources. This gives us 231 time series TS_X where the ith point of such time series indicates the amount of sources, observed on all platforms, located in country X. We represent by TS_L1 the set of all these Level 1 time series. To reduce the computational cost, we keep only the countries from which we have seen at least 10 sources on at least one day. This enables us to focus on 85 (the set of corresponding countries is called $big_{countries}$), instead of 231, time series. We represent by TS_L1' this refined set of Level 1 time series. Then, we split each of these time series by cluster to produce the final set of time series $\Phi_{[0-800],c_i,country_j} \forall c_i$ and $\forall country_j \in big_{countries}$. The ith point of the time series $\Phi_{[0-800],X,Y}$ indicates the amount of sources originating from country Y that have been observed on day i attacking any of our platforms thanks to the attack defined by means of the cluster X. We represent by TS_L2 the set of all these Level 2 time series. In this case $|TS\_L2|$ is equal to 436,756 which corresponds to 3,284,551 sources. As explained in [27], time series that barely vary in amplitude over the 800 days are meaningless to identify attack events and we can get rid of them. Therefore, we only keep the time series that highlight important variations during the 800 days period. We represent by TS_L2' this refined set of Level 2 time series. In this case $|TS\_L2'|$ is equal to 2,420 which corresponds to 2,330,244 sources. We have done the very same splitting and filtering by looking at the traces on a per platform basis instead of on a per country of origin basis. The corresponding results are given in Table 6.4.

Table 6.4 dataset description: TS: *all sources observed on the period under study, OVP: observation view point, TS_L1: set of time series at country/platform level, TS_L1': set of significant time series in TS_L1, TS_L2 : set of all cluster time series, TS_L2' set of strongly varying cluster time series*

TS consists of 3,477,976 sources		
OVP	country	platform
$|TS\_L1|$	231	40
$|TS\_L1'|$	85	40
	(94,4% TS)	(100% TS)
$|TS\_L2|$	436,756	395,712
$|TS\_L2'|$	2,420	2,127
sources	2,330,244	2,538,922
	(67% of TS)	(73% of TS)

6.5.1.3 Results on Attack Event Detection

We have applied the techniques presented in [26] to identify the attack events existing in our 2 distinct datasets, namely $TS_{country}$ and $TS_{platform}$. For the time series in $TS_{country}$ (resp. $TS_{platform}$), we have found 592 (resp. 690) attack events which correspond to 574,125 (resp. 578,372) sources. The results are given in Table 6.5

---

[2] The geographical location is given to us thanks to the Maxmind product, based on the IP address. However, some IPs can not be mapped to any real country and are attached to labels not corresponding to any country, e.g. EU,A1,..

Table 6.5 Result on Attack Event Detection

AE-set-I($TS_{country}$)		AE-set-II($TS_{platform}$)	
No.AEs	No.sources	No.AEs	No.sources
592	574,125	690	578,372

No.AEs: amount of attack events

6.5.2 Armies of Zombies

So far, we have identified what we have called attack events which highlight the existence of coordinated attacks launched by a group of compromised machines, i.e. a zombie army. It would be interesting to see if the very same army manifests itself in more than one attack event. To do this, we propose to compute what we call the *action sets*. An *action set* is a set of attack events that are likely due to same army. In this Section, we show how to build these action sets and what information we can derive from them regarding the size and the lifetime of the zombie armies.

6.5.2.1 Identification of the armies

Similarity Measures: In its simplest form, a zombie army is a classical botnet. It can also be made of several botnets. That is, several groups of machines listening to a distinct *C&C*. This is invisible to us and irrelevant. All that matters is that all the machines do act in a coordinated way. As time passes, it is reasonable to expect members of an army to be cured while others join. Hence, if the same army attacks our honeypots twice over distinct periods of time, one simple way to link the two attack events together is by observing that they have a large amount of IP addresses in common. More formally, we measure the likelihood of two attacks events e_1 and e_2 to be linked to the same zombie army by means of their similarity defined as follows:

$$sim(e_1, e_2) = \begin{cases} max(\frac{|e_1 \cap e_2|}{|e_1|}, \frac{|e_1 \cap e_2|}{|e_2|}) & \text{if } |e_1 \cap e_2| < 200 \\ 1 & \text{otherwise} \end{cases}$$

In which, $|e_1|$ (resp. $|e_2|$) represents the number of distinct IP addresses of attack event e_1 (resp. e_2) and $|e_1 \cap e_2|$ represents the number of IP addresses in common of attack events e_1 and e_2. We conclude that e_1 and e_2 are caused by the same zombie army if and only if $sim(e_1, e_2) > 10\%$. Called P_{e_1,e_2} is the probability that two attack events e_1 and e_2 share n IP addresses in common by chance. We also verify that $|e_1 \cap e_2| > n$, in which the corresponding $P_{e_1,e_2} <= 10^{-9}$.

Action Sets: We now use the $sim()$ function to group together attack events into action sets. To do so, we build a simple graph where the nodes are the attack events. There is an arc between two nodes e_1 and e_2 if and only if $sim(e_1, e_2) > \delta$. All nodes that are connected by at least one path end up in the same action set. In other words, we have as many action sets as we have disconnected graphs made of at least two nodes; singleton sets are not counted as action sets.

We note that our approach is such that we can have an action set made of three attack events e_1, e_2 and e_3 where $sim(e_1, e_2) > \delta$ and $sim(e_2, e_3) > \delta$ but where $sim(e_1, e_3) < \delta$. This is consistent with our intuition that armies can evolve over time in such a way that the machines present in the army can, eventually, be very different from the ones found the first time we have seen the same army in action.

Results: we have identified 40 (resp. 33) zombie armies from AE-set-I (resp. AE-set-II) which have issued a total of 193 (resp. 247) attack events. Figure 6.8 (Left) represents the distribution of attack events per zombie army. Its top (resp. bottom) plot represents the distribution obtained from AE-set-I(resp. AE-set-II). We can see that the largest amount of attack events for an army is 53 (resp. 47) whereas 28 (resp. 20) armies have been observed only two times.

6.5.2.2 Main Characteristics of the Zombie armies

Lifetime of Zombie Army.

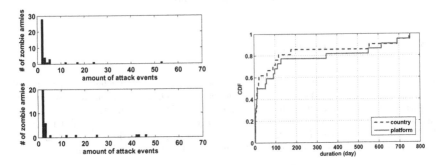

Fig. 6.8 Left: Zombie Army Size. Right: Cumulative Distribution Function (CDF) of the durations of zombie armies.

Figure 6.8 (Right) represents the cumulative distribution of minimum lifetime of zombie armies obtained from $TS_{platform}$ and $TS_{country}$ (see Section 6.5.1). According to the plot, around 20% of zombie armies have existed for more than 200 days. In the extreme case, two armies seems to have survived for 700 days! Such result seems to indicate that either *i)* it takes a long time to cure compromised machines or that *ii)* armies are able to stay active for long periods of time, despite the fact that some of their members disappear, by continuously compromising new ones.

Lifetime of Infected Host in Zombie Armies

We can classify the armies into two classes as mentioned in the previous Section. For instance, Figure 6.9a represents the similarity matrix of zombie army 33, ZA33. To build this matrix, we first order its 42 attack events according to their occurred time. Then, we represent their similarity relation under an 42×42 similarity matrix $\mathcal{M}$. The cell (i,j) represents the value of *sim*() of the ordered attack event i^{th} and j^{th}. Since, $\mathcal{M}$ is a symmetric matrix, for the visibility, we represent only half of it.

As one can see, we have a very high similarity measure between almost all the attacks events (i.e., around 60%). This is also true between the very first and the very last attack events. It is important to notice the time interval between the first and the last activities observed from this army is 753 days!

Figure 6.9b represents an opposite case, the zombie army 31, ZA31, consisting of 46 attack events. We proceed as above to build its similarity matrix. One can see that the important values are surrounded around the main diagonal of $\mathcal{M}$. It means that the attack event i^{th} has the same subset of infected machines with only few attack events happening not far from it in terms of time. Another important point to be noticed is that this army changes its attack vectors over time. In fact, it moves from attack against 4662 TCP, to 1025 TCP, then 5900 TCP, 1443 TCP, 2967 TCP, 445 TCP,...And the lifetime of this army is 563 days! It is clear, from these two cases, that the composition of armies evolves over time in different ways. More work remains to be done in order to understand the reasons behind these various strategies.

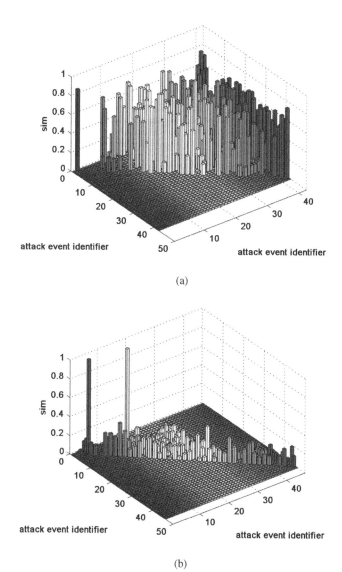

(a)

(b)

Fig. 6.9 Renewal rate of zombie armies

6.5.3 Impact of Observation View Point

6.5.3.1 Analysis

Table 6.5 highlights the fact that depending on how we decompose the initial set of traces of attacks (i.e the initial time series TS), namely by splitting it by countries of origin of the attackers or by platforms attacked, different attacks events show up. To assess the overlap between attack events detected from different observation view points, we use the *common source ratio, namely csr,* measure as follows:

$$csr(e,AE_{op'}) = \frac{\sum_{\forall e' \in AE_{op'}} |e \cap e'|}{|e|}$$

in which $e \in AE_{op}$ and $|e|$ is the amount of sources in attack event e, AE_{op} is *AE-set-I* and $AE_{op'}$ is *AE-set-II* (or vice versa).

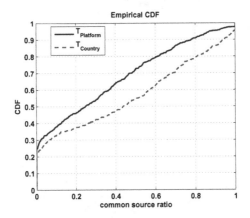

Fig. 6.10 CDF common source ratio.

Figure 6.10 represents the two cumulative distribution functions corresponding to this measure. The point (x,y) on the curve means that there are $y*100\%$ of attack events obtained thanks to $T_{country}$ (resp $T_{platforms}$) that have less than $x*100\%$ of sources in common with all attack events obtained thanks to $T_{platforms}$ (resp $T_{country}$). The $T_{country}$ curve represents the cumulative distribution obtained in this first case and the $T_{platforms}$ one represents the CDF obtained when starting from the attacks events obtained with the intial $T_{platforms}$ set of time series. As we can notice, around 23% (resp. 25%) of attack events obtained by starting from the $T_{country}$ (resp. $T_{platform}$) set of time series do not share any sources in common with any attack events obtained when starting the attack even identification process from the $T_{platform}$ (resp. $T_{country}$) set of time series. This corresponds to 136 (16,919 sources) and 171 (75,920 sources) attack events not being detected. In total, there are 288,825 (resp. 293,132) sources present in AE-Set-I (resp. AE-Set-II), but not in AE-Set-II (resp. AE-Set-I).

6.5.3.2 Explanation

There are good reasons why we can not rely on a single viewpoint to detect all attacks events. We elaborate on these reasons in the following discussion.

Split by country: Suppose we have one botnet B made of machines that are located within the set of countries $\{X, Y, Z\}$. Suppose that, from time to time, these machines attack our platforms leaving traces that are also assigned to a cluster C. Suppose also that this cluster C is a very *popular* one, that is, many other machines from all over the world continuously leave traces on our platforms that are assigned to this cluster. As a result, the activities specifically linked to the botnet B are lost in the noise of all other machines leaving traces belonging to C. This is certainly true for the cluster time series (as defined earlier) related to C and this can also be true for the time series obtained by splitting it by platform, $\Phi_{[0-800),C,platform_i} \forall platform_i \in 1..40$. However, by splitting the time series corresponding to cluster C by countries of origins of the sources, then it is quite likely that the time series $\Phi_{[0-800),C,country_i} \forall country_i \in \{X, Y, Z\}$ will be highly correlated during the periods in which the botnet present in these countries will be active against our platforms. This will lead to the identification of one or several attack events.

Split by platform: Similarly, suppose we have a botnet B' made of machines located all over the world. Suppose that, from time to time, these machines attack a specific set of platforms $\{X, Y, Z\}$ leaving traces that are assigned to a cluster C. Suppose also that this cluster C is a very *popular* one, that is, many other machines from all over the world continuously leave traces on all our platforms that are assigned to this cluster. As a result, the activities specifically linked to the botnet B' are lost in the noise of all other machines leaving traces belonging to C. This is certainly true for the cluster time series (as defined earlier) related to C and this can also be true for the time series obtained by splitting it by countries, $\Phi_{[0-800),C,country_i} \forall country_i \in big_{countries}$. However, by splitting the time series corresponding to cluster C by platforms attacked, then it is quite likely that the time series $\Phi_{[0-800),C,platform_i} \forall platform_i \in \{X, Y, Z\}$ will be highly correlated during the periods in which the botnet influences the traces left on the sole platforms concerned by its attack. This will lead to the identification of one or several attack events.

The top plot of Figure 6.11 represents the attack event 79. In this case, we see that the traces due to the cluster 175309 are highly correlated when we group them by platform attacked. In fact, there are 9 platforms involved in this case, accounting for a total of 870 sources. If we group the same set of traces by country of origin of the sources, we end up with the bottom curves of Figure 6.11 where the specific attack event identified previously can barely be seen. This highlights the existence of a botnet made of machines located all over the world that target a specific subset of the Internet.

6.6 Multi-Dimensional Analysis of Attack Events

6.6.1 Methodology

Analogous to criminal forensics, the security analyst needs to synthesize different pieces of evidence in order to investigate the root causes of global attack phenomena on the Internet. This task can be a tedious, lengthy and informal process mostly relying on the analyst's expertise, and involving many different dimensions characteristics of attack events. For those reasons, we seek to develop a multi-dimensional knowledge discovery and data mining methodology that should help us to improve, in a more systematic way, our understandings of emerging Internet threats, so as to achieve a better cyber situational awareness.

Our idea consists of *i)* extracting relevant nuggets of knowledge by mining a dataset of attack events according to different relevant characteristics; and in *ii)* combining systematically those pieces of knowledge so as to create higher-level concepts able to explain more clearly the underly-

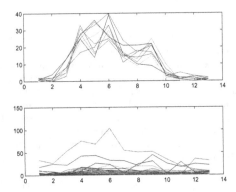

Fig. 6.11 Top plot represents the attack event 79 related to cluster 17309 on 9 platforms. The bottom plot represents the evolution of this cluster by country. Noise of the attacks to other platforms decrease significantly the correlation of observed cluster time series when split by country.

ing phenomena that might be the root cause of the suspicious traffic. Each step is further explained in the next sections.

6.6.2 Clique-based Clustering

6.6.2.1 Principles

The first component of our knowledge mining methodology involves an unsupervised graph-theoretic correlation process which aims at grouping similar "events" (through their corresponding feature vectors) in a reliable and consistent manner.

Typical clustering tasks involve the following steps [16]: *i)* feature selection and/or extraction, and pattern representation; *ii)* definition of a similarity measure between pairs of patterns; *iii)* grouping similar patterns; *iv)* data abstraction (if needed), to provide a compact representation of each cluster; and *v)* the assessment of the clusters quality and coherence (also when needed).

In any clustering, we must select salient features that may provide meaningful *patterns* from the data (e.g., from attack events in our case). Those patterns are represented with *feature vectors*, which are for instance the geographical distributions, subnet distributions, attack time series, etc.

In the second step, we need to measure the similarity between two such defined patterns or input vectors. For that purpose, several types of similarity distances are available (e.g., Pearson correlations, Minkowski, Jackknife, etc.). Clearly, the choice of a similarity metric has an impact on the properties of the clusters, such as their size, quality, or consistency. To reliably compare the empirical distributions mentioned here above, we rely on strong statistical distances that are based on non-parametric statistical tests, such as Pearson's χ^2 and Kolmogorov-Smirnov, whose resulting *p-value* is then validated against the Kullback-Leibler divergence. Those methods are amongst the most commonly used ones to determine whether two underlying one-dimensional probability distributions differ in a significant way.

Finally, we take advantage of those similarity measures to group all pattack events whose patterns look very similar. We simply use an unsupervised graph-theoretic approach to formulate the problem: the vertices of the graph represent the patterns (or feature vectors) of each attack event, and the edges (or the arcs) express the similarity relationships between those vertices. Then, the clustering is performed by extracting so-called *maximal weighted cliques* (MWC) from the graph, where a maximal *clique* is defined as an induced sub-graph in which the vertices are fully connected and it is not contained within any other clique. Since it is a NP-hard problem [4], several approximate algorithms for solving the MWC problem have been developed. We refer the interested reader to [38, 39] for a more detailed description of this clique-based clustering technique applied to honeynet traces.

6.6.2.2 Some Experimental Results.

We applied our clique-based clustering on a honeynet dataset made of 351 attack events comprising 282,363 IP sources, which were collected on the Internet in a period spanning from Sep 2006 until June 2008. These events were observed on 36 platforms located in 20 different subnets, and belonging to 18 different class A-subnets. In terms of network activities, all sources could be classified in no more than 136 attack clusters

Table 6.6 presents a high-level overview of the cliques obtained for each attack dimension separately. As one can see, a relatively high volume of sources could be classified into cliques in each dimension. The high proportion of correlated sources with respect to the attack time series suggests that a majority of the attack events collected in this dataset were actually coordinated, or at least synchronized, on different honeypots. Among the targeted port sequences, we can observe some commonly targeted ports (e.g., Windows ports used for SMB or RPC, or SQL and VNC ports), but also a large number of uncommon high TCP ports that are normally unused on standard (and clean) machines. A non-negligeable volume of sources is also due to UDP spammers targeting Windows Messenger popup service (ports 1026-1028 UDP).

Table 6.6 Some experimental clique results obtained from a one year-honeynet dataset

Attack Dimension	Nr of Cliques	Volume of sources (%)	Most targeted port sequences
Geolocation	45	66.4	1027U, I, 1433T, 1026U, I445T, 5900T, 1028U, 9763T, I445T80T, 15264T, 29188T, 6134T, 6769T, 1755T, 64264T, 1028U1027U1026U, 32878T, 64783T, 4152T, 25083T, 9661T, 25618T, ...
IP Subnets (Class A)	30	56.0	1027U, I, 1433T, 1026U, I445T, 5900T, 1028U, 9763T, 15264T, 29188T, 6134T, 6769T, 1755T, 50656T, 64264T, 1028U1027U1026U, 32878T, 64783T, 18462T, 4152T, 25083T, 9661T, 25618T, 7690T, ...
Targeted platforms	17	70.1	I, 1433T, I445T, 1025T, 5900T, 1026U, I445T139T445T139T445T, 4662T, 9763T, 1008T, 6211T, I445T80T, 15264T, 29188T, 12293T, 33018T, 6134T, 6769T, 1755T, 2968T, 26912T, 50656T, 64264T, 32878T, ...
Attack time series	82	92.2	135T, I, 1433T, I445T, 5900T, 1026U, I445T139T445T139T445T, I445T80T, 6769T, 1028U1027U1026U, 50286T, 2967T, ...

6.6.2.3 Visualizing Cliques of Attackers.

In order to assess the consistency of the resulting cliques of attack events, it can be useful to see them charted on a two-dimensional map so as to *i)* verify the proximities among clique members (intra-clique consistency), and *ii)* to understand potential relationships between *different* cliques that are somehow related (i.e. inter-clique relationships). Note that a clique can be considered as a stricter definition of a cluster. Moreover, the statistical distances used to compute those cliques make them intrinsically coherent, which means that certain cliques of events may be somehow related to each other, although they were separated by the clique algorithm.

Since most of the feature vectors we are dealing with have a high number of variables (e.g., a geographical vector has more than 200 country variables), obviously the structure of such high-dimensional data set cannot be displayed directly on a 2D map. Multidimensional scaling (MDS) is a set of methods that can help to address this type of problem. MDS is based on dimensionality reduction techniques, which aim at converting a high-dimensional dataset into a two or three-dimensional representation that can be displayed, for example, in a scatter plot. As a result, MDS allows an analyst to visualize how near observations are to each other for many kinds of distance or dissimilarity measures, which in turn can deliver insights into the underlying structure of the high-dimensional dataset.

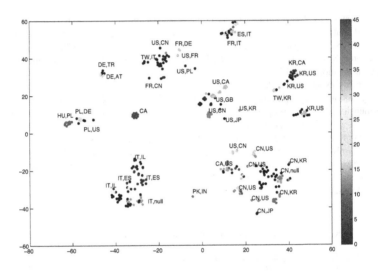

Fig. 6.12 Visualization of geographical cliques of attackers. The coloring refers to the different clique Id's. The superposed text labels show the two top attacking countries for some of the data points.

Because of the intrinsic non-linearity of real-world datasets, and the induced feature vectors, we applied a recent MDS technique called *t-SNE* to visualize each dimension of the dataset and to assess the consistency of the cliques results. t-SNE [40] is a variation of *Stochastic Neighbour Embedding* (SNE); it produces significantly better visualizations than other MDS techniques by reducing the tendency to crowd points together in the centre of the map. Moreover, this technique has proven to perform better in retaining both the local and global structure of real, high-dimensional data in a single map, in comparison to other non linear dimensionality reduction techniques such as Sammon mapping, Isomaps or Laplacian Eigenmaps.

Figure 6.12 shows the resulting two-dimensional plot obtained by mapping the geographical vectors on a 2D map using t-SNE. Each datapoint on the map represents the geographical vector of given attack event, and its coloring refers to its clique membership as obtained previously by applying the clique-based clustering. It can be easily verified that two adjacent events on this map have highly similar geographical distributions (even from a statistical viewpoint), while two distant events have clearly nothing in common in terms of originating countries. Quite surprisingly, the resulting mapping is far from being chaotic; it presents a relatively sparse structure with clear data-point groupings, which means also that most of those attack events present very tight relationships regarding their origins. Due to the strict statistical distances used to calculate cliques, this kind of correlation can hardly be obtained by chance only.

Similar "semantic mapping" can naturally be obtained for other dimensions considered (e.g., subnets, platforms, etc), so as to help assessing the quality of other cliques of attackers. To conclude this illustration, on Figure 6.13 we have indicated also some of the port sequences for several geographical cliques of attackers. This can help to visualize unobvious relationships among different types of activities and their origins.

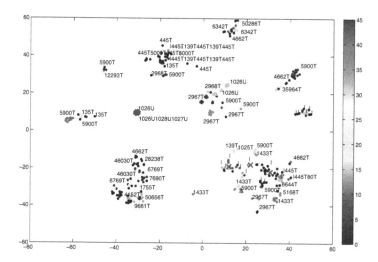

Fig. 6.13 Same visualization of the geographical cliques of attackers as Fig 6.12, but here the superposed text labels indicate the port sequences made by the attackers.

6.6.3 Combining Cliques of Attackers

The second component of our methodology is similar to a dynamic data fusion process. Starting from all sets of cliques, the idea is to combine k sets out of the N attack dimensions, with $k = 2, ..., N$, in order to discover higher-level knowledge about certain phenomena and their root cause (e.g., a set of attack events belonging to a same botnet or worm family, the evolution of a botnet IP location, etc). As such, each clique pattern can hold a piece of interesting knowledge about an attack phenomenon; but in many cases the security analyst will have to synthesize different pieces of evidence in order to perform a root cause analysis, and to really understand what happened. Therefore, we can take advantage of all one-dimensional cliques to construct higher-level concepts by simply combining different sets of cliques. Based on the phenomenon under scrutiny, the practitioner may include any number of dimensions in order to create "concepts" containing more or less semantics. In practice, we observe that the number of concepts obtained by combining any number of dimensions is not excessive. So, while the analysis of raw network traces (composed of thousands of packets) on each sensor would definitively be impractical, now the analysis of a limited number of combined concepts can provide a better insight into the real-world phenomena that have caused the attack traffic.

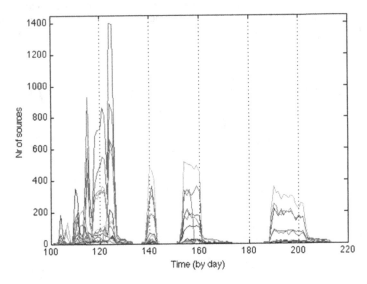

Fig. 6.14 Time series (i.e., nr of distinct sources by day) of a large scale phenomenon related to a botnet activity, made of 67 attack events observed from Dec 06 until April 07.

Illustration of Multi-dimensional analysis.

When we apply the multi-dimensional analysis on the examples given in 6.3.4, now we find out that those attack events were actually involved in a large-scale phenomenon assumed to be related to a botnet activity. This phenomenon has been active in a time period spanning from 1-Dec-06 until 31-Mar-07, during which we observed about 67 attack events that can be grouped into 4 distinct waves (see Fig 6.14) thanks to the temporal dimension. The platform correlations indicate that all attack events have hit exactly the same set of platforms (mostly in Belgium and in UK). Regarding the origins of the attacks (e.g., countries and subnets of origin), our method can clearly highlight two communities of attackers: one large group of "scanners" (performing almost only ICMP scanning on all honeypot IP's), and one smaller group of "attackers" (performing ICMP followed by attacks on Windows ports 445T or 139T). Interestingly, the attackers seem to "know" which honeypots are emulating a Windows machine, as they hit almost exclusively those IP addresses. The last finding deals with the dynamic evolution of the botnet population (in terms of IP blocks) between each botnet attack wave, which can be observed from the mapping of the different cliques of attackers. The scanner community has indeed been split into a few different cliques; but when looking at the geographical mapping (Fig 6.13 - see the regions indicated by the three red crosses in the lower-right part of the map), we can observe that those cliques appear in the same neighborhood.

6.7 Beyond Events Correlation: Exploring the epsilon-gamma-pi-mu space

In the previous Sections we took advantage of correlation techniques to analyze and correlate the available information to infer meaningful facts on the identity and on the behavior of the clients responsible for the observed events. We have left out until now the analysis of the *effects* of these activities on the victims. Many of these activities are likely to be exploitation attempts carried on by self propagating malware. Gathering intelligence on the nature of these activities and studying their structure is an important step towards a better understanding of the Internet threats. As explained in Section 6.4, such analysis requires an increase of the level of interaction, requirement that motivated our efforts in the development of the SGNET deployment.

The SGNET deployment was designed around the phase separation introduced by the epsilon-gamma-pi-mu model: each of the phases of a generic code injection attack is handled by a different entity of the distributed system. The emulation of these phases generates information on the characteristics of the specific instance. For instance, the network interaction involved in the exploit phase ε is associated to a traversal identifier in ScriptGen's FSM models. All the information generated by the different components of the SGNET deployment is collected and stored in the central database. Similarly to the Leurré.com case, this information is then enriched through different analysis tools. For instance, all the malware collected by SGNET is submit to the Anubis sandbox [3] to retrieve information on its behavior. The SGNET dataset puts at our disposal a variety of information on the observed exploits (ε), shellcodes (π) and malware samples (μ).[3]

Following the epsilon-gamma-pi-mu model, we model an attack as a tuple (ε, π, μ), assigning to each dimension a coordinate representative for a given "type" of interaction in the model. The relationship and the correlation among the dimensions of this three-dimensional space offer a perspective over the structure and the amount of code reuse present in nowadays exploitation attempts.

The identification of the interaction "type" is not always a straightforward task, since it needs to cope with the increasing usage of polymorphic techniques in malware and shellcode.

Malware families such as the Allaple one [15] take advantage of polymorphism to generate a new variant of themselves at each propagation attempt. Such a technique ensures each malware sample to completely mutate its binary content at every generation, making its detection much more complex to AV vendors. From our standpoint, the employment of such techniques leads to the proliferation of unique samples (downloaded only once) and makes the problem of attribution of two events to the activity of the same malware type much more complicated. How to define two completely different binaries to be *similar* and thus attribute two different code injections to the activity of the same malware?

The intuition that helped us in solving the problem is that any polymorphic technique can be used by attackers to randomize only *some* of the characteristics of a certain observed event. A polymorphic technique such as that previously mentioned will indeed succeed in randomizing the content of the injected malware (and consequently its MD5 hash), but might not succeed in randomizing other characteristics, such as its structure or its behavior. By looking at a sufficient amount of samples of the same activity type, it will be always possible to identify the invariant characteristics and reduce the activity classification problem to a pattern generation process.

For each of the 29283 code injection attacks observed by the SGNET honeypots in a period of 8 months ranging from January to August 2008, we have considered the set of characteristics described in Table 6.7. For each dimension, we have considered the corresponding characteristics vector, discovered *frequent* patterns and used these patterns to cluster them. In the rest of this work, we will refer to the name e-clusters, p-clusters and m-clusters to refer to the clusters of activities along the epsilon, pi and mu dimensions respectively.

---

[3] While theoretically possible, the prototype deployment did not collect sufficient information on the control flow hijack itself to include the dimension γ in the analysis

Table 6.7 Information taken into account

Exploit	Destination port
	Traversal identifier
	Alerts generated by Snort
Shellcode	Hash of the binary shellcode
	Interaction with the terminal emulator, if any
	Type of malware download (pushed by the attacker or pulled by the victim)
	Protocol used in the malware download
	Host involved in the download (the attacker itself or a central malware repository)
	Port involved in the download
Malware	Hash of the binary sample
	Size of the sample
	Number of created mutexes
	Name of the created processes
	Number of sections declared in the PE header
	Linker version declared in the PE header
	Packer name as detected by the PEiD database
	Number of sections in the PE header marked as both writable and executable

6.7.1 Degrees of freedom

We tried to get a very high level view over the relationship between the three (e,p,m) dimensions by quantifying the number of different combinations witnessed by the honeypot deployment in the 8 months observation period. We have thus counted the number of generated clusters, and the number of combinations over two or three dimensions. In the multi-dimensional case, we have compared the number of combinations witnessed by the honeypots with the maximum achievable number to have a rough estimate of the amount of variability over that combination.

As it possible to see from the table here under, most of the variability is introduced by the combinations of exploits and payloads: 20 different exploits have been combined with 58 different payloads in 107 different ways accounting for approximately 9% of all possible combinations.

e-clusters	20
p-clusters	58
m-clusters	74
(e,p) combinations	107 (9.22%)
(p,m) combinations	186 (4.33%)
(e,p,m) combinations	290 (0.33%)

The previous results seem to suggest a considerable reuse of exploitation code in different malware variants and eventually combined with personalized payloads. Indeed, in the 8 months of observation period, each e-cluster was combined in average with 5.9 different p-clusters and 21.2 different m-clusters. The same payload type was also often used by different malware families: in average, each payload type was used to upload 6.2 different m-clusters.

6.7.2 Interesting cases

It is interesting to look more in depth at different subsets of the epsilon-gamma-pi-mu space to better evaluate the impact of this variability in some practical cases. We have thus focused our attention on three interesting cases, associated to the usage of two specific vulnerability types and to the propagation strategies employed by a specific malware family associated to an m-cluster.

6.7.2.1 ASN.1 vulnerability

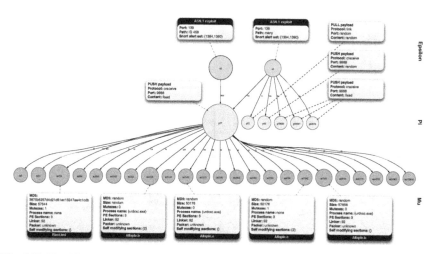

Fig. 6.15 The ASN.1 exploit (port 139)

Figure 6.15 provides an overview of all the observed code injections associated with the exploitation of the ASN.1 vulnerability (MS04-007) on TCP port 139.

In this specific case, there is a very low level of correlation between the first two dimensions. The totality of the *e2* exploits always pushes to the victim a single type of payload (*p57*). The payload involved in these exploits runs a small downloader that binds itself to TCP port 9988 and runs any content received upon connection from the attacker. Such download behavior is easy to identify and block: it is hard to identify a legitimate case in which a host should be allowed to accept inbound connections on a high port, and TCP port 9988 is not associated to any legitimate service. Despite its simplicity and its potentially low success rate, this payload is responsible for pushing to the honeypots a large number of m-clusters. For each of these clusters, we reported in Figure 6.15 the label associated with the malware samples by Kaspersky antivirus.

Many of the m-clusters involved in this propagation strategy are related to different variants of the Allaple worm, previously mentioned as example of polymorphic malware. These different variants are all sharing the same propagation strategy despite differences in the overall behavior of the worm. The same propagation strategy is also used by different malware types that are not directly related to the Allaple worm, such as the m-cluster 732, associated to the Rbot.bni IRC bot.

6.7.2.2 Rbot.bni malware family

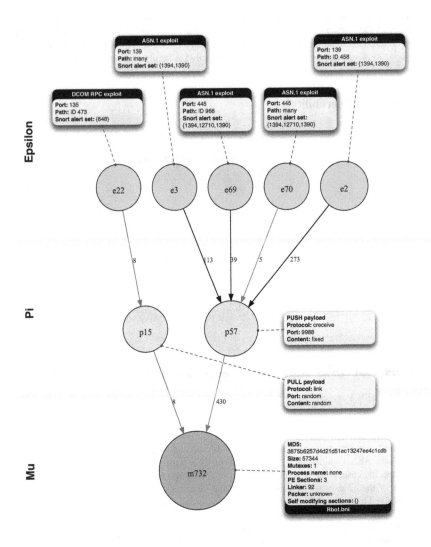

Fig. 6.16 Propagation ability for mu group m732

The propagation strategy used by Rbot.bni is shown in Figure 6.15. Interestingly, while most of the infections associated to it were witnessed through the previously analyzed ASN.1 exploit on port 139, SGNET honeypots observed a more diversified propagation strategy. This malware family was in fact also witnessed exploiting the ASN.1 exploit on port 445 and the DCOM RPC exploit on port 135. While all the ASN.1 exploits took advantage of the payload *p57* previously described, the RPC DCOM exploit (*e22*) took advantage of a completely different download strategy. The exploits on this vulnerability forced in fact the victim to actively open a connection and download the malware from the attacker on a random port.

6.7.2.3 DCOM RPC vulnerability

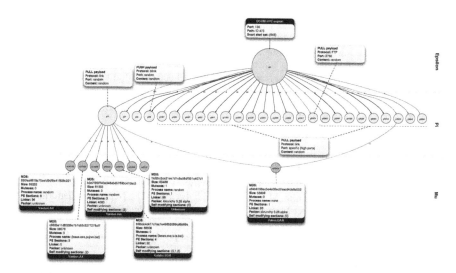

Fig. 6.17 The DCOM RPC exploit

We previously analyzed a case of high correlation between the exploitation type and the corresponding payload. Figure 6.17 takes into consideration a different vulnerability to show a completely different scenario. The vulnerability taken into consideration is the DCOM RPC vulnerability on port 135, used as "secondary" propagation vector by the Rbot.bni malware previously taken into consideration. The difference with Figure 6.15 is striking: in this case, a very high level of variability exists between the exploitation type and the payload involved.

Three different classes of payloads can be identified: a PULL payload (*p24073*) forces the download of malware from the attacker on port 2755; a PUSH payload (*p258*) forces the victim to accept the malware on a random port using the protocol *blink*; finally, there is a proliferation of clusters related to PULL payloads taking advantage of the protocol *link*.

The variability in terms of payloads is also reflected by a variability in terms of malware variants pushed through these combinations of epsilon and pi. While none of the mu clusters in Figure 6.17 correspond to polymorphic malware, all of them are associated with IRC-based C&C channels.

6.8 Conclusions

In this chapter, we have presented in detail Leurré.com, a worldwide distributed system of honeypots running since 2003. We have extensively described its architecture used for collecting meaningful data about emerging attack processes observed at various places on the Internet.

Several examples have been given throughout the text to illustrate the richness of our central data repository and the flexibility of its design, enabling a large diversity of analyses to be carried out on it. It is not the main purpose of this chapter to report on a specific analysis. Other publications have focused on some of these issues and some more work is ongoing. Instead, we have shown by means of simple examples that this database helps in discovering trends in the attacks and in characterizing them quite precisely. Next to this, we have also presented the important improvements we made to our infrastructure by deploying high-interaction ScriptGen sensors, which enable us to collect even more precise and valuable information about malicious activities. In the light of those promising results, we showed that this entire data collection infrastructure holds a great potential in augmenting our threats intelligence capability on the Internet. Being able to conduct in-depth analyses on this huge data collection, in a systematic way, will hopefully help us to make some advances towards the creation of early warning information systems.

So, it is our wish to share the data contained in this database with those interested in carrying some research on it. The authors can be reached by mail to get detailed information on how to join the project in order to gain access to the database.

References

1. ALMODE Security. Home page of disco at at http://www.altmode.com/disco/.
2. P. Baecher, M. Koetter, T. Holz, M. Dornseif, and F. Freiling. The Nepenthes Platform: An Efficient Approach to Collect Malware. *Proceedings of the 9th International Symposium on Recent Advances in Intrusion Detection (RAID)*, September 2006.
3. U. Bayer, C. Kruegel, and E. Kirda. *TTAnalyze: A Tool for Analyzing Malware*. PhD thesis, Master's Thesis, Technical University of Vienna, 2005.
4. I. Bomze, M. Budinich, P. Pardalos, and M. Pelillo. The maximum clique problem. In *Handbook of Combinatorial Optimization*, volume 4. Kluwer Academic Publishers, Boston, MA, 1999.
5. F. M. C. R. Center. Web security trends report q1/2008, http://www.finjan.com/content.aspx?id=827, sep 2008.
6. CERT. Advisory CA-2003-20 W32/Blaster worm, August 2003.
7. Z. Chen, L. Gao, and K. Kwiat. Modeling the spread of active worms. In *Proceedings of IEEE INFOCOM*, 2003.
8. M. P. Collins, T. J. Shimeall, S. Faber, J. Janies, R. Weaver, M. D. Shon, and J. Kadane. Using uncleanliness to predict future botnet addresses. In *IMC '07: Proceedings of the 7th ACM SIGCOMM conference on Internet measurement*, pages 93–104, New York, NY, USA, 2007. ACM.
9. E. Cooke, M. Bailey, Z. M. Mao, D. Watson, F. Jahanian, and D. McPherson. Toward understanding distributed blackhole placement. In *WORM '04: Proceedings of the 2004 ACM workshop on Rapid malcode*, pages 54–64, New York, NY, USA, 2004. ACM Press.
10. J. Crandall, S. Wu, and F. Chong. Experiences using Minos as a tool for capturing and analyzing novel worms for unknown vulnerabilities. *Proceedings of GI SIG SIDAR Conference on Detection of Intrusions and Malware and Vulnerability Assessment (DIMVA)*, 2005.
11. M. Dacier, F. Pouget, and H. Debar. Attack processes found on the internet. In *NATO Symposium IST-041/RSY-013*, Toulouse, France, April 2004.
12. M. Dacier, F. Pouget, and H. Debar. Honeypots, a practical mean to validate malicious fault assumptions. In *Proceedings of the 10th Pacific Ream Dependable Computing Conference (PRDC04)*, Tahiti, February 2004.
13. M. Dacier, F. Pouget, and H. Debar. Leurre.com: On the advantages of deploying a large scale distributed honeypot platform. In *Proceedings of the E-Crime and Computer Conference 2005 (ECCE'05)*, Monaco, March 2005.
14. DShield. Distributed Intrusion Detection System, www.dshield.org, 2007.

15. F-Secure. Malware information pages: Allaple.a, http://www.f-secure.com/v-descs/allaplea.shtml, December 2006.
16. A. Jain and R. Dubes. *Algorithms for Clustering Data*. Prentice-Hall advanced reference series, 1988.
17. C. Leita and M. Dacier. Sgnet: a worldwide deployable framework to support the analysis of malware threat models. In *Proceedings of the 7th European Dependable Computing Conference (EDCC 2008)*, May 2008.
18. C. Leita and M. Dacier. SGNET: Implementation Insights. In *IEEE/IFIP Network Operations and Management Symposium*, April 2008.
19. C. Leita, M. Dacier, and F. Massicotte. Automatic handling of protocol dependencies and reaction to 0-day attacks with ScriptGen based honeypots. In *RAID 2006, 9th International Symposium on Recent Advances in Intrusion Detection, September 20-22, 2006, Hamburg, Germany - Also published as Lecture Notes in Computer Science Volume 4219/2006*, Sep 2006.
20. C. Leita, K. Mermoud, and M. Dacier. Scriptgen: an automated script generation tool for honeyd. In *Proceedings of the 21st Annual Computer Security Applications Conference*, December 2005.
21. C. Leita, V. Pham, . Thonnard, E. Ramirez-Silva, F. Pouget, E. Kirda, and M. Dacier. The Leurre.com Project: Collecting Internet Threats Information using a Worldwide Distributed Honeynet. In *1st WOMBAT open workshop*, April 2008.
22. Maxmind Product. Home page ot the maxmind company at http://www.maxmind.com.
23. D. Moore, C. Shannon, G. Voelker, and S. Savage. Network telescopes: Technical report. *CAIDA, April*, 2004.
24. S. Needleman and C. Wunsch. *A general method applicable to the search for similarities in the amino acid sequence of two proteins*. J Mol Biol. 48(3):443-53, 1970.
25. Netgeo Product. Home page of the netgeo company at http://www.netgeo.com/.
26. V.-H. Pham and M. Dacier. Honeypot traces forensics: The observation view point matters. Technical report, EURECOM, 2009.
27. V.-H. Pham, M. Dacier, G. Urvoy Keller, and T. En Najjary. The quest for multi-headed worms. In *DIMVA 2008, 5th Conference on Detection of Intrusions and Malware & Vulnerability Assessment, July 10-11th, 2008, Paris, France*, Jul 2008.
28. G. Portokalidis, A. Slowinska, and H. Bos. Argos: an emulator for fingerprinting zero-day attacks. *Proc. ACM SIGOPS EUROSYS*, 2006.
29. F. Pouget, M. Dacier, and V. H. Pham. Understanding threats: a prerequisite to enhance survivability of computing systems. In *IISW'04, International Infrastructure Survivability Workshop 2004, in conjunction with the 25th IEEE International Real-Time Systems Symposium (RTSS 04) December 5-8, 2004 Lisbonne, Portugal*, Dec 2004.
30. T. C. D. Project. http://www.cymru.com/darknet/.
31. N. Provos. A virtual honeypot framework. In *Proceedings of the 12th USENIX Security Symposium*, pages 1–14, August 2004.
32. M. Rajab, J. Zarfoss, F. Monrose, and A. Terzis. A multifaceted approach to understanding the botnet phenomenon. In *ACM SIGCOMM/USENIX Internet Measurement Conference*, October 2006.
33. E. Ramirez-Silva and M. Dacier. Empirical study of the impact of metasploit-related attacks in 4 years of attack traces. In *12th Annual Asian Computing Conference focusing on computer and network security (ASIAN07)*, December 2007.
34. J. Riordan, D. Zamboni, and Y. Duponchel. Building and deploying billy goat, a worm detection system. In *Proceedings of the 18th Annual FIRST Conference*, 2006.
35. I. M. Sensor. http://ims.eecs.umich.edu/.
36. TCPDUMP Project. Home page of the tcpdump project at http://www.tcpdump.org/.
37. The Metasploit Project. www.metasploit.org, 2007.
38. O. Thonnard and M. Dacier. A framework for attack patterns' discovery in honeynet data. *DFRWS 2008, 8th Digital Forensics Research Conference, August 11- 13, 2008, Baltimore, USA*, 2008.

39. O. Thonnard and M. Dacier. Actionable knowledge discovery for threats intelligence support using a multi-dimensional data mining methodology. In *ICDM'08, 8th IEEE International Conference on Data Mining series, December 15-19, 2008, Pisa, Italy*, Dec 2008.

40. L. van der Maaten and G. Hinton. Visualizing data using t-sne. *Journal of Machine Learning Research*, 9:2579–2605, November 2008.

41. T. Werner. Honeytrap. http://honeytrap.mwcollect.org/.

42. M. Zalewski. Home page of p0f at http://lcamtuf.coredump.cx/p0f.shtml.

Part IV
Enterprise Cyber Situational Awareness

Chapter 7
Topological Vulnerability Analysis

Sushil Jajodia and Steven Noel

Traditionally, network administrators rely on labor-intensive processes for tracking network configurations and vulnerabilities. This requires a great deal of expertise, and is error prone because of the complexity of networks and associated security data. The interdependencies of network vulnerabilities make traditional point-wise vulnerability analysis inadequate. We describe a Topological Vulnerability Analysis (TVA) approach that analyzes vulnerability dependencies and shows all possible attack paths into a network. From models of the network vulnerabilities and potential attacker exploits, we compute attack graphs that convey the impact of individual and combined vulnerabilities on overall security. TVA finds potential paths of vulnerability through a network, showing exactly how attackers may penetrate a network. From this, we identify key vulnerabilities and provide strategies for protection of critical network assets. TVA provides predictive context for network hardening, intrusion detection deployment and alarm correlation, and optimal attack response. Further, it employs efficient algorithms that scale well to larger networks.

7.1 Introduction

By their very nature, security concerns on networks are highly interdependent. Each machine's susceptibility to attack depends on the vulnerabilities of the other machines in the network. Attackers can combine vulnerabilities in unexpected ways, allowing them to incrementally penetrate a network and compromise critical systems. To protect our critical infrastructure networks, we must understand not only our individual system vulnerabilities, but also their interdependencies.

While we cannot predict the origin and timing of attacks, we can reduce their impact by knowing the possible attack paths through our networks. We need to transform raw security data into roadmaps that let us proactively prepare for attacks, manage vulnerability risks, and have real-time situational awareness. We cannot rely on manual processes and mental models. We need automated tools to analyze and visualize vulnerability dependencies and attack paths, so we can understand our overall security posture, providing context over the full security life cycle.

Our approach to such full-context security is called Topological Vulnerability Analysis (TVA) [1][2]. TVA monitors the state of network assets, maintains models of network vulnerabilities and residual risk, and combines these to produce models that convey the impact of individual and

Center for Secure Information Systems, George Mason University, Fairfax, VA 22030-4444, USA, e-mail: {jajodia, snoel}@gmu.edu

S. Jajodia et al., (eds.), *Cyber Situational Awareness*,
Advances in Information Security 46, DOI 10.1007/978-1-4419-0140-8_7,
© Springer Science+Business Media, LLC 2010

combined vulnerabilities on overall security posture. The central product of this tool is an attack graph showing all possible ways an attacker can penetrate the network.

Our TVA approach provides a unique new capability, transforming raw security data into a roadmap that lets one proactively prepare for attacks, manage vulnerability risks, and have real-time situational awareness. It supports both offensive (e.g., penetration testing) and defensive (e.g., network hardening) applications. The mapping of attack paths through a network via TVA provides a concrete understanding of how individual and combined vulnerabilities impact overall network security. For example, we can

- Compare possible expenditures of resources to determine which will have the greatest impact on overall security
- Determine how much a new vulnerability will impact overall security
- Determine whether risk-mitigating efforts have a significant impact on overall security
- Analyze how changes to individual machines may increase overall risk to the enterprise

We have implemented our approach as a security tool that transforms raw security data into a model of all possible network attack paths. In developing this tool, we have met key technical challenges, including the design of appropriate models, efficient model population, effective visualizations and decision support tools, and the development of scalable mathematical representations and algorithms. The result is a working software tool that offers truly unique capabilities.

In the design of computers and networks, security is often not given adequate priority. This is compounded by the fact that each machine's exposure to attack depends on the vulnerabilities of the other machines in the network. Attackers can combine vulnerabilities in unexpected ways, allowing them to incrementally penetrate a network and compromise critical systems.

To protect critical networks, we must understand not only individual system vulnerabilities, but also their interdependencies. TVA places vulnerabilities and their protective measures within the context of overall network security by modeling their interdependencies via attack graphs. The analysis of attack graphs provides alternative sets of protective measures that guarantee safety of critical systems. Through this unique new capability, administrators are able to determine the best sets of protective measures that should be applied in their environment.

Still, we must understand that not all attacks can be averted in advance, and there must usually remain some residual vulnerability even after reasonable protective measures have been applied. We then rely on the detect phase to identify actual attack instances. But the detection process needs to be tied to residual vulnerabilities, especially ones that lie on paths to critical network resources as discovered by TVA.

Once attacks are detected, comprehensive capabilities are needed to react to them. TVA can reduce the impact of attacks by providing knowledge of the possible vulnerability paths through the network. TVA attack graphs can be used to correlate and aggregate network attack events, across platforms as well as across the network. These attack graphs also provide the necessary context for optimal response to attacks.

The next section shows the architecture of our TVA tool. Section 7.3 illustrates the TVA approach through a simple example. Section 7.4 describes the process for building models of the security environment for TVA, for generating multi-step attack graphs. Section 7.5 explains the visualization and analysis of TVA attack graphs. Section 7.6 examines scalability of TVA. Section 7.7 reviews related work, and Section 7.8 summarizes our approach.

7.2 System Architecture

Because of vulnerability interdependencies across networks, a topological attack graph approach is needed for defense against multi-step attacks. The traditional approach that treats network data and events in isolation without the context provided by attack graphs is clearly insufficient. TVA combines vulnerabilities in ways that real attackers might do, discovering all attack paths through a network.

Figure 7.1 shows the architecture of our software tool for TVA attack graph analysis. *Network Capture* builds a model of the network, in terms of relevant security attributes. *Vulnerability Database* represents a comprehensive repository of reported vulnerabilities, with each vulnerability record listing the affected software (and hardware).

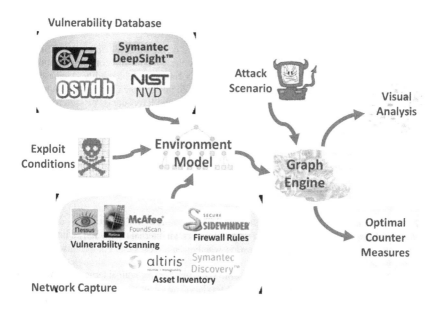

Fig. 7.1 Topological Vulnerability Analysis (TVA). Data from network scans and known vulnerabilities are combined into a model of the network security environment. Multi-step attack graph for this environment provides context for overall network security.

The *Exploit Specifications* encode how each vulnerability may be exploited (preconditions) and the result of its exploitation (postconditions). Network Capture represents data collection for a network to be defended, in terms of corresponding elements in *Vulnerability Reporting* and *Exploit Specifications*. Together, all these inputs are used to build an *Environment Model* for multi-step attack graph simulation.

In particular, the *Graph Engine* uses the *Environment Model* to simulate multi-step attacks through the network, for a given user-defined *Attack Scenario*. This engine analyzes vulnerability dependencies, matching exploit preconditions and postconditions, thus generating all possible paths through the network for a given attack scenario. The scenario may define particular starting and/or ending points for the attack, so that the graph is constrained to lie between them, or may be completely unconstrained (all possible starting and ending points).

The TVA tool provides sophisticated capabilities for interactive *Visual Analysis* of attack graphs [3]. It also computes *Optimal Counter Measures*, e.g., minimum number of network changes to thwart the attack scenario [4]. TVA attack graphs can also support proactive planning for optimal responses to attacks, based on known paths of residual vulnerability through the network. For example, attack graphs can guide the placement of intrusion detection sensors to cover all attack paths, while minimizing sensors redundancy [5].

TVA attack graphs can filter false intrusion alarms, based on known paths of residual vulnerability. They also provide the context for correlating isolated alarms as part of a larger multi-step attack penetration [6]. The attack graph shows the next possible vulnerabilities that could be exploited by an attacker. This in turn supports optimal planning and response against attacks, while minimizing effects of false alarms and attacker misdirection.

As shown in Figure 7.1, our TVA tool integrates with vulnerability scanners Nessus [7], Retina [8], and FoundScan [9] for populating its network model. TVA processes data from the Sidewinder firewall [10] to capture network connectivity to vulnerable host services. TVA also integrates with host-based asset inventory technology, such as Centennial Discovery [11] and Symantec Altiris [12].

TVA matches the network model against a database of reported vulnerabilities. There are a number of such vulnerability databases, maintained by the government, commercial companies, and the security community. Examples include NIST's National Vulnerability Database (NVD) [13], the Bugtraq security database [14], Symantec DeepSight [15], the Open Source Vulnerability Database (OSVDB) [16], and the Common Vulnerabilities and Exposure (CVE) referencing standard [17]. We can thus leverage a storehouse of knowledge gathered by security researchers around the world, rather than being limited to vulnerabilities detected by a single tool like Nessus.

7.3 Illustrative Example

In Figure 7.2, a network is separated from the Internet by a firewall. The network is divided into 3 subnets, with one host in each subnet: a DMZ web server, an internal client, and an internal server. We wish to generate an attack graph showing whether an attacker can compromise the internal server from the Internet.

The DMZ web server is running Microsoft Windows Server, with Internet Information Services (IIS), Apache/MySQL/PHP, and Tomcat servlets. The client is running Microsoft Windows XP, client security software, an office productivity suite, and other utilities. The internal server is running Apache/ MySQL/PHP, the Symantec Discovery asset inventory server, and Altiris Inventory Solution with associated software (e.g., IIS, Microsoft SQL Server). The Altiris Agent is deployed on each internal machine to collect asset inventory data.

The firewall blocks direct access to the internal server and client subnets from the Internet. Thus, from the outside, network vulnerability scanners such as Nessus are unable to detect any vulnerabilities on the internal server and client. In fact, if the firewall has network address translation (NAT) enabled, Nessus cannot even discover the existence of machines on these 2 subnets.

From the outside of the firewall, the only machine exposed is the DMZ server. In particular, the firewall blocks all traffic except HTTP to the DMZ server's TCP port 80. From behind the firewall, Nessus shows a variety of vulnerabilities on the DMZ server. But from the Internet, only the web server vulnerability is exposed. A Nessus scan from the DMZ to the internal subnets identifies any internal vulnerabilities permitted through the firewall. In our network, MySQL traffic is permitted between the DMZ web server and the internal server, and two exposed MySQL vulnerabilities allow an attacker to access the internal server (from the DMZ web server).

The question is whether an attacker can compromise the internal server from the Internet. Figure 7.3 shows the resulting attack graph for this network, using a TVA model populated by Nessus scans alone. This shows that an attacker starting on the Internet can first penetrate through the firewall and compromise the DMZ server, exploiting a vulnerability on its web server installation. Then, from the DMZ server, the attacker can access the internal server via exploitation of the two vulnerabilities.

A Nessus scan from the Internet would reveal no vulnerabilities on the internal server or client, so that there is no direct attack from the Internet to the internal machines. Because the firewall

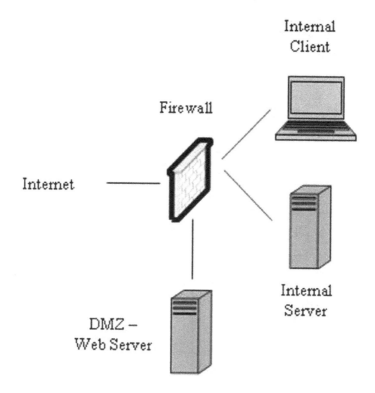

Fig. 7.2 Example network. Firewall is intended to protect network from Internet attackers.

blocks traffic originating from the server subnet to the client subnet, and blocks all traffic from the DMZ to the client subnet, there is no attack path to the client at all. That is, a Nessus scan from the DMZ to the client reveals no vulnerabilities. In this case, a Nessus scan of the client within its own subnet (no intervening firewalls) detects no vulnerabilities (or even open ports), because of the client's personal firewall (part of the security suite).

We then augment the Nessus-based model, using software inventory data from Altiris. In particular, we compare products and versions from Altiris against a vulnerability database to determine the vulnerabilities associated with each application. For Microsoft products, this correlation process involves an extra step. We first determine how many vulnerabilities are associated with the Microsoft product and version installed, and then compare the Microsoft patches and hotfixes installed (collected by Altiris). This determines which Microsoft vulnerabilities are unpatched.

So, for example, while there are almost 200 vulnerabilities associated with Microsoft Windows XP SP2, many of the older vulnerabilities are patched on the client machine. On the other hand, no Microsoft hotfixes are applied on the client for Microsoft Office components after Office SP2. Thus all of the dozens of vulnerabilities associated with that version of Microsoft Office are relevant to the client.

These client-side vulnerabilities are associated with software that has no network service running. Still, these vulnerabilities represent vectors by which an attacker might obtain access to the client machine. Significant numbers of vulnerabilities are associated with web browsers and plug-ins. The typical scenario for these increasingly widespread vulnerabilities is that a user running a vulnerable web browser or plug-in visits a web site with malicious content that exploits the

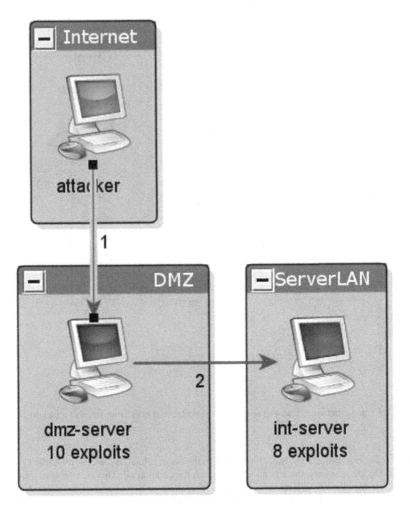

Fig. 7.3 Attack graph from internet attacker to internal server. The network model is populated from Nessus vulnerability scans.

client-side vulnerability. Another important class of vulnerabilities is associated with document processing applications, e.g., infected documents via e-mail.

Figure 7.4 shows the attack graph augmented with Altiris data. This shows that it is actually possible to attack the client directly from the Internet, via 12 different client-side vulnerabilities. Strictly speaking, the client needs to make an outbound connection (e.g., web site visit) to a compromised server. But the firewall allows this, so it is correct to model the server as the attacker and the client as the victim. The attacker on the client can then compromise the internal server, through a firewall hole allowing access from client to server.

This example illustrates the importance of accounting for such client-side vulnerabilities. Services on an internal server would typically be exposed to internal clients, and may be vulnerable. In this case, our augmented model has uncovered attack paths that would have otherwise been undetected by a vulnerability scanner.

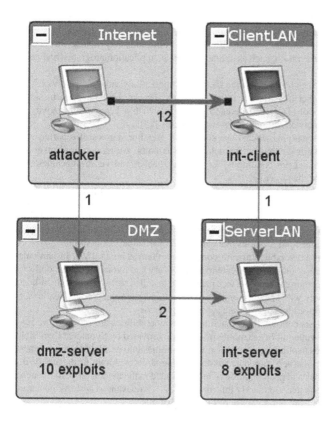

Fig. 7.4 Attack graph augmented with Altiris data. The host-based asset inventory uncovers additional client-side vulnerabilities.

Our attack graphs show how hosts on a network can be exploited through multiple steps, even when the attacker cannot access them directly. It is not directly possible to compromise the internal server from the outside because of the policy enforced by the firewall. But TVA shows that the attack goal can be reached indirectly, through two different attack paths. While it may be possible for an experienced analyst to find such paths manually for a small network, for enterprise networks an automated tool is needed.

7.4 Network Attack Modeling

In TVA, the environment model includes aspects of the network configuration relevant to attack penetration, as well as a set of potential attacker exploits that match attributes of the configuration. The TVA approach can apply to many different types of attack models (even non-cyber models) as long as a common schema is employed across the model.

Typically, we model a network as machines and collections of machines into protection domains. Protection domains capture the idea that the set of machines in a domain have (implicitly) unrestricted access to one another's vulnerable services. A machine may include attributes for modeling network attack penetration, such as operating system, application programs, and connections to vulnerable services.

A connection describes how a machine connects to potentially vulnerable services across the network, to ports on other machines or to its own ports. This mirrors the Transmission Control Protocol/Internet Protocol (TCP/IP) reference model, in which a layered connectivity structure represents the various network architectures and protocols [18].

To keep pace with emerging threats, we continually monitor sources of reported vulnerabilities, and add those to our database of modeled TVA exploits. We model an attacker exploit in terms of preconditions and postconditions, for generic attacker and victim machines, which are subsequently mapped to the target network.

The detection of a host vulnerability (e.g., via Nessus) represents a precondition for a corresponding TVA modeled exploit. In reality, the vulnerability exists because of a particular combination of software components. A detected vulnerability is thus a convenient higher level abstraction, in comparison to the combination of components that causes it. There are usually many possible software components and configurations that can cause a particular vulnerability.

We can thus model vulnerable software components themselves in TVA. In particular, host-based asset management solutions like Centennial Discovery and Symantec Altiris collect specific information such as operating system, service packs, and installed software through on-host agents. Many exploits work only with specific versions of operating systems and/or applications, and vulnerabilities can be removed by applying the appropriate patches.

To keep TVA exploits continually updated as new vulnerabilities are reported, we may leverage the component-to-vulnerability mapping information provided by Symantec DeepSight. Also, while TVA incorporates exploits against known vulnerabilities into its analysis, it is a general modeling approach that can also accommodate unknown vulnerabilities. Anything that can be described in terms of preconditions and postconditions can be included in the model. Also, tools such as Nessus generate many alerts that are merely informational, i.e., irrelevant to network penetration. We carefully exclude these from our database of modeled exploits.

One important class of vulnerabilities detected by our approach is client applications. Client-side vulnerabilities have a major impact on enterprise network security posture, a trend that will no doubt continue. For example, web applications (an important source of client-side vulnerabilities) represent about 60% of vulnerabilities documented in 2007 [19].

In our approach, the correctness of attack graphs depends on the quality of the input datasets. The network scanning tools must have a complete and current database of detected software and/or vulnerabilities. Standardization efforts such as Security Content Automation Protocol (SCAP) [20] help facilitate the management of mapping data between asset inventory and vulnerabilities. Otherwise, each tool may use its own naming conventions. Within SCAP, the Common Platform Enumeration (CPE) [21] provides standard naming of operating systems and applications, and CVE provides mappings to CPE for vulnerable software. The OVAL Language [22] standardizes the vulnerability assessment process and results. Adoption of such standards among tool vendors will greatly facilitate the building of attack models for TVA.

The purpose of modeling network configuration in TVA is to support preconditions of modeled attacker exploits. Machines are explicitly included in the model only if they offer services over the network that can be exploited. The effects of other network devices such as routers and firewalls is captured implicitly, in the way that connectivity is modeled at the various network layers, i.e., in the way that they provide/restrict connectivity to vulnerable services on other machines.

For remote (versus host-based) scanners such as Nessus, Retina, and FoundScan, we can capture the implicit effects of devices such as firewalls by scanning from different network vantage points, targeting hosts through the firewall. We can then combine multiple scans from various network locations, building a complete map of connectivity to vulnerable services throughout the network. Alternatively, we can analyze firewall rules directly, adding the resulting vulnerable connections to the model, eliminating the need for scanning through firewalls.

7.5 Analysis and Visualization

Based on a given attack scenario, the attack graph may be constrained by specific starting and ending points. The scenario may also be less constrained, such as finding all possible attack starts leading to one or more goals, or finding all possible paths from particular starting points. For example, one may wish to know how a particular critical system can be compromised from all possible starting points. Or, one may want to know all systems that could be compromised from a particular starting point, or even from all possible starting points. Our TVA tool supports each combination of specified/unspecified attack start/goal.

In their raw form, attack graphs can be much too complex for easy understanding. Figure 7.5 is an example of such a raw attack graph, for a network of only 20 hosts in four subnets. Computational complexity for this graph is quadratic in the number of hosts, and we compute it in a fraction of a second. Still, it is difficult to for an analyst to understand its complexity. To help manage this, we aggregate attack graphs, providing better situational awareness at higher levels of abstraction. We define multiple levels of abstraction by recursively aggregating elements from one level to the next, forming a hierarchy of abstraction levels.

Figure 7.6 illustrates our hierarchy of attack graph abstractions. From the bottom, the preconditions or postconditions for an exploit are aggregated into a condition set. This provides the higher-level viewpoint that exploits depend on one another, without showing the particular conditions that cause the dependency.

Sets of conditions for a machine are aggregated into a machine abstraction, so that one can consider a machine without knowing its particular conditions. Exploits, with their preconditions and postconditions, are aggregated if they involve the same pair of attacker/victim machines. This shows that there are exploits from one machine to another, while hiding the details about them.

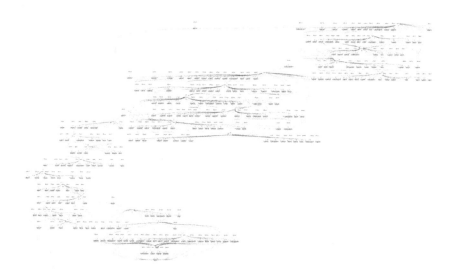

Fig. 7.5 Raw attack graph. This graph is computed quickly, but cannot be quickly understood.

An important high-level abstraction in TVA is the protection domain, which represents a set of machines that have full access to one another's vulnerabilities. In general, connectivity can be restricted across a network through a variety of mechanisms, such as firewalls, trust relationships, etc. But within a protection domain, implicitly there are no connectivity limitations among machines. Thus all of a machine's vulnerabilities are potentially exploitable from anywhere within the protection domain.

In a raw non-aggregated form, the attack graph is fully connected within a protection domain. Through this implicit full connectivity, we employ a much more efficient representation. The machines in a domain are listed, along with exploits against each of their vulnerabilities. Then implicitly, once an attacker takes control of a machine within a protection domain, he can exploit all vulnerabilities on machines within it. In this way, we avoid explicitly listing every n^2 (fully-connected) exploit dependency within the protection domain. Thus, within each domain, complexity is linear in the number of hosts.

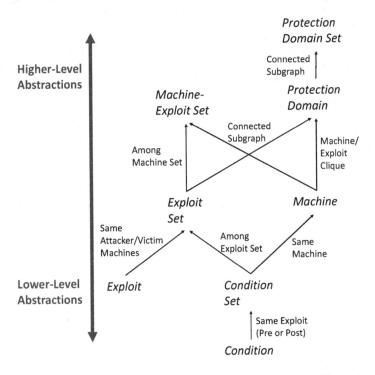

Fig. 7.6 Levels of attack graph aggregation. Lower-level details are aggregated into progressively summarized sets.

Figure 7.7 demonstrates the effectiveness of our graph aggregation approach. This is an attack graph for a network of six subnets, with 150 hosts. In its raw form, this attack graph is actually much more complex than Figure 7.5. But through our graph aggregation, the flow of the attack paths is clear. Individual machines appear within protection domains, and are visible when a domain is expanded. Graph edges from one machine to another represent the set of exploits from attacker to victim machine. Graph edges between domains are aggregated exploit sets between domain pairs.

Our TVA software tool includes a full-featured attack graph visualization interface. In this interface, a high-level view clearly displays attack relationships among protection domains, which can be opened individually or in groups for deeper views of attack properties and relationships. In this process, no graph information is lost; one has merely to expand a folder to acquire information at a lower level.

A complete listing of exploits and associated details for any selected component is available at all times. This supports in-depth analysis of exploit details, while overall topology and network relationships are kept simple and understandable within the main graph view.

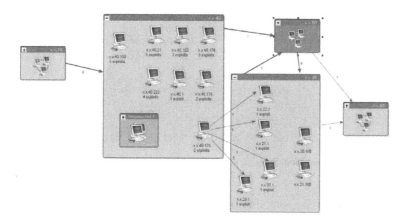

Fig. 7.7 Aggregated attack graph. This is much easier to understand overall attack flow.

Our TVA tool also emulates the hardening of machines and exploitable vulnerabilities to study the effects of remediation and what-if scenarios. Exploring the attack graph, the analyst is often faced with multiple options for remediation. This involves choosing a machine or set of machines to protect (harden), or identifying specific exploits to protect against.

We display the attack graph effects that occur when a specific machine or protection domain is hardened or when a specific exploit is neutralized. Hardened elements are maintained in a log, e.g., for reporting. The TVA tool also generates recommendations automatically, i.e., first layer (from start), last layer (from goal), and minimum set that that separates start from goal.

To aid user navigation, the TVA tool maintains a global overview of the entire attack graph at all times, which can be used to pan the main graph view. The tool also has a graphical (tree) attack dictionary of all graph elements. The various graph views are linked, so that selecting an element in one view cause it to be selected in all view. A variety of toolbars are available for commonly used tools. This includes a suite of interactive layout tools, with manual repositioning as well as full-scale layout algorithms, continuously available to restructure the display.

7.6 Scalability

For computing attack graphs for larger networks, we need scalable mathematical representations and algorithms. We assume the attacker's control over the network increases monotonically over time. This corresponds to the conservative assumption that once an attacker gains control of a network resource, there is no need to relinquish it to further advance the attack.

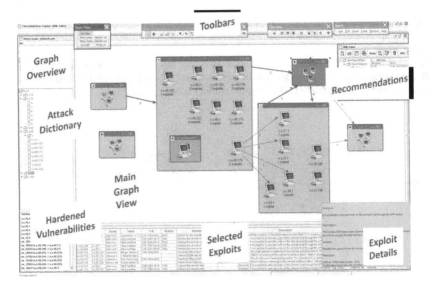

Fig. 7.8 Attack graph visualization. Supports graph navigation with high-level overviews and detail drilldowns.

Under this monotonicity, it is sufficient to represent the dependencies among exploits, rather than explicitly enumerating every sequence of exploits [23]. The resulting exploit-dependency attack graphs grow quadratically rather than exponentially [24]. In particular, worst-case complexity for n network hosts is $O(n^2)$ By grouping hosts into protection domains, complexity is reduced to $O(n)$ within each domain. In terms of the database of potential attacker exploits, complexity is $O(e)$, for e exploits.

Figure 7.9 shows attack graph computation times for networks of various sizes. In each case, a subnet contains 200 hosts, and each host has 5 vulnerabilities. Each subnet has incoming vulnerable connections from 2 other subnets, and symmetrically, outgoing vulnerable connections to 2 other subnets. This is a ring topology, in which the number of network connections grows linearly with the number of subnets.

From one subnet to another, there are 500 connections to vulnerabilities in the victim subnet. Thus there are 2 * 500=1,000 incoming and 2 * 500=1,000 outgoing vulnerable connections (a grand total of 2,000) for each subnet. Computation times (total run time in seconds) are based on increasing numbers of subnets, from 20 subnets (4,000 hosts) to 200 subnets (40,000 hosts). Run times are for a quad-core Intel Xeon CPU at 1.86 GHz, with 4 GB RAM.

In this experiment, overall network size (number of vulnerable connections) grows linearly with the number of subnets (and hosts). This clearly shows how graph generation time depends proportionally on the size of the input network. This excludes any time for generating the input model (network and exploits) itself, although this has the same worse-case complexity, and these can be pre-computed.

Graph visual layout performance is a separate issue, and is not included in the execution times of Figure 7.9. For example, Figure 7.10 shows a layout of the 20-subnet case (4,000 hosts) of Figure 7.9. Computing this layout only a few seconds, but computing layout for the 100-subnets case (20,000 hosts) takes 14 minutes. But in all cases, once the initial layout is computed, performance of user interaction (repositioning, drilldown, etc.) is immediate.

Visual layout computation is needed for a cyber view of network attack graphs. Such layout induces spatial coordinates onto an abstract information graph. But in some situations, understanding the actual physical location of attacks may be important. We can embed the attack graph in a geo-spatial visualization, as illustrated in Figure 7.11. When spatial coordinates are given, no

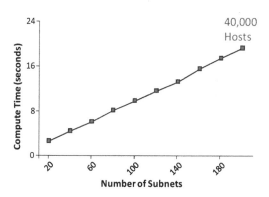

Fig. 7.9 Computation time for attack graph generation. Network complexity grows linearly with the number of subnets. Attack graph generation time is proportional to the size of the network.

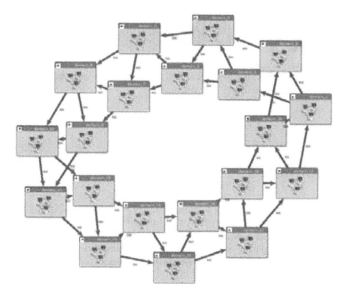

Fig. 7.10 Attack graph layout solution. For this 20-subnet case (4,000 hosts), graph visual layout is computed in only a few seconds.

additional graph layout computation is needed. In such cases, visualizing complex attack graphs is much faster than for abstract cyber views.

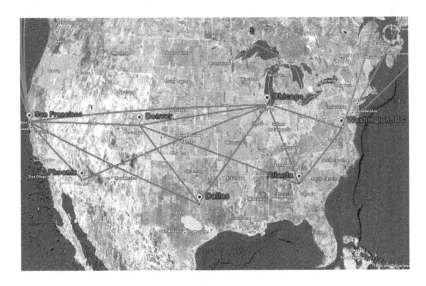

Fig. 7.11 Geo-spatial attack graph visualization. When spatial coordinates are given, computational requirements are reduced.

7.7 Related Work

In early attack graph formalisms, algorithmic complexity is exponential [25][26][27] [28] because paths are explicitly enumerated. Under reasonable assumptions attack graph analysis can be formulated as monotonic logic, making it unnecessary to explicitly enumerate states. This leads to polynomial rather than exponential complexity [29]. Our protection domain abstraction reduces complexity further, to linear within each domain [30]. Complexity can be further reduced based on host configuration regularities [31].

Attack graph research has largely focused on scalability, with relatively little work on aspects of model population. Notable exceptions include [18][32][33], although these are more theoretical frameworks than practical model population. Commercial capabilities for attack graph analysis remain limited, especially in the area of visualization for large-scale graphs [34][35]. A review of attack graph research circa 2005 is given in [36].

7.8 Summary

TVA shows paths of vulnerability allowing attackers to penetrate through a network. It identifies critical vulnerabilities and provides strategies for protection of critical network assets. This allows us to harden networks before attacks occur, and handle intrusion detection more effectively, and respond appropriately to attacks.

TVA captures the network configuration, including software, their vulnerabilities, and connectivity to vulnerable services. It then matches the network configuration against a database of modeled attacker exploits for simulating multi-step attack penetration.

During simulation, the attack graph can be constrained according to user-defined attack scenarios. From the resulting attack graphs, TVA computes recommendations for optimal network hardening. It also provides sophisticated visualization capabilities for interactive attack graph exploration and what-if analysis. TVA employs algorithms with worst-case quadratic complexity in the number of network hosts.

Further, TVA attack graphs then provide the necessary context for correlating and prioritizing intrusion alerts, based on known paths of vulnerability through the network. Overall, TVA offers powerful capabilities for proactive network defense, transforming raw security data into actionable intelligence.

Acknowledgements

This material is based upon work supported by Homeland Security Advanced Research Projects Agency under the contract FA8750-05-C-0212 administered by the Air Force Research Laboratory/Rome; by Air Force Research Laboratory/Rome under the contract FA8750-06-C-0246; by Federal Aviation Administration under the contract DTFAWA-08-F-GMU18; by Air Force Office of Scientific Research under grant FA9550-07-1-0527 and FA9550-08-1-0157; and by the National Science Foundation under grants CT-0716567, CT-0716323, and CT-0627493. Any opinions, findings, and conclusions or recommendations expressed in this material are those of the authors and do not necessarily reflect the views of the sponsoring organizations.

References

[1] S. Jajodia, S. Noel, and B. O'Berry, "Topological Analysis of Network Attack Vulnerability," in *Managing Cyber Threats: Issues, Approaches and Challenges*, V. Kumar, J. Srivastava, A. Lazarevic (eds.), Kluwer Academic Publisher, 2005, pages 248-266.

[2] S. Jajodia, S. Noel, "Topological Vulnerability Analysis: A Powerful New Approach for Network Attack Prevention, Detection, and Response," in *Algorithms, Architectures and Information Systems Security (Indian Statistical Institute Platinum Jubilee Series)*, B. B. Bhattacharya, S. Sur-Kolay, S. C. Nandy, A. Bagchi, eds., World Scientific, New Jersey, 2009, pages 285–305.

[3] S. Noel, M. Jacobs, P. Kalapa. S. Jajodia, "Multiple Coordinated Views for Network Attack Graphs," in *IEEE Workshop on Visualization for Computer Security (VizSEC2005)*, Minneapolis, MN, October, 2005, pages 99–106.

[4] L. Wang, S. Noel, S. Jajodia, "Minimum-Cost Network Hardening Using Attack Graphs," *Computer Communications*, 29(18), 2006, pages 3812–3824.

[5] S. Noel, S. Jajodia, "Optimal IDS Sensor Placement and Alert Prioritization Using Attack Graphs," *Journal of Network and Systems Management*, 16(3), 2008, pages 259–275.

[6] S. Noel, E. Robertson, S. Jajodia, "Correlating Intrusion Events and Building Attack Scenarios through Attack Graph Distances," in *Proceedings of the 20th Annual Computer Security Applications Conference (ACSAC)*, 2004, pages 350–359.

[7] R. Deraison, *Nessus*, http://www.nessus.org.

[8] eEye Digital Security, *Retina Network Security Scanner*, http://www.eeye.com/html/Products/Retina/index.html.

[9] Foundstone, *FoundScan Frequently Asked Questions*, http://www.foundstone.com/us/index.asp.

[10] Secure Computing, Sidewinder Firewall Device, http://www.securecomputing.com/.

[11] Centennial Software, Discovery Asset Management, http://www.centennial-software.com/.

[12] Symantec, Altiris, http://www.altiris.com/.

[13] NIST, National Vulnerability Database (NVD), http://nvd.nist.gov/.

[14] Security Focus, *Bugtraq Vulnerabilities*, http://www.securityfocus.com/vulnerabilities.

[15] Symantec Corporation, *Symantec DeepSight Threat Management System*, https://tms.symantec.com/Default.aspx.

[16] Open Source Vulnerability Database, http://osvdb.org/.

[17] MITRE Corporation, *CVE - Common Vulnerabilities and Exposures*, http://cve.mitre.org/.

[18] R. Ritchey, B. O'Berry, S. Noel, "Representing TCP/IP Connectivity for Topological Analysis of Network Security," in *Proceedings of the 18th Annual Computer Security Applications Conference (ACSAC)*, 2002, pages 156–165.

[19] D. Turner, M. Fossi, E. Johnson, T. Mack, J. Blackbird, S. Entwisle, M. K. Low, D. McKinney, C. Wueest, *Symantec Global Internet Security Threat Report Trends*, 2008.

[20] NIST, Security Content Automation Protocol (SCAP), http://nvd.nist.gov/scap.cfm.

[21] MITRE, Common Platform Enumeration (CPE), http://cpe.mitre.org/.

[22] MITRE, Oval Language, http://oval.mitre.org/.

[23] P. Ammann, D. Wijesekera, S. Kaushik, "Scalable, Graph-Based Network Vulnerability Analysis," in *Proceedings of the 9th ACM Conference on Computer and Communications Security*, Washington, DC, pages 217–224.

[24] S. Noel, J. Jajodia, "Understanding Complex Network Attack Graphs through Clustered Adjacency Matrices," in *Proceedings of the 21st Annual Computer Security Applications Conference (ACSAC)*, 2005, pages 160–169.

[25] D. Zerkle, K. Levitt, "Netkuang: A Multi-Host Configuration Vulnerability Checker," in Proceedings of the 6th USENIX Unix Security Symposium, 1996.

[26] R. Ritchey, P. Ammann, "Using Model Checking to Analyze Network Vulnerabilities," in Proceedings of the IEEE Symposium on Security and Privacy, 2000.

[27] L. Swiler, C. Phillips, D. Ellis, S. Chakerian, "Computer-Attack Graph Generation Tool," in Proceedings of the DARPA Information Survivability Conference & Exposition II, 2001.

[28] O. Sheyner, J. Haines, S. Jha, R. Lippmann, J. Wing, "Automated Generation and Analysis of Attack Graphs," in *Proceedings of the IEEE Symposium on Security and Privacy*, Oakland, CA.

[29] R. Lippmann, K. Ingols, C. Scott, K. Piwowarski, K. Kratkiewicz, M. Artz, R. Cunningham, "Validating and Restoring Defense in Depth Using Attack Graphs," in Proceedings of the MILCOM Military Communications Conference, 2006.

[30] S. Noel, S. Jajodia, "Managing Attack Graph Complexity through Visual Hierarchical Aggregation," in *Proceedings of the ACM CCS Workshop on Visualization and Data Mining for Computer Security* Fairfax, Virginia.

[31] W. Li, An Approach to Graph-Based Modeling of Network Exploitations, PhD dissertation, Department of Computer Science, Mississippi State University, 2005.

[32] F. Cuppens, R. Ortalo, "LAMBDA: A Language to Model a Database for Detection of Attacks," in 3rd International Workshop on Recent Advances in Intrusion Detection, 2000.

[33] S. Templeton, K. Levitt, "A Requires/Provides Model for Computer Attacks," in New Security Paradigms Workshop, 2000.

[34] Skybox Security, http://www.skyboxsecurity.com/.

[35] RedSeal Systems, http://www.redseal.net/.

[36] R. Lippmann, K. Ingols, An Annotated Review of Past Papers on Attack Graphs, Lincoln Laboratory, Technical Report ESC-TR-2005-054, 2005.

Chapter 8
Cross-Layer Damage Assessment for Cyber Situational Awareness

Peng Liu, Xiaoqi Jia, Shengzhi Zhang, Xi Xiong, Yoon-Chan Jhi, Kun Bai, and Jason Li

Abstract Damage assessment plays a very important role in securing enterprise networks and systems. Gaining good awareness about the effects and impact of cyber attack actions would enable security officers to make the right cyber defense decisions and take the right cyber defense actions. A good number of damage assessment techniques have been proposed in the literature, but they typically focus on a single abstraction level (of the software system in concern). As a result, existing damage assessment techniques and tools are still very limited in satisfying the needs of *comprehensive* damage assessment which should not result in any "blind spots".

This chapter presents a generic multi-level damage assessment framework, which captures several fundamental characteristics of the damage assessment problem, points out the necessity and importance of cross-layer damage assessment, and identifies the key component techniques of a systematic damage assessment solution. To demonstrate the feasibility, merits and applicability of this framework, we propose a concrete virtual machine (VM) approach to do damage assessment across two fundamental abstraction levels: instruction level and OS level. This approach will integrate the damage assessment operations at the instruction level and the OS process level. This approach leads to a novel production-environment damage assessment architecture. Although this approach does not cover all of the abstraction levels, it shows that *across-level* damage assessment could be done in complex software systems.

8.1 INTRODUCTION

Damage assessment plays a very important role in securing enterprise networks and systems. Gaining good awareness about cyber attack situations would enable security officers to make the right cyber defense decisions and take the right cyber defense actions. To gain full cyber situational awareness under severe cyber attacks, the security analysts need to go through three basic awareness gaining stages: Situation Perception, Situation Comprehension, and Situation Projection. Being a main part of impact assessment and situation assessment, damage assessment is an essential component of the Situation Comprehension stage. In addition, predictive damage assessment, which assesses the damage that is going to be caused in (near) future, could play an important role at the Situation Projection stage.

Peng Liu, Xiaoqi Jia, Shengzhi Zhang, Xi Xiong, Yoon-Chan Jhi, Kun Bai, Pennsylvania State University, University Park · Jason Li, IAI Inc.

S. Jajodia et al., (eds.), *Cyber Situational Awareness*,
Advances in Information Security 46, DOI 10.1007/978-1-4419-0140-8_8,
© Springer Science+Business Media, LLC 2010

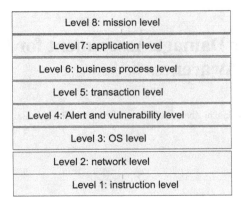

Fig. 8.1 Damage Semantics at Multiple Abstraction Levels

8.1.1 A Multi-Level Damage Assessment Framework

Fundamentally, the goal of damage assessment is to develop techniques and tools to identify and assess compromised and damaged information assets. For mission-critical or business-critical enterprise information systems and cyber infrastructures, damage assessment is an indispensable part of situation awareness and security/risk management. Since a computer software system handles only *two* types of information assets: *data* and *code* (note that network packets are data), so only two things could be damaged: data or code. However, due to at least three observations, damage assessment is still a hard problem:

- Observation 1: A piece of damaged data or code has different semantics at different levels.
- Observation 2: Damage can propagate.
- Observation 3: Damage assessment has two dimensions: time dimension vs. space dimension.

Due to Observation 1, we cannot ignore semantics (of damaged data or code elements). For example, when a data record is corrupted by SQL injection attack, we could observe the following *abstraction levels* of damage semantics:

- Level 1 Instruction level semantics: a specific memory unit is tainted.
- Level 2 Network level semantics: the network session (or flow) which sends the malicious SQL query to the victim host is tainted.
- Level 3 OS level semantics: the OS process (code) executing the malicious SQL query is doing bad things.
- Level 4 Alert and vulnerability level semantics: a SQL injection attack alert is raised by the intrusion detection system.
- Level 5 Transaction level semantics: there is a *malicious interest rate adjusting* transaction, and a data record is corrupted.
- Level 6 Business process level: the *interest rate management* business process is causing damage.
- Level 7 Application level semantics: the loan management application is causing $80 million cascading financial loss.
- Level 8 Mission level semantics: the mission of protecting the organization's finance infrastructure is affected.

Figure 8.1 shows the set of abstraction levels. Instruction level semantics tell how processors execute individual instructions. Network level semantics tell the type of network protocols (e.g., TCP,

UDP) and the associated protocol automata, network flows, connection status, packets, and events. Besides processes and threads, the OS level semantics also include (a) bugs and bug exploitation inside device driver code and other kernel code entities, and (b) Rootkits. Alert and vulnerability level semantics include alerts (raised by intrusion detection tools such as Snort), known vulnerabilities, reports generated by vulnerability analysis tools (e.g., Nessus), and attack graphs that "predict" how vulnerabilities could be exploited by multi-step attacks. Transaction level semantics capture the transaction processing model and the read/write operations of business transactions. Business process level semantics capture business workflows which could involve a sequence of transactions.

The example above shows that the same damage can exhibit different "looks" at different abstraction levels. Hence, if we only examine the damage (caused by a piece of tainted data or code) at one or two abstraction levels, we won't be able to gain complete knowledge of the damage. A lot useful information about the damage (and its cause) exists at the other levels, and they should not be ignored. Accordingly, Observation 1 demands multilevel, bidirectional damage assessment. This means that when we collect the *manifestations* of a piece of damaged data or code, we should not only study how the damage changes its manifestations (or looks) from higher abstraction levels to lower abstraction levels, but also study how the damage changes its manifestations from lower abstraction levels to higher abstraction levels. In general, bottom-up damage assessment helps the security analyst understand the *impact* of the damage (on applications and missions), while top-down damage assessment helps the security analyst understand the *causality* of security accidents observed at a higher level. In addition, top-down analysis could also serve two other relevant purposes: *forensics* and *what-if analysis*.

Observation 2 implies the importance of *dependences* (or causality relationships) in damage assessment. In principle, we can classify all damage into two categories: *direct* damage vs. *indirect* damage. Direct damage is directly caused by intrusion actions, e.g., SQL injection actions can make a data record modified. In contrast, indirect damage is indirectly caused by *damage propagation*, e.g., a corrupted file X is used by an innocent program to corrupt file Y. It is clear that damage propagation is caused by dependences between actions. It is safe to say that if there were no dependences, there won't be any damage propagation.

Intrusion detection systems can identify a lot of direct damage; however, they are not designed to handle indirect damage. *Damage assessment is fundamentally about identifying and tracking the relevant dependences.* The relevant causality relationships either exist within a single abstraction level or exist across two (or more) abstraction levels. Integrating Observation 1 and Observation 2 indicates the importance of *cross-level* damage assessment. In particular, it is not hard to see that damage propagation is simultaneously happening at multiple abstraction levels. For example, when write-read dependence happens between a tainted instruction X and a good instruction Y belonging to two applications, not only does the damage propagate from X's writes to Y's writes, the damage will also propagate from the process that executes X to the process that executes Y, from the transaction that executes X to the transaction that executes Y, from the business process that executes X to the business process that executes Y, and from the application that executes X to the application that executes Y.

Accordingly, although many damage assessment jobs can be done within a single abstraction level, some important damage assessment tasks must be performed in a cross-level style.

Observation 3 indicates the importance of the *time angle* in damage assessment. As shown in Figure 8.2, the whole process of damage assessment and repair has a sequence of key events:

- At time t1, the intrusion happens and the damage starts to propagate. However, the intrusion time is typically not the time when the system (including its users) "feels" that something is going wrong.
- At time t2, some effects and attack actions are identified by intrusion detection "sensors" or sensors that monitor the "health" of the whole system. Note that "effects" and "attack actions" are not equivalent notations. On one hand, effects are not always directly caused by attack actions, that is, they often represent indirect damage instead of direct damage. On the other hand, knowing what the attack actions does not automatically produce the knowledge about

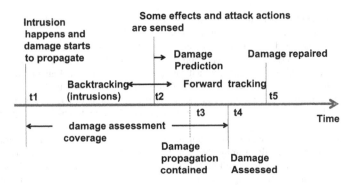

Fig. 8.2 The Time Angle of Damage Assessment

what all the effects are. The intrusion detection sensors tell what the attack actions are, but these sensors are not designed to track damage propagation, which is necessary to know what all the effects are.

- Due to the limitations of both intrusion detection sensors and effect identification sensors, at time t2 the security analyst has only very limited knowledge about the damage that has been caused. In order to gain full knowledge, the security analyst usually needs to do both *backward intrusion action tracking* and *forward damage propagation tracking*:
  - The purpose of *backward intrusion action tracking* is to back-track the intruding actions that have caused the identified effects through direct damage causing or indirect damage propagation.
  - The purpose of *forward damage propagation tracking* is to track the damage propagation traces starting from the detected attack actions or the identified attack effects. Since the detected attack actions usually happen at a time earlier than t2, forward tracking should start with the log records taken since the happening time(s) of the detected attack actions instead of t2.
- At time t2, not all the damage that has been caused is known to the security analyst. So damage prediction could be needed for the security analyst to quickly know the scale of the security accident (and its impact) before concrete damage assessment reports can be generated through a much more time-consuming process. Damage prediction has two aspects: (a) predict the damage that has already been caused but are still unknown to the analyst; (b) predict the damage that would be caused in the future.

- At time t3, the on-going damage propagation is contained. That is, after this time, no new legitimate operations or actions can further propagate the damage caused to the system. Damage containment is automatically achieved if the system is shut down during damage assessment and repair; however, this may not be acceptable in information systems that demand high availability. For non-stop 24*7 systems, damage containment is possible when a superset of the system's data or code entities can be identified on-the-fly to guarantee that it contains all the damaged items. Once this superset is identified, access controls can be enforced to prevent information from "leaking" outside of the superset. If the superset is not very large, the system will still be able to provide very good availability. As soon as an entity in the superset is identified innocent or repaired, the entity can be moved out of the superset to further increase system availability.
- At time t4, the damage assessment task is finished. Note that this task starts at time t2, note that this task involves co-working of both forward damage propagation tracking and backward intrusion action tracking. In particular, whenever the backward tracking process identified a

new intruding action, a new thread of the forward tracking process will start to check whether this action has caused any unknown damage. Similarly, whenever the forward tracking process identified a damage entity from known attack effects, a new thread of the backward tracking process will start to check whether the new effects have been caused by an unknown attacking action.

- At time t5, the damage identified during time window t2-t4 will be repaired. Note that the damage repair process starts at time t2 instead of t4. Note also that the damage repair process gradually reduces the scope of damage containment.

8.1.2 Existing Damage Assessment Techniques

In the literature, most if not all of the existing damage assessment techniques focus on a single abstraction level. At the instruction level, the well-known and widely used dynamic taint analysis technique is proposed in [19]. Given a taint seed, which is typically a data item originating from or arithmetically derived from an intruding event (e.g., a remote exploit from the network), the dynamic taint analysis technique can track how the instructions executed in the system (after the taint need is born) propagate the taint to other data items through *data dependences*. (For example, when an instruction uses a tainted data item x to calculate the value of data item y, y will become tainted.) As a result, all the data items tainted through this taint propagation tracking processing can be viewed as damaged. Nevertheless, it should be noticed that dynamic taint analysis typically requires the being assessed system to run on top of a CPU emulator such as QEMU [7], and all CPU emulators cause significant performance degradation.

At the network level, the damage caused by an intruding network event is typically assessed through the event's impact on the host system, and such impact is typically assessed through damage assessment activities at the other abstraction levels.

At the OS level, in [17] a novel backward intrusion action tracking technique called Back-Tracker is proposed. This technique works by observing OS-level objects (e.g., files, file names, processes) and events (e.g., system calls). BackTracker uses three types of dependency relationships between OS-level objects: process/process dependencies, process/file dependencies, and process/filename dependencies. (So both data dependences and control dependences are taken into consideration.) BackTracker logs the relevant OS-level objects and events during run time through a virtual-machine monitor (VMM) extension so that the being assessed system (including OS and applications) is running inside a virtual machine and any system call issued inside the virtual machine could trigger BackTracker to do some logging. Using the logged OS-level objects and events, BackTracker builds the corresponding dependency graphs backwardly starting from a single detection point (e.g., a suspicious file). In these graphs, nodes represent OS-level objects and edges represent one of the three aforementioned types of dependencies. The root nodes of these dependency graphs often represent the intruding events.

Besides backward intrusion tracking, forward damage propagation tracking techniques are also proposed at the OS level. In [12], the authors use roughly the same types of dependencies as used in [17], but their techniques do forward damage propagation tracking instead of backward tracking. In particular, they build forward damage propagation dependency graphs and use such graphs to track how damage propagates insides a file system.

At the alert and vulnerabilities level, attack graphs [5], [14], [15], [21], [26], [30] and alert correlation tools [10], [20] can be integrated to do damage assessment. Alert correlation tools can "glue" scattered alerts of a specific multi-step attack together so that the attack's strategy and intent are made much clearer to the security officer. However, due to false negatives and false positives, the results of alert correlation can be incomplete or even erroneous. To address such problems, attack graphs generated through offline vulnerability analysis can be used as a "reference" to fix the results of alert correlation. Since attack graphs capture all the possible multi-step attacks enabled by known vulnerabilities, known attacks reported by alert correlation tools should match the corresponding attack graph, and mismatches should be good indicators of the mistakes made by alert correlation tools. Finally, it should be noticed that this approach can capture the direct effects of (multi-step) attacks on OS level objects such as files and programs, but it cannot capture the indirect effects of attacks on OS level objects due to instruction level and OS level damage propagation.

At the transaction level, a large amount of work has been done on damage assessment. In general, damage assessment at this level can be done in two possible ways: either *data-oriented* (e.g., [22]) or *transaction-oriented* (e.g., [4], [6]). Transaction-oriented methods assess and repair the damage by identifying and backing out affected transactions. In particular, they work as follows: given an execution history that includes (a) the operations of both legitimate transactions and malicious transactions, and (b) the serialization order between these transactions, they build the dependency graph for the set of malicious transactions detected. Since this dependency graph captures the data dependences between every pair of transactions in the history, the dependency graph consists of all and only the affected or tainted transactions that have "contributed" to damage propagation. Assuming that read operations are logged together with write operations, it is not difficult to build the dependency graph. It is shown in [4] that the log can be scanned forward only once (i.e., one-pass) from the entry where the first malicious transaction starts to locate every affected transaction.

In contrast, data-oriented methods use the read and write operations of transactions to trace the damage spreading from one data object to another, and compose a specific piece of code to repair each damaged data object. In particular, data-oriented methods work as follows: they construct a specific damage propagation graph in which each node is a (corrupted) data object while each directed edge from node x to y is a transaction T such that T reads x and writes y. The damage propagation graph can be built by one-pass scanning of the log.

Data-oriented methods are more flexible and better at handling blind writes, however, composing cleaning code for each data object can be time consuming and prone to errors. Transaction-oriented methods use a cleaning transaction, which can be easily composed, to repair multiple data objects at the same time, thus they are more robust and efficient.

At the business process level (a.k.a. the *workflow* level), a novel damage assessment technique is proposed in [32]. While transaction level damage assessment techniques can completely rely on data dependency relationships, workflow level damage assessment techniques must taken control dependences into consideration. Otherwise, the damage assessment results would be wrong in many situations. In [32], both data dependences and control dependences are identified and used to correctly track damage propagation across workflows.

Finally, due to the need to address the specific application and mission semantics, generic application level and mission level damage assessment techniques have not been thoroughly investigated in the literature.

8.1.3 Focus of This Work: Damage Assessment Cross Instruction Level and OS Level

The multi-level damage assessment framework presented in Section 1.1 suggests the needs and benefits of doing coordinated cross-level damage assessment; however, as shown in Section 1.2 almost all existing damage assessment techniques focus on a single abstraction level. As a result, existing damage assessment techniques and tools are still very limited in satisfying the needs of *comprehensive* damage assessment which should not result in any "blind spots". In this work, we propose a virtual machine (VM) approach to do damage assessment across two fundamental abstraction levels: instruction level and OS level. This approach will integrate the damage assessment operations at the instruction level and the OS process level. Although this approach does not cover all of the eight levels shown in Figure 8.1, it shows that *across-level* damage assessment could be done in complex software systems. To the best of our knowledge, it is the first work that does damage assessment across instruction level and OS level.

Software systems handle two types of information assets: data and code. Damaged data is often denoted as "tainted" data or "corrupted" data. Damaged code includes Malware (e.g., worm, bots, and Trojan horses), injected malicious code, and legitimate code executed for malicious purposes. In this work, we propose a framework that uses virtual machines to do cross-layer damage assessment. To resolve the conflict between fine-grained damage assessment and the response time requirements of service requests, we present a novel architecture doing production environment damage assessment, in which expensive fine-grained information-flow-based damage propagation tracking operations are decoupled from online execution of the production virtual machine without letting the correctness be hurt by the "fidelity" challenge. We have implemented the fine-grained information-flow-based damage propagation tracking (and analysis) portion of the architecture (atop QEMU) and done preliminary evaluation. The merits of our system include combining instruction and OS level taint tracking, and efficient "what-if" damage assessment methods.

The rest of this chapter is organized as follows. The problem is made clear in Section 2 and Section 3. The design and implementation of our system are described in Section 4. In Section 5, some preliminary evaluation results are presented. In Section 6, we discuss the related work. In Section 7, we point out the next steps. We conclude the chapter in Section 8.

8.2 PEDA: An Architecture For Fine-Grained Damage Assessment In A Production Environment

In a real world production environment (e.g., 24*7 business processing), the need to do fine-grained damage assessment and the need to satisfy the response time requirements of service requests often *conflict* with each other. In particular, fine-grained information-flow tracking damage assessment usually involves binary instruction instrumentation (or CPU emulation), which can significantly decrease the response time of production (server) systems. As we will show shortly in Section 5, implementation of a fine-grained information-flow-based damage propagation tracking mechanism atop QEMU, a widely used CPU emulator, could cause as much as 100X response time degradation compared with the native performance (without any instrumentation). Such response time degradation is typically too significant for a production system to deploy any fine-grained damage propagation tracking mechanism.

To resolve this conflict, one idea is to do damage propagation tracking at a higher abstraction level, since damage-propagation dependency logging at a higher abstraction level can be significantly more efficient than information-flow tracking. One attractive higher abstraction level is the system call level, and nice system call level dependency analysis mechanisms are proposed in such works as [17] and [12]. However, system call level analysis cannot satisfy all the fine-grained damage assessment requirements. A main limitation is that system call level dependence analysis cannot capture every taint propagation information flow, e.g., taint propagation information flows via (memory) write instructions cannot be "observed" by system call level monitors. Hence, we believe that complete system damage assessment requires microscopic instruction level analysis, such as information flow analysis.

To resolve this conflict, another idea is to do offline fine-grained damage assessment. Offline damage assessment does not need the production system to do fine-grained information-flow-based damage propagation tracking, so the logs generated during execution of the production system will no longer be sufficient for fine-grained damage assessment. Because the logs are insufficient, offline re-execution of the production system is actually required during which information-flow-based damage propagation tracking can be done without worrying about the response time constraints. However, this approach would face a daunting challenge: we call it the "fidelity" challenge. Intuitively, the "fidelity" challenge is about how to make sure that the *exact same* damage as

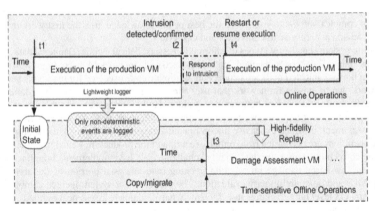

Fig. 8.3 PEDA Architecture

what had happened to the production system will re-happen during offline re-execution of the production system. This is a daunting challenge because due to non-determinism and its impact [11], ad-hoc system activity replaying mechanisms, such as replaying the logged service requests, could generate very wrong damage assessment reports.

To address the "fidelity" challenge while avoiding the aforementioned conflict, we propose the PEDA architecture, which is shown in Figure 8.3. PEDA shares the same basic idea proposed in [9], but it was independently proposed by us. A main difference between PDEA and the work done in [9] is that [9] focuses on generic analysis decoupling while PEDA is motivated by specific damage assessment and recovery needs.

As shown in Figure 8.3, PEDA consists of both online executions of the production system and offline damage assessment operations performed on a separate virtual machine "behind the curtain" (Note that the damage assessment operations are invisible and insensible to customers). The online portion of PEDA is very typical (except that the associated lightweight logging subsystem logs every non-deterministic event): we assume the business application is executed on a native speed or near-native speed virtual machine (e.g., Xen, Hyper-V) so that the response time requirements can be satisfied. When a serious intrusion is detected and confirmed, it could be too risky to let the application be continuously executed: so at time t_2, the system may want to quickly reconfigure itself to mitigate the risk. For example, the system may want to restart the application (from a clean disk) on a rebooted virtual machine at time t_4. For availability and business continuity, the service interruption caused by such reconfiguration is usually minimized. To satisfy the response time requirements, PEDA does not let the production system do fine-grained information-flow-based damage propagation tracking. To address the "fidelity" challenge, PEDA lets the Lightweight Logger logs every non-deterministic event. As shown in [9], such logging activities introduce negligible runtime overhead.

The offline portion of PEDA addresses the "fidelity" challenge and does time-sensitive offline damage assessment against a specific *execution history* of the production system between t_1 and t_2 as shown in Figure 8.3. Its fidelity argument is supported by the fidelity claim made in Revirt [11]: the same initial machine state and a complete set of non-deterministic events can guarantee identical re-execution (or replay). Motivated by this key observation, PEDA migrates the *initial state* of the production system to a virtual machine (i.e., QEMU) that does instruction instrumentation, then lets the damage assessment virtual machine use the non-deterministic events logged during execution of the production system to faithfully replay the designated execution history. A fundamental difference between the damage assessment virtual machine and the production virtual machine is that the damage assessment virtual machine will do fine-grained information-flow-based damage propagation tracking.

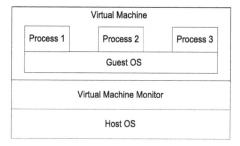

Fig. 8.4 Basic System Model

Several intriguing challenges need to be addressed by PEDA. First, since the damage assessment virtual machine and the production virtual machine are two very different types of virtual machines, compatibility will be a major issue when replaying the non-deterministic events on the damage assessment virtual machine. In [9], this challenge has been well addressed and it is shown that such compatibility hurdles can be overcome with careful analysis. Second, the tension between "fidelity" replay and instruction-instrumentation based damage propagation tracking must not be overlooked. Instruction instrumentation might hurt the fidelity of replay, and the interleaving between replay and instruction instrumentation must be carefully done.

8.3 VM-Based Cross-Layer Damage Assessment: An Overview

Although our PEDA architecture includes both the non-deterministic event logging/replay part and the fine-grained information-flow-based damage propagation tracking/analysis part, we have so far completed the implementation of only the second part. Hence, in the rest of this paper, we will present only the second part. To evaluate our implementation of the second part, we have used emulated execution of the being-protected application (or service) processes and their underneath OS software to simulate the effects of high-fidelity replay of the production VM during a specific damage-causing execution history.

8.3.1 System Model

The system model of the Damage Assessment VM of PEDA is shown in Figure 8.4. A virtual machine monitor (VMM) is a layer of software that emulates the hardware of a computer system [13]. We re-run service processes within a virtual machine (VM), which is simulated by the VMM. The operating system running inside the VM is called *guest OS*, while the operating system on which VMM works is called *host OS*. Since the problem is caused by service-oriented attacks, we neglect the attacks aiming at the VMM or host OS and simply assume that the VMM is trusted. Nevertheless, since the guest kernel is not really more secure than the services, we assume that the guest kernel's data or code entities could be compromised.

We concentrate on attacks through malicious input messages towards service processes. We denote such malicious input messages as *bad seed*. The bad seed and the data infected by the seed inside the VM are called *bad data*. The bad data may include both memory states of the VM and other system states such as files. The bad data may also include code or instructions. Furthermore, due to the reason that some input messages cannot be identified as malicious, but only suspicious at the beginning, and ignoring these unidentified malicious messages will disable one to track their effects on system activities, we define the looking-like-bad-seeds yet unidentified suspicious input messages sent to the services as *tainted seed*. Similar to bad data, we define tainted seed and the data infected by the seed inside the VM as *tainted data* (In Sections 4.1.2, we will show how the tainted seed may "affect" other data through both data and control flows). Note that due to false positives raised by the IDS system (associated with the production VM in Figure 8.3), the tainted data could include some good data. Moreover, we define the memory (either physical memory or swap space) containing the tainted data as *tainted memory*.

In order to model the secondary effects of a bad seed on a VM, we define the relevant (semantic) *relationships* between two processes, and between processes and files. First, we define two types of relation between processes. (A1) Parent and child relationship: A parent process may fork a child process; (A2) Two processes may communicate with each other using inter process communications, such as shared memory, pipes, sockets, message queues, and semaphores.

Second, we define five *relationships* between processes and files. (B1) A process may write data to a file (including file name, contents or attributes); (B2) A process may read data from a file (file name, contents or attributes); (B3) A file may be executed to generate a process.

Now we define a file that contains any bad data as a *bad file*. The definition of bad process is a little complex. Firstly, a process whose memory space contains bad data should no doubt be a *bad process*. Secondly, any process having any one of (B2) and (B3) relationships with a bad file is a *bad process*. Last, any process having (A2) relationship with a bad process, or forked by a bad process is also a *bad process*. Obviously, other processes besides bad processes are all called *good processes*. Finally, the guest kernel's data or code entities might be indirectly compromised via service-oriented attacks, or by exploiting the bugs owned by kernel code entities. Based on this observation, we focus on service-oriented attacks and their effects on (user space) processes, and extend our solution to handle compromised kernel data structures and code entities.

8.3.2 Problem Statement

Motivating Example. Suppose one intends to record the web-surfing hobbies of a group of individuals to provide information for social network research analysis. He may use a web proxy, a statistics process, and several analysis processes to achieve his goal. For example, when the individuals access the internet through the proxy, the proxy can forward each web request to the statistics process. The statistics process will maintain all the statistical information gathered from the proxy, such as a sequence of web requests from individuals and the time of each web request. The analysis processes will fetch information of their interest from the statistics process, and then analyze these data records for their purposes. However, any software may have vulnerabilities, which could be exploited by the remote malicious programs. As for our motivating example, the attackers may compromise the proxy program for different purposes. They could freeze the proxy leading to a denial of service, steal or even modify private web request information of individuals. Therefore, the statistics process would malfunction by receiving the modified information from the proxy, such as losing previous accuracy of statistical information. Then these analysis processes cannot obtain their desired analysis results by fetching the compromised data records from the statistics process. Therefore, we can conclude that the bad data from attackers has propagated from the proxy to the statistics process and all the analysis processes, thus destroying the accuracy of the analysis results.

More seriously, the attackers could do more beyond above in reality. By executing malicious programs which exploit software defects on a selected victim, the attacking programs could obtain and send out valuable sensitive information of the victim, or execute their codes to open a backdoor to bypass authorized privileges. Furthermore, the bad data at the attacked process could be sent to other processes through inter process communication, thus propagating the infection.

The Damage Assessment Needs. First, to gain awareness of the indirect damage caused during a cyber attack (e.g., the indirect damage caused on the statistics process in the motivating example), intrusion detection is insufficient and damage assessment is necessary. Second, since some taint propagation information flows could evade higher level damage propagation trackers, complete system damage assessment requires microscopic instruction level analysis, such as information flow analysis. Third, since in a large enterprise different stake holders are usually interested in the damage semantics at different abstraction levels, damage assessment at multiple abstraction levels is highly desired.

Problem Statement. In order to address the damage assessment needs mentioned above, two basic damage assessment problems are listed below.

- (1) How to use an integrated mechanism to do damage assessment cross the boundaries between the instruction level and the process/thread level so that the damage semantics at both layers can be obtained?
- (2) How to figure out what would have happened if the attack request were not sent to the server?

8.3.3 Overview of Our Approach

In this work, we propose an OS-blind, replay-based, offline time-sensitive damage assessment technique to to audit and track the damage propagation activities happening on an infected virtual machine in a fine-grained fashion without interrupting the online services. By modifying the source code of the VMM, our system "extends" the VMM to "monitor" and track damage/infection/taint propagation throughout the VM, and record necessary state information for (application) state repair and efficient what-if damage assessment. By replaying the compromised virtual machine with recorded checkpoint and non-deterministic events on our fine-grained dependency analysis system, we could generate an accurate and complete damage assessment report.

We assume the IDS (associated with the production VM shown in Figure 8.3) will inform us the compromised source of the infected virtual machine, which is regarded as tainted seed. By monitoring the instruction flow, the dependency analysis (refer to Section 4.1.2) could identify all the tainted data. In order to maintain a mapping between instruction level taint analysis and process level semantics, reconstruction (refer to Section 4.1.1) is required. By implementing reconstruction, which process the tainted data belongs to can be easily known, thus enabling us to get a picture of taint propagation at the process level. Furthermore, to deal with the compromised guest kernel, the reconstruction also needs to get the semantics of all the kernel data structures (refer to Section 4.2). In sum, no matter the guest kernel is compromised or not, taking advantage of reconstruction and multi-level dependency analysis, people can process the dependency log to generate human-cognition-friendly graphical representations of the damage at both instruction and process levels, which clearly show the damage caused by the attacks.

8.4 Design And Implementation

We designed and implemented our offline damage assessment system by modifying the source code of QEMU, a VMM, on which we installed Linux Version 2.6.20. QEMU works as a dynamic translator, which performs a runtime conversion of the VM instructions into the host instruction set [7], which enables us to monitor each instruction executed for the VM.

```
struct rq {
            .
            .
            .
    unsigned int nr_running;
    unsigned long nr_uninterruptible;
    unsigned long expired_timestamp;
            .
            .
            .
    struct task_struct *curr, *idle;
    struct prio_array *active, *expired, arrays[2];
            .
            .
            .
}
```

Fig. 8.5 The *rq* Structure

8.4.1 Cross-Layer Damage Assessment when the Guest Kernel is Not Compromised

8.4.1.1 Reconstruction

Reconstruction provides valuable semantic information for the other components. There exists a semantic gap [8] between the view outside and inside the VM. For example, from the view of QEMU, we could only read bytes residing in the physical memory or disk of the VM. We have no way to understand the semantics of them, such as whether they represent for process data, process code, kernel stacks, kernel data structures, page tables, or others. Therefore, the reconstruction component is needed to maintain such a mapping between the bytes and semantics that we could monitor everything happened inside the VM in a semantic way on the VMM level.

There are in general two ways to achieve this goal. The first one is to modify guest OS, such as developing a kernel module inside the guest OS [19], which will send the OS level semantics to VMM. However, this kernel module could be compromised, so that our proposed system may malfunction. The second one is to implement the reconstruction totally at the VMM level without any awareness of the guest OS. Since the VMM is assumed to be trusted in our system model, the reconstruction will always be secure and reliable.

We implement the reconstruction component at the QEMU level as security is our most significant concern. QEMU defines a structure *env* to emulate the target CPU of the VM. From *env*, we can obtain all the registers of the target CPU. Through register *tr*, we can locate the kernel stack of the currently running process. At the bottom of kernel stack resides the *thread_info* structure, which includes a pointer to the *task descriptor* (defined as *task_struct* in Linux). Through the *task_struct*, we can obtain all the information related to one process, such as the structures describing the virtual memory, scheduling status, files, and inter process communications. Furthermore, from the pointer *tasks* in the *task_struct*, we can locate all the processes in the VM, and then we can get all the relative information of them. At last, we can also get all the management information of the guest OS, such as scheduling information and memory management information. For example, from the pointer *array* in the *task_struct*, we can locate the address of the kernel run queue structure *rq*, through which, all the currently runnable processes in the VM can be located. From the *rq* structure 8.5, we can obtain two arrays (active and expired), each of which consists of 140 priority *runlists*, shown in Figure 8.6. Each runnable process must reside in one *runlist* of either of the two arrays, waiting for CPU scheduler. Besides the runnable processes, the processes blocked on a resource such as a file, semaphore or a device can be located in wait queue list, the address of which can be obtained in a similar way.

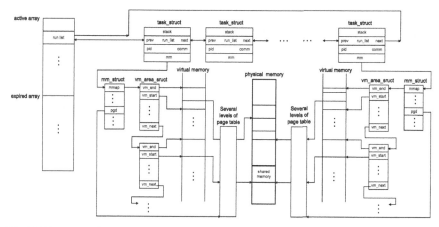

Fig. 8.6 Reconstruction From Out-Of-Box

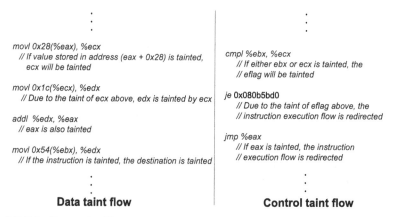

Data taint flow   **Control taint flow**

Fig. 8.7 Taint Propagation Flows

8.4.1.2 Cross-Layer Dependency Analysis

In order to pinpoint all infected part of the VM, we need to log system activity and do dependency or taint analysis. The existing approaches audit all the system calls either by adding a kernel module [12] or by using a VMM such as XEN [23]; then they do system call level dependency analysis. Although they can get result of which processes are tainted, the exact location of the tainted date inside the processes' memory space and how the tainted data propagates inside the kernel are unknown. To solve these problems, we do multi-level dynamic taint analysis, through which we can obtain a fine-grained taint propagation graph of the VM including both instruction level views and process level views.

Instruction level dependency analysis. We analyzed the source and destination of each instruction. Figure 8.7 shows two kinds of taint propagation flows in a VM: data taint flow and control taint flow. For the data flow, for an instruction involving a source operand and a destination operand, we will taint the destination if the data stored in the source is tainted (e.g., the first and the third instructions in data taint flow), the value used to find the source/destination is tainted (e.g., the second instruction in data taint flow), or the instruction itself is tainted (e.g., the fourth instruction in data taint flow). For the control flow, if the destination address of the redirection is tainted (e.g., the third instruction in the control taint flow), or the condition of the currently executing instruction is tainted (e.g., the second instruction in the control taint flow), we will taint the corresponding event of the control flow redirection. By analyzing each executed instruction, we can gradually construct an instruction level dependency graph. If there is an intrusion detector such as [16], which can notify us part of the bad data, we can obtain all the bad data by tracking the taint propagation traces in the dependency graph. In principle, our instruction level dependency analysis method is the same as dynamic taint analysis [19], but serving a different purpose, the way we maintain and use the dependency graph is different.

Process level dependency analysis. Since the reconstruction component can provide us the semantic information of instructions, with the integration of reconstruction and instruction level dependency graph, we can also construct a process level dependency graph. When an intrusion is confirmed, we can obtain all the bad processes through this graph. Since the instruction level dependency is fine-grained, our process level dependency graph can record all the different ways of inter process communications, such as pipes, messages, sockets, and shared memory regions. The major difference between our approach and [17], which also does process level dependency analysis, is that we do reconstruction but they do not.

8.4.2 Cross-Layer Damage Assessment when the Guest Kernel is Compromised

In the real world, the OS kernel is not always secure, sometimes it will be compromised. Because our instruction level taint analysis does not depend on OS level information, no matter the kernel is compromised or not, it will be completed correctly (regarding the identified taint seeds). After obtaining the fine-grained damage information, we need to generate the semantic damage assessment information by doing reconstruction. Since the impact of compromised guest kernel on reconstruction is heavily dependent upon whether the initial state (or checkpoint) (see Figure 8.3) of the guest kernel is clean or not, we will discuss two different situations in the rest of this section: the situation when the initial state of the guest kernel is clean, and the situation when the initial state is not clean.

The first condition is when we start damage assessment from a good checkpoint in which the guest system is not compromised. We mark the suspicious non-deterministic event as tainted seed and track the damage propagation in the same way as in Section 4.1. At instruction level, if the taint propagation affects the kernel data structure, we will record the original value of the modified part. When we do out-of-box reconstruction for damage assessment, although the guest kernel is compromised, we can use the latest pre-tainting version of the corresponding kernel data structure instead of the corrupted version to do the reconstruction. Hence, we can obtain the correct OS level damage information (or semantics) even if the Guest kernel is compromised.

The second condition is when we can not start damage assessment from a good checkpoint or can not know all the tainted seeds before kernel is compromised. So we can not record the original value of every guest kernel footprint modification due to damage propagation. Under this situation, (1) if the modified kernel part is not related to our reconstruction component, we will be able to handle it to get the right high level information such as which part of kernel, process or file is compromised. For example, an attack modifies the system call table or system call handler will not prevent us from obtaining the right high level information. (2) If the modified kernel part is related to our reconstruction component, but the necessary correct information used for reconstruction can somehow be obtained by analyzing the whole memory, execution information and checkpoint information, we can still do reconstruction correctly. For example, an attack modifying the related task list pointers to hide a process cannot prevent us from obtaining the process information through analyzing the memory and execution information. (3) If the modified kernel part is related to our reconstruction component, and the necessary correct information used for reconstruction can not be obtained by analyzing the whole memory, execution information and checkpoint information, then our reconstruction will malfunction. Fortunately, this does not cause lots of problem now, because to the best of our knowledge, most kinds of the existing kernel-infecting attacks do not cause this problem.

8.4.3 *"What-if" Damage Assessment*

A main purpose of offline intrusion assessment is to figure out what would have happened if the attack request were not sent to the server. To have this functionality, we should resort to not only reconstruction, but also checkpoint and state rollback (Currently we assume the kernel is not compromised when doing state rollback).

8.4.3.1 Checkpointing

Our per process checkpointing information will be directly used for the state rollback and what-if damage assessment purposes. We propose three requirements for checkpointing information when doing state rollback:

- (1) The process should not crash when its state is rolled back to a checkpoint;
- (2) The repaired process could resume execution and run correctly from the checkpoint;
- (3) There should be no abnormality in the system caused by rollback.

To satisfy these requirements, we let each process *execution state* be determined by three different domains: its own execution, interaction with kernel, and communication with other processes. Therefore, CPU registers, all the kernel structures, memory pages, kernel stack, and inter processes communications related to a process should be recorded to represent the execution state of it. Firstly, we checkpoint all the CPU registers stored in *env* structure. Secondly with the help of reconstruction component, we checkpoint all the other parts of execution state. For example, as shown in Figure 8.6, to checkpoint the memory information of one process, we need to record the *mm_struct*, *vm_area_struct*, and each physical page the virtual memory blocks are mapped to. To consistently maintain the mapping between the virtual memory and physical memory when recovery component does repairs, we also need to checkpoint the page table.

Whenever we do checkpointing, the corresponding checkpoint is directly stored in the host OS memory, which is more secure than storing it in the VM and faster than storing it in files of host OS. We crafted a process of host OS, responsible for writing the checkpointing information to files of host OS. To save storage space, we do incremental, periodical checkpointing instead of simply periodical checkpointing. Whenever we do checkpointing, we only record the differences from the last checkpointing. Moreover, we only checkpoint the runnable processes; for the process blocked on a resource, we keep monitoring it until it becomes runnable, then we do checkpointing.

8.4.3.2 State Rollback

By implementing state rollback functionality, a process can be rolled back to a *most recently healthy checkpoint*, from which it could resume execution correctly. The most recently healthy checkpoint means that the process should not have been infected at the checkpoint, but must have been infected at the following one. By analyzing the taint propagation graph, we can easily know at which very point the bad data infected the bad process. Therefore, the checkpoint taken before that point is the most recently healthy checkpoint of that process. Afterwards, we can rollback the execution state of that process based on the information recorded in the most recently healthy checkpoint. Note that we should terminate some bad processes, if they are forked by a bad process after its most recently healthy checkpoint, because the child processes are born bad.

To maintain the consistency of the VM, we also need to modify management information of guest OS after switching the execution state of the bad process. For example, among different execution states (of the same process), the number of memory pages used by one process and the mapping between the virtual pages and physical pages may change, so we need to rebuild page table for the re-execution of that process based on page table currently used by it and page table recorded in the most recently healthy checkpoint.

Afterwards, to resume the execution of a bad process, we need to add it to its original *runlist* waiting to be scheduled from the most recently healthy checkpoint. Note that the related information of the VM should be maintained, such as increasing the number of the runnable processes. After resuming execution, we can remove all the checkpointing information later than the most recently healthy checkpoint, since it is all infected and can not be used anymore.

8.4.3.3 Approach.

Having the reconstruction, checkpoint, and state rollback functionality in hand, we could figure out what would have happened if the attack request were not sent to the server. To characterize what would have happened, the values of a set of specific variables, denoted *key variables*, are usually used. When the key variables can capture all the curiosity of the security manager, the problem is reduced to determining the "correct" values that would have been held by the key variables at the end of the (being-analyzed) execution history (see Figure 8.3) if the attack request were not sent to the server.

To solve this problem, the naive approach is to firstly rollback the system to a pre-attack checkpoint, then replay all the network requests except for the attack request. However, this approach could consume too much time to enable the executives to make timely risk mitigation decisions, especially when there are a very large number of need-to-replay requests. In this sense, we say that the proposed damage assessment mechanisms are *time-sensitive*. A more efficient approach is partial replay (Currently the partial replay is not fully completed and still under implementation). However, successful partial replay would require two pre-conditions: (1) be able to know the subset of key variables that have not been affected by the attack; (2) be able to know the processes that have not been affected by the attack.

It is clear our multi-level dependency analysis scheme can meet both of the two pre-conditions. Now we are ready to present the partial replay method:

Step 1. For the processes that have not been affected by the attack, their *newest* checkpoints can be used unless when certain inter-process synchronization constraints are violated. Once we resume these processes from their newest (set of synchronized) checkpoints, we may replay the logged yet un-processed network requests (towards only these processes) in their original order. Once every unprocessed request is processed, the newest values of the set of unaffected key variables represent one part of the answer to question "Would have happened if the attack request were not sent to the server?"

Step 2. Regarding the key variables that have been affected by the attack, to see what would be their correct values if the attack request were not sent to the server, we need to firstly rollback the states of the affected processes to a synchronized set of pre-attack checkpoints. Then, we replay the logged yet un-processed network requests (towards only the affected processes) in their original order. Once every unprocessed request is processed, the newest values of the set of affected key variables may represent the other part of the answer.

Regarding the partial replay method, (a) it should be noticed that due to the nice properties of our multi-level dependency analysis scheme, replaying the unaffected processes typically will not

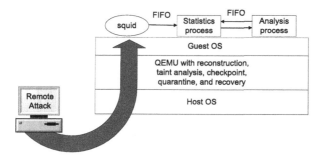

Fig. 8.8 Compromised Process Experiment

"touch" the execution of any affected process, since the process states, the execution environment, and the requests are the same as in the original execution of the unaffected processes. (b) It should be noticed that replaying the affected processes, however, might "touch" an affected process or an unaffected key variable, since the attack request will no longer be replayed and the process state of affected process X before reprocessing request R could be different from the corresponding state in the original execution of X. If such situations happen, the correctness of partial replay will be threatened, and it may be a good idea to use the naive approach.

In sum, the partial replay method shows one merit of checkpointing and state rollback in offline intrusion assessment.

8.5 Preliminary Evaluation

8.5.1 Compromised Process Damage Assessment Experiment

In our experiments, we evaluated the runtime overhead and damage reduction of the proposed system. We installed the *squid* web proxy [1] (version 2.4.STABLE1) on guest OS running on QEMU. Currently we use QEMU single step without translation cache (refer to Section 7). As our motivating example, we modified squid to forward its current web request messages to the statistics process. The statistics process will group the web requests based on domain name of each request. During the emulated re-execution of the production VM, the analysis process will periodically set up a named pipe with the statistics process, send a request message to it, and then close the named pipe. Upon receiving a request, the statistics process will set up another named pipe with the analysis process, forward its group information to the analysis process, and then close the named pipe. When the analysis process receives messages, it will do a simple computation to find the hottest website. To trigger the damage propagation activities, we exploited a buffer overflow vulnerability of squid [2] and crafted an attacking program compromising squid to send bad data to the statistics process.

For the runtime overhead, we use software WAPT (trial version 4.0) [3] to simulate 10 users, each of whom continues surfing the Internet through the squid web proxy with an average of 8 web requests per minute. We set up three different experiment environments with squid, the statistics process, and the analysis process (1) installed directly in host OS, (2) installed in VM on QEMU without our proposed system components, and (3) installed in VM on QEMU with our proposed system components (as shown in Figure 8.8). Each experiment lasts for 1 hour, and is repeated up to 10 runs. For QEMU with our system components, the period of checkpointing is set at 10 minutes.

command: vi

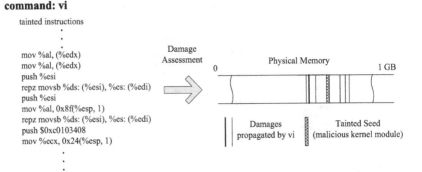

Fig. 8.9 Experiment Results

Table 8.1 Response Time For Each Website

Response times	On host OS	On QEMU without our system	On QEMU with our system
www.yahoo.com	0.05s	4.31s	5.37s
www.aol.com	0.25s	6.07s	7.31s
www.youtube.com	0.39s	5.17s	5.85s
www.facebook.com	0.31s	4.95s	5.51s

We simulate 60 suspicious packets evenly spread in each run. In Table 1, we record the average response time of each request for the same website in the three different experiment environments. Table 1 shows that the ratio of response times between the third and fourth column is far less than that between the second and third column. We can conclude that the response delay is mainly introduced by QEMU instead of our system components.

For the damage reduction, if squid and the statistics process are restarted after the intrusion detection alarm is raised, the statistics process will lose all the previous data records. With our state rollback components, the squid and the statistics process are rolled back to the most recently healthy checkpoint. Thus, the statistics process can still maintain the previous data records at that time. These "saved" data records (and other relevant application state information) could be merged into the production VM in a proper on-the-fly way to reduce the amount of damage that would have otherwise been caused by the attack (see Figure 8.3).

8.5.2 Malicious Kernel Module Experiment

In this experiment, we want to demonstrate the damage assessment when the guest kernel is compromised. We assume a malicious kernel module is intalled in the guest OS. The damage assessment (i.e., the information-flow-based damage propagation tracking) starts after the IDS detects and reports the address of the malicious kernel module. We implemented an experimental kernel module that intercepts the write system calls by altering the interrupt descriptor table handler and the sysenter instruction handler.Whenever the write system call is invoked, the malicious kernel module changes the contents to be written to the target file and passes the modified data to the original write system call handler. Other system calls are executed as usual.

To run a test, we use *vi* to open a file, modify the contents, and store it to the file. When we save the file, the malicious kernel module intercepts the write system call and stores contaminated contents to the file. Starting with tainting the destination of every instruction executed by the malicious kernel module, our damage assessment keeps track of the propagation of damages. We observed our damage assessment successfully identified all the damaged memory cells shown as shadowed regions in Figure 8.9.

8.6 RELATED WORK

From the systems security's point of view, there are in general three sorts of related work: prevention, detection, response. Since not all the attacks can be prevented and intrusion detection is only the starting point instead of the finish line of resolution, response techniques have seized more and more attention. First, the seminal Revirt work [11] shows that re-playable systems can be built. However, Revirt is not designed to distinguish true secondary attack effects from infection-free effects. In addition, Revirt is not designed to replay only the infected processes. Finally, it should be noticed that Revirt does full system replay but the "rewindable" feature of Mac OS seems not. Second, process checkpointing (e.g., Flashback [29]) has been researched for many years. However, rolling back the attacked process to the latest pre-attack checkpoint could result in the inconsistency among interactive processes, and the secondary infection effects caused by the attack is not repaired. Third, motivated by the limitations of the above response technologies, a set of self-healing solutions have been recently proposed, including error virtualization [27], oblivious computing [25], Rx (bug evading by environment alteration) [24], and DIRA (rollback of memory updates) [28]. All these approaches (a) do some sort of checkpointing, and (b) do detection. When a fault/attack is detected, they do not terminate the process. Instead, they first rollback the process to a safe checkpoint (or rescue point) and then make some necessary changes. Then the process can be re-executed (since the checkpoint) as if the fault/attack has never happened. "The first two approaches may cause a semantically incorrect continuation of execution" [18]. This problem is addressed by Rx, in which the consistency between the in-memory states and data in files is also well maintained. This problem is also addressed in [18]: behavior profiling and policy-driven methods are added to [27] to guide the semantic correctness. However, focusing on a single service process, these three approaches do not maintain the consistency among interactive processes. In terms of how memory states are repaired, DIRA [28] is more advanced than our approach: DIRA can log individual memory updates and use the log to locate and restore the nearest pre-intrusion restart point. Nevertheless, our approach and DIRA have several major differences: (a) DIRA does not consider the problem of cascading rollback; (b) DIRA does source code instrumentation while our approach can directly work on binaries.

Sharing the benefit of taint analysis technique, our proposed damage assessment system and Panorama [31] have the following major differences in terms of how well the taint analysis facilities are protected and the purposes of such information flow analyses.

In-the-box vs Out-of-the-box taint analysis. As mentioned above, we must maintain a mapping between the bytes and semantics so that we could monitor everything happened inside the virtual machine. Panorama proposed to load a kernel module, module notifier, into the Guest OS to collect such information. However, as Panorama admitted, the attacker may attempt to tamper with the module notifier, especially when the attacker obtains the kernel privilege. If compromised, the module cannot provide the OS level semantics for the taint analysis component and can even give unrealistic semantics information, thus losing the key to the following malware analysis or damage assessment. Therefore, we do the reconstruction which bridges the gap between the bytes and semantics outside VM. Even if the attacker gains the kernel privilege to compromise and modify the kernel data structures, we will still succeed in tracking the taint flow in the semantics level by recording which kernel structure has been compromised by the tainted instructions.

Purpose. Our system uses the dynamic taint analysis technique to do the damage assessment during replaying the whole VM, while Panorama [31] does the offline malware detection and analysis during the execution of the malware.

8.7 LIMITATIONS

First, only the damage propagation tracking/analysis part of the PEDA architecture (see Figure 8.3) has been implemented so far, the non-deterministic event logging/replay part is yet to be implemented and evaluated. Second, implementation of the information-flow-based damage propagation tracking mechanism is yet to be optimized. The efficiency can be substantially improved by turning on QEMU translation cache to speed up the VM, which needs to implement the instruction dependency buffer first. Third, the proposed what-if damage assessment methods are yet to be implemented and evaluated. Fourth, the evaluation done in Section 6 is still preliminary, comprehensive evaluation is needed to complete this research.

8.8 Conclusion

In this chapter, we present a generic multi-level damage assessment framework, which captures several fundamental characteristics of the damage assessment problem, points out the necessity and importance of cross-layer damage assessment, and identifies the key component techniques of a systematic damage assessment solution. To demonstrate the feasibility, merits and applicability of this framework, we propose a concrete virtual machine (VM) approach to do damage assessment across two fundamental abstraction levels: instruction level and OS level. This approach will integrate the damage assessment operations at the instruction level and the OS process level. This approach leads to a novel production-environment damage assessment architecture. Although this approach does not cover all of the abstraction levels, it shows that *across-level* damage assessment could be done in complex software systems.

Acknowledgements This work was supported by NSF CNS-0716479, AFOSR MURI: Autonomic Recovery of Enterprise-wide Systems after Attack or Failure with Forward Correction, AFRL award FA8750-08-C-0137, and ARO MURI: Computer-aided Human Centric Cyber Situation Awareness.

References

1. http://www.squid-cache.org.
2. http://www.milw0rm.com/exploits/347.
3. http://www.loadtestingtool.com/.
4. P. Ammann, S. Jajodia, and P. Liu. Recovery from malicious transactions. 14(5):1167–1185, 2002.
5. P. Ammann, D. Wijesekera, and S. Kaushik. Scalable, graph-based network vulnerability analysis. In *CCS '02: Proceedings of the 9th ACM conference on Computer and communications security*, pages 217–224, Washington, DC, USA, 2002. ACM.
6. Kun Bai and Peng Liu. A data damage tracking quarantine and recovery (dtqr) scheme for mission-critical database systems. pages 720–731, 2009.

7. F Bellard. Qemu, a fast and portable dynamic translator. In *USENIX Annual Technical Conference*, pages 41–46, 2005.
8. Peter M. Chen and Brian D. Noble. When virtual is better than real hotos. In *Hot Topics in Operating Systems*, pages 133– 138, 2001.
9. Jim Chow, Tal Garfinkel, , and Peter M. Chen. Decoupling dynamic program analysis from execution in virtual environments. In *USENIX Annual Technical Conference*, pages 1–14, Boston, Massachusetts, USA, 2008.
10. F. Cuppens and A. Miege. Alert correlation in a cooperative intrusion detection framework. In *In Proceedings of the 2002 IEEE Symposium on Security and Privacy*, pages 202–215. IEEE, 2002.
11. George W. Dunlap, Samuel T. King, Sukru Cinar, Murtaza A. Basrai, and Peter M. Chen. Revirt: enabling intrusion analysis through virtual-machine logging and replay. In *OSDI '02: Proceedings of the 5th symposium on Operating systems design and implementation*, pages 211–224, Boston, Massachusetts, USA, 2002. ACM.
12. A. Goel, K. Farhadi K. Po, Z. Li, and E de Lara. The taser intrusion recovery system. In *SOSP '05: Proceedings of the twentieth ACM symposium on Operating systems principles*, pages 23–26, Brighton, United Kingdom, 2005. ACM.
13. R. P. Goldberg. Survey of virtual machine research. In *IEEE Computer*, pages 34–45, june 1974.
14. K. Ingols, R. Lippmann, and K. Piwowarski. Practical attack graph generation for network defense. In *In 22nd Annual Computer Security Applications Conference (ACSAC)*, pages 121–130, Miami Beach, Florida, USA, 2006. IEEE.
15. S. Jajodia, S. Noel, and B. O'Berry. Topological analysis of network attack vulnerability. In *Proceedings of the 2nd ACM symposium on Information, computer and communications security*, pages 2–2, Singapore, 2007. ACM.
16. Xuxian Jiang, Xinyuan Wang, and Dongyan Xu. Stealthy malware detection through vmm-based "out-of-the-box" semantic view reconstruction. In *CCS '07: Proceedings of the 14th ACM conference on Computer and communications security*, pages 128–138, Alexandria, Virginia, USA, 2007. ACM.
17. Samuel T. King and Peter M. Chen. Backtracking intrusions. pages 223–236, 2003.
18. Michael E. Locasto, Angelos Stavrou, Gabriela F. Cretu, and Angelos D. Keromytis. From stem to sead: Speculative execution for automated defense. In *USENIX Annual Technical Conference*, pages 219–232, 2007.
19. J. NEWSOME and D. SONG. Dynamic taint analysis for automatic detection and analysis and signature generation of exploits commodity software. In *Proceedings of the 12th Symposium on Network and Distributed System Security (NDSS)*, pages 196–206, San Diego, CA, USA, feb 2005.
20. Peng Ning, Yun Cui, and Douglas S. Reeves. Constructing attack scenarios through correlation of intrusion alerts. In *CCS '02: Proceedings of the 9th ACM conference on Computer and communications security*, pages 245–254, Washington, DC, USA, 2002. ACM.
21. X. Ou, W. F. Boyer, and M. A. McQueen. A scalable approach to attack graph generation. In *CCS '06: Proceedings of the 13th ACM conference on Computer and communications security*, pages 336–345. ACM, 2006.
22. B. Panda and J. Giordano. Reconstructing the database after electronic attacks. In *The 12th IFIP 11.3 Working Conference on Database Security*, pages 143–156, Greece, Italy, 1998.
23. Bryan D. Payne, Martim Carbone, Monirul Sharif, and Wenke Lee. Lares: an architecture for secure active monitoring using virtualization. In *Proceedings of the IEEE Symposium on Security and Privacy*, pages 233–247, 2008.
24. Feng Qin, Joseph Tucek, Jagadeesan Sundaresan, and Yuanyuan Zhou. Rx: treating bugs as allergies—a safe method to survive software failures. pages 235–248, 2005.
25. Martin Rinard, Cristian Cadar, Daniel Dumitran, Daniel M. Roy, Tudor Leu, and Jr. William S. Beebee. Enhancing server availability and security through failure-oblivious computing. In *OSDI'04: Proceedings of the 6th conference on Symposium on Opearting Systems Design & Implementation*, pages 21–21, San Francisco, CA, USA, 2004. USENIX Association.

26. O. Sheyner, J. Haines, R. Lippmann S. Jha, and J. M. Wing. Automated generation and analysis of attack graphs. In *In Proceedings of the 2002 IEEE Symposium on Security and Privacy*, pages 273–284. IEEE, 2002.

27. Stelios Sidiroglou, Michael E. Locasto, Stephen W. Boyd, and Angelos D. Keromytis. Building a reactive immune system for software services. In *ATEC '05: Proceedings of the annual conference on USENIX Annual Technical Conference*, pages 11–11, Anaheim, CA, USA, 2005. USENIX Association.

28. A. Smirnov and T. Chiueh. Dira: Automatic detection and identification and repair of control-hijacking attacks. In *Proceedings of the 12th Symposium on Network and Distributed System Security (NDSS)*, San Diego, CA, USA, feb 2005.

29. Sudarshan Srinivasan, Christopher Andrews, Srikanth Kandula, and Yuanyuan Zhou. Flashback: A light-weight extension for rollback and deterministic replay for software debugging. In *Proceedings of the annual Usenix technical conference*, 2004.

30. L. P. Swiler, C. Phillips, D. Ellis, and S. Chakerian. Computer-attack graph generation tool. In *In DARPA Information Survivability Conference and Exposition II (DISCEX '01)*, volume 2, pages 307–321, June 2001.

31. Heng Yin, Dawn Song, Manuel Egele, Christopher Kruegel, and Engin Kirda. Panorama: Capturing system-wide information flow for malware detection and analysis. In *CCS '07: Proceedings of the 14th ACM conference on Computer and communications security*, pages 116–127, Alexandria, Virginia, USA, 2007. ACM.

32. M. Yu, P. Liu, and W. Zang. Self healing workflow systems under attacks. In *Proc. 24th IEEE International Conference on Distributed Computing Systems (ICDCS'04)*, pages 418–425, Tokyo, Japan, 2004. IEEE.

Part V
Microscopic Cyber Situational Awareness

Chapter 9
A Declarative Framework for Intrusion Analysis

Matt Fredrikson, Mihai Christodorescu, Jonathon Giffin, and Somesh Jha

Abstract We consider the problems of computer intrusion analysis and understanding. We begin by presenting a survey of the literature in this area and extrapolate a set of common principles and characteristics present in the most promising techniques. Using these principles, we develop a comprehensive analysis solution based on a variety of system events and the causal dependencies among them. We then present a declarative language that gives a system administrator the facilities required to analyze the event information present in system logs, and we identify the subset of the event information pertinent to an intrusion in a vastly simplified view. Finally, we demonstrate the ability of the language to accurately return a simplified view of the relevant events in a realistic intrusion case study.

9.1 Introduction

A recent study by the CERT coordination center indicates that despite the best efforts of network administrators to prevent network intrusions, the number of successful attacks is on the rise [6]. Among the potential causes for this trend, the authors cite an increase in automated attacks, increasing sophistication in attack tools, faster discovery of critical software vulnerabilities, and an increasing focus on infrastructure attacks. From a practical standpoint, this means that network administrators need effective tools to make the task of understanding and recovering from attacks more manageable.

After an intrusion has been discovered, the task of a network administrator is twofold. First, the source of the intrusion must be identified; if the system component that allowed the intrusion to

Matt Fredrikson
Computer Sciences Department, University of Wisconsin, Madison, e-mail: `mfredrik@cs.wisc.edu`

Mihai Christodorescu
IBM T.J. Watson Research Center, e-mail: `mihai@us.ibm.com`

Jonathon Giffin
School of Computer Science, Georgia Institute of Technology, e-mail: `giffin@cc.gatech.edu`

Somesh Jha
Computer Sciences Department, University of Wisconsin, Madison, e-mail: `jha@cs.wisc.edu`

S. Jajodia et al., (eds.), *Cyber Situational Awareness*,
Advances in Information Security 46, DOI 10.1007/978-1-4419-0140-8_9,
© Springer Science+Business Media, LLC 2010

take place is not removed or patched in a timely manner, then additional intrusions are inevitable. Second, a prudent administrator will attempt to identify all files, processes, and other artifacts on the system that were created or affected by the intrusion in some way. For even a moderately sized organization, these tasks can require a substantial amount of effort. Without the appropriate tools and information, it is difficult to provide any assurances that an administrator's efforts are sufficient.

The primary difficulty with these problems is the large amount of potentially relevant information that must be analyzed and summarized. In a typical network setting, an administrator may have numerous sources of relevant information available, including application logs, intrusion detection logs at both the host and network level, and the entire state of the persistent store. There has been a fair amount of research concerned with the general problems of collecting, storing, and analyzing the audit information needed to solve these problems. However, the field has progressed in a piecemeal way, with each contribution focusing on a specific type of attack or information source. As a result, the current body of work is disjoint and fragmented, lacking any unifying principles or logic despite their common goal. This limits the impact and utility of these contributions, as new innovations must be developed to apply similar techniques in new settings.

In this paper, we survey some of the major contributions to the area of intrusion analysis and recovery, and we postulate that much of the work that has been done in this area can be framed as systems that *(1)* correlate and calculate dependencies among recorded events, and *(2)* use the resulting information to select subsets of events and system components that are directly involved in an intrusion. Using the principles inferred from our literature survey, we then introduce a logic and corresponding language to reason about events and relationships among events in a coherent way. We present a case study involving a simulated intrusion and demonstrate the use of our language for analyzing the artifacts left behind by the intruder, providing important information about the intrusion.

9.2 A Survey of Related Work

Computer systems collect a large amount of information as they process data. System logs and applications logs grow to contain timestamped evidence of events as they occur in the system, be it only one computer or multiple computers networked together. The large amount of information buried in these can be useful in understanding how a particular input maliciously affected the system and determining how to remediate the system. Here we focus primarily on tools and techniques for analyzing intrusions and for recovering from intrusions, with additional information on preventing and detecting intrusions.

9.2.1 Forensic Analysis of Intrusions

Several projects have produced forensic analysis systems designed to determine how an installed attack initially entered the system. ReVirt allowed an analyst to study the execution of an intrusion in order to gain comprehension of the malicious software's behavior [14], and BackTracker automated the ReVirt analysis [26]. Starting from evidence of an intrusion, such as a malicious file, BackTracker identified files and processes that could have affected the detection point. Working backward through log information, the system determined the attack's entry point into the system. In BackTracker, the authors introduced the idea of using dependencies among events for the problem of intrusion analysis and presented tools for collecting the relevant information, analyzing the information, and producing dependence graphs. BackTracker is limited in that it cannot reason about dependencies in general, as it works only with a custom designed event-logging utility, and does not allow a user to specify additional notions of event dependence.

Observing that the graphs produced by BackTracker may still be too large for timely manual analysis, Sitaraman *et al.* extended its logging and dependence analysis facilities with additional information that allowed them to produce smaller and more concise graphs [41]. Specifically, when computing dependencies involving filesystem operations, they took into account the offset intervals of read and write operations to avoid calculating spurious dependencies. Additionally, they computed instruction-level dynamic slices within individual processes to precisely determine the feasibility of dependencies among the various objects accessed by the process. While the authors claimed that these extensions greatly reduced the size of the resultant dependence graphs, they did not provide a detailed performance analysis of their system. Furthermore, the overhead introduced by collecting the information needed to compute dynamic program slices is prohibitive for many usage scenarios, both in terms of time and space.

Goel *et al.* presented Forensix, a system for high-precision forensic discovery and history reconstruction on commodity operating systems [19]. They performed event monitoring inside the kernel to collect detailed, application-independent information. As Forensix collected events, it sent them to an append-only store in a database on a secure remote machine. When history information is needed, the database was queried using standard declarative query languages. As with BackTracker, subsequent analysis of the database then revealed how attacks operated. In subsequent work, Goel *et al.* created dependency rules among files, processes, and sockets based on information in the Forensix logs to characterize data flows in a manner similar to our dependency graph [20]. These rules then propagated data from a manually specified set of unsafe processes to files in the file system. By reverting the file system to an earlier, clean state and replaying all non-malicious events recorded in the log, the authors could then rebuild the clean file system.

Whitaker *et al.* approached the problem of diagnosing system failures using the time-tested technique of searching the parameter space for an optimal selection [48]. However, whereas previous work used system models to evaluate candidate solutions in the search, Whitaker proposed the use of virtual machines that simply revert state for this task. Aside from being a novel use of system history information, this work is interesting in that this type of search can be applied to forensic analysis to accomplish many of the same goals as BackTracker. For example, identifying the parameter at fault for a particular failure is equivalent to doing a backward, causal slice to find the process or file that led to an intrusion.

Goel *et al.* developed an operating system-level auditing system that records a fine-granularity history of a system so that detailed analysis can be performed if an intrusion is detected [18]. The novelty of their technique lies in a technique to deal with the potentially overwhelming amount of data present in realistic logs. Rather than attempting to trim potentially irrelevant data from the log files, a task that is fraught with the possibility of discarding critical information, the information was organized in a manner that allowed efficient reconstruction of state. The data in the logs was organized into *interval tables* that index the state of the system by properties that are likely to be referenced in queries. For example, one interface table might list the owner of a file at all given points in the history of the system. The authors showed that many different types of analysis, such as data dependence analysis and process I/O analysis, can be effectively encoded using this mechanism.

Khanna *et al.* addressed the problem of diagnosing failures in distributed environments [25]. Citing the complex, layered construction of modern systems and the interactions among their components, they proposed to treat the components as blackboxes and focused entirely on the protocol interactions among them. As design principles, they sought to build a system that can work asynchronously with the target network, so as to impose reasonable performance overhead, and to avoid any changes to the functionality or makeup of the target network. To meet these requirements, they proposed a hierarchical system composed of two parts. *Local* monitors snoop on the message-passing behaviors of individual applications and use a set of predefined rules to diagnose failure. *Intermediate* monitors match a second set of rules, based on messages that are passed up from the set of local monitors. The authors evaluated the effectiveness of their system on a large campus network and observed a trade-off between diagnostic accuracy and latency. This work is interesting for several reasons. First, the nature of their problem is fault diagnosis in a distributed setting, which is an instance of forensic discovery applied to software reliability. Second, the analysis performed by the system is based entirely on the causal relationships of a group of interacting entities on a network. The authors demonstrated that this blackbox technique could be applied to real problems by specifying domain-specific invariants in terms of these relationships.

9.2.2 Recovery From and Remediation of Intrusions

Jain *et al.* addressed the problem of intrusion remediation using application-level isolation [22]. The authors observed that the main difficulty with remediation on modern systems was that the effects of the intrusion were eventually intertwined with the effects of normal system operation in complex ways, so reversing the malicious effects was never as trivial as it might seem. To implement isolation for untrusted applications, a copy-on-write filesystem was used. If an application was found to be malicious, all of its side effects could be removed easily from the operating system due to the copy-on-write mechanism. However, if trusted applications were found to have interacted with the malicious application, then data dependency analysis was used to track and remove all compromised system state. This work is a good example of the use of data dependencies inferred from logged system information to reconstruct historical state on a system. Although the authors did not deal directly with situational awareness or forensic discovery, the techniques they developed could be applied directly to problems in this domain.

A large body of research focused on constructing environments in which any unwanted executions can be rolled back and their effects undone. Many mechanisms have been proposed, from virtual machines [7, 49], to transactional and versioned file systems [32, 37], to one-way isolation for processes [29, 43]. These mechanisms are powerful, as they can track changes throughout the system, but they lack the fine-grained information about which changes should be undone when only part of the execution was malicious. In other words, oftentimes these rollback and recovery mechanisms are an all-or-nothing proposition due to lack of dependency information, giving little flexibility to a system operator.

9.2.3 Intrusion Detection

Recently, there have been a number of systems that utilize taint tracking to reason about information flows dynamically for the purpose of exploit detection and repair [34]. These tools use information flows proactively in real-time online analyses of specific problems, whereas we are concerned primarily with their utility in comprehensive analysis and overall understanding of events after they occur.

Closer to the type of information flows considered in our work are those used by Kruger *et al.* for the purpose of detecting privacy violations in application-level software [27]. In that work, the authors used dynamic data equivalence with type information to infer dependencies among events but did not use *def* and *use* information explicitly as in our work to allow fine-grained control over the inference process. They did not consider the problem of integrating multiple sources of event information explicitly as we do. Finally, Kruger *et al.* used dependence information as much for real-time policy enforcement as for post-mortem analysis, which we do not consider in our work.

Jiang *et al.* used taint analysis to detect worms propagating in real time [23, 24]. That system, which must execute before the worm infection begins, identified attacks that self-propagate by exploiting vulnerabilities in network service software.

Lakkaraju *et al.* took a visual approach to network situational awareness with their tool NVisionIP [28]. To deal with the large amount of data needed to effectively diagnose certain network intrusion and failure scenarios, the authors developed lossless, compact visual representations of various aspects of network operation. For example, by visualizing source-destination flows between specific ports on the two-dimensional plane, portscans could be trivially identified by human analysts as a line or rectangle.

Gu *et al.* used correlation across events from multiple network intrusion-detection systems (IDS) to detect machines infected by malware (in particular, by bot software) [21]. Their system, called BotHunter, combines alert events from three classes of IDSes to identify the various phases of malware lifecycle: target scanning, infection exploitation, binary egg download and execution, command and control channel establishment, and outbound scanning. The correlation of events is based on a bot model in which malware-lifecycle events occur in an given order.

Debar and Wesbi observed that intrusion-detection systems are often prone to flooding the users with false alarms, do not present enough context to validate an alarm as true, and do not scale [13]. They solved these issues in an architecture for aggregating and correlating IDS alerts. The architecture aggregated similar events to allow the user to evaluate the progress of the attacker and the knowledge he has gained. The correlation mechanism focused on identifying and removing duplicate alerts, a common problem when using multiple IDSes, and the inference of alert chains (called "consequences"). These alert chains simplified the amount of data presented to the user and often described the path of the attacker through a distributed system.

Analyzing system-call sequences is a well-studied and powerful technique for intrusion detection, where the actual system calls invoked by a program are checked against a model of expected system calls. Giffin *et al.* observed that the accuracy of system-call-based intrusion detectors can be improved significantly by validating system-call arguments in relation to the execution environment and to previous system calls [16]. While their work used static analysis to derive these relationships over system-call arguments, Bhatkar *et al.* proposed a learning technique to derive the flow of security-sensitive data through various system-call arguments [2]. In both cases, the intrusion-detection technique relies not only on a log of the system calls made by the program, but also on the temporal and data dependencies among these system calls, as expressed by their arguments.

9.2.4 Security Analysis

Panorama used a software program's information access and processing behavior to identify malware [51]. The research observed that a fundamental property of privacy-breaching malware, such as spyware, key loggers, sniffers, backdoors, and rootkits, was their suspicious use of confidential data. The system detected malware with that trait by executing suspect software in a clean environment, providing test inputs to the environment meant to represent secret data, and monitoring the software's execution to see if it spied on the data. In a similar way, BotSwat used coarse information flow analysis to detect bots based on their command-response behavior [42]. The system used taint analysis to determine if data input from the network to a suspect program is passed as an argument to a subsequent system call. Panorama and BotSwat are malware analysis systems used as detectors of privacy violating software and command-response malware.

Other uses of taint analysis have been explored. TaintBochs augmented the Bochs emulator with taint analysis to determine the length of time that confidential data remained in memory [8]. Newsome and Song developed TaintCheck, a system that can detect exploits against software flaws and, with the aid of the exploit instance, can then create an intrusion detection signature that prevents further use of the exploit [34]. Yin *et al.* developed HookFinder, a system to identify hooking points of interest to malware [50]. To this end, they use taint tracking to connect "impact" events to control-flow leading into the malware through a chain of relationships.

Christodorescu *et al.* introduced techniques to construct specifications of malicious behavior automatically, by analyzing execution traces of both malicious and benign programs [9]. They applied a dependency-inference algorithm on the collected system-call traces and then used graph-mining techniques to derive a specification (described in terms of system calls and dependencies among them) that uniquely described a malware sample.

9.2.5 Event Collection and Processing Infrastructure

Using logs to reconstruct security-relevant information places trust on these logs and on the mechanisms used to collect the log data. Additionally, the feasibility of storing and manipulating these logs must be addressed in practice. Thus, logs have to be protected against tampering during and after data collection, they have to be compact, and they have to provide an expressive way to query the log data.

9.2.5.1 Log Resilience to Tampering

Systems reliant upon event logs must ensure that log information is free from tampering. Forensix monitored all actions on a system in a manner similar to ReVirt and BackTracker, but it used offsite storage for log security [19].

Schneier *et al.* addressed the problem of securely storing log files on systems that are not assumed to be immune from compromise [38]. The goals of their work were to ensure that *(1)* an attacker who gains control of the system at a particular time cannot view entries in the log before that time, and *(2)* an attacker cannot forge, remove, or otherwise modify entries in the log from before the time of compromise. To accomplish this, they assumed the existence of a second trusted system that cannot be compromised as well as a shared secret between the two machines. From this shared secret, a chain of authentication and encryption keys were derived and used to secure the log files.

Buchholz *et al.* addressed a technique commonly used by hackers to cover their tracks, wherein network connections are laundered through a series of intermediary connections under the assumption that current logging mechanisms do not allow the original source to be identified [4]. The authors proposed minor modifications to the host operating systems to allow on-line and forensic analyses to correlate incoming and outgoing network flows.

9.2.5.2 Log Compression and Summarization

Marzullo *et al.* logged general function calls to perform forensic analysis much in the same way system calls had been used in the past [31]. They found that although valuable forensic information could be calculated using historical function-call information, the amount of data needed to accomplish this reliably was overwhelming in certain cases, thus limiting the application of this technique.

Verbowski *et al.* tackled the problem of logging application interactions with the persistent store [45]. This problem was of course made difficult by the extremely large amount of data that must be maintained to accomplish this in most modern systems. Their system, called *Flight Data Recorder* (FDR), is purportedly capable of analyzing 1000 days of logs, which works out to more than 25 billion recorded events, in less than 30 minutes. Furthermore, they show that their system can potentially scale to provide trace collection and storage services for very large networks of thousands of machines. The insight that makes FDR feasible is to exploit common characteristics of persistent state workloads and key aspects of typical log queries to construct a highly-efficient domain-specific log format. Despite having its roots firmly in the domain of research systems, this system shipped with Microsoft Windows Vista.

Jiang *et al.* presented Collapsar, a virtual machine based architecture for managing an array of high-interaction honeypots. A large number of virtual machines can be easily managed by a single central authority, but they provide an approximation of a decentralized view as each virtual machine appears to an attacker as a distinct entity. The authors largely focused on the technical challenges of simulating a decentralized honeyfarm in a setting that enables easy centralized control, rather than developing novel event correlation or situational awareness mechanisms.

Huang *et al.* presented a general-purpose framework for efficiently tracking interactions between various applications and the operating system. The authors restricted their monitoring and logging facilities to events that modified the persistent state, as well as events that resulted in communication with external hosts. Furthermore, a mechanism for event summary was included to simplify the presentation and analysis of logged events. However, in its current form, the only summary discussed by the authors combined adjacent memory operations into equivalent atomic operations. The authors evaluated the performance of their logging mechanism by comparing the number of log entries produced to that of previous work. The most interesting part of this work is the event summarization component. This allowed log files produced by fine-granularity events to be used for high-level analysis of the history of a system.

Burtscher developed an algorithm that employed value predictors to amplify patterns in program execution logs, thereby allowing traditional compression algorithms to compress them more effectively [5]. Specifically, a set of value predictors were applied to each data element in a program trace (register values, operands, etc.). If one of the predictors was correct, then the predictor's unique index number, rather than the operand value, was stored in the log rather. As the range of index numbers is significantly smaller than the data value range, the bit savings can be quite substantial. Additionally, further regularities were introduced into the log in this way, enabling a post-compression stage with more traditional algorithms to further reduce the size. Burtscher's experiments revealed substantially higher compression rates as well as faster compression and decompression times.

9.2.5.3 Log Querying

Citing the difficulties of monitoring distributed systems due to heterogeneity of information and the distribution of resources and tools, Conradie *et al.* applied principles from the study of relational databases to the problem [10]. The authors considered a situation where similar information was collected on a number of hosts, possibly using different tools. The authors combined the information produced by these disparate sources into a relational table. Furthermore, they asserted that the operations needed to combine and analyze the information can be expressed in terms of queries on such a table, for instance in the relational algebra. Thus, the crux of their work is in developing *flexible agents* that translate information produced by system monitoring tools on end hosts into entries in the relation. The flexible agents also take part in query processing operations, as they are distributed among the end hosts rather then centralized. As a case study, the authors implemented a prototype of their system and showed that it can be used to effectively monitor resource usage on a distributed, heterogeneous set of hosts.

Reynolds *et al.* developed Pip, a tool for understanding and debugging distributed systems [35]. The insight that set this work apart was that Pip allowed the analyst to express their expectations of the system in a declarative language and compare the monitored behavior of the actual system against them. Using libraries provided by Pip, applications of interest were compiled to generate log files containing events and resource measurements as they executed. The log files were collected and compared against analyst expectations offline. Expectations of two types could be specified: *recognizers* validated individual program runs, and *aggregates* asserted properties of multiple program runs and dependencies among various applications. Finally, Pip provided a tool that allowed the analyst to visualize the application behavior recorded in the logs. To evaluate the system, the authors applied it to a number of popular distributed applications and were able to detect and correct several latent bugs. From an awareness and forensics perspective, this work is interesting for two reasons. First, it allowed the analyst to ignore the irrelevant aspects of system history by specifying his expectation of *normal* or *acceptable* behavior, and it then presented only the aspects that deviate from this notion. Second, the analysis was distributed among multiple layers of conceptual abstraction; the analyst could give his expectation of individual applications, as well as collections of interacting applications. These properties seemed to make it scale well to the distributed setting.

Mysore *et al.* observed that modern systems are composed of several different abstraction layers and frequently distributed across networked machines [33]. This situation can create problems when an analyst needs to understand the nature of interactions among different systems or layers of abstraction, particularly when some components cross abstraction boundaries. They proposed a mechanism dubbed *data-flow tomography* that leveraged the inherent information flow characteristics of these systems to help visualize the interactions among interacting components. With this technique, data elements entering the system are "tagged", and their progress through individual hosts and the larger network is tracked to create visualizations of the whole system. They applied this technique to several problems related to forensic discovery, including identification of data uses (forward slicing), provenance (backward slicing), and mapping the boundaries of system components by observing tag collisions. This work appears to offer much of the same functionality as BackTracker [26] but tracks information flow at a much finer granularity and in a more general manner. Methods for reducing the amount of information produced were not discussed.

Cretu *et al.* described a system for collecting, storing, visualizing, and analyzing performance logs of large clusters running datacenter services [11]. The primary feature of this system was the use of a relational schema to connected logs from different parts of the data center. On top of this relational database of logs, queries and statistical analyses can help a user understand and trace the source of problems in the cluster.

9.2.6 Common Characteristics of Existing Techniques

All of the techniques discussed above share a common theme. They collect event information into logs, analyze the logs to establish relationships among the events, and then query the logs to determine which of these relationships are relevant to the intrusion of interest. A major limitation of these approaches is the top-down manner in which the solutions are constructed. For example, BackTracker was primarily designed to analyze intrusions caused by network input and which manifest themselves at the file system and process level. As a result, BackTracker uses a custom event logging utility, which both complements and overlaps the existing system and application logs, and can only reason about dependencies among events in this custom log. There is no way for a user to specify additional notions of dependence as in our work and the facilities used for event simplification involve lossy filters, as discussed in Section 9.4.3. These are major design limitations of most existing techniques, both in terms of security and in terms of extensibility and scalability, and a major part of the inspiration for this work.

We wish to develop a generic log-based security analysis model in a principled manner, built with the issues of extensibility and scalability in mind from the beginning. The model we present separates the logging concerns about which events are collected, to what amount of detail, and with what kind of security guarantees, from the analysis concerns about which events are relevant to an intrusion. This separation is achieved with the help of a declarative language to express log events and relationships among them. The underlying logging mechanism must be powerful enough to collect data in support of this language, and the analysis technique must rely only on this language to access the log data.

In previous work, Singh *et al.* made a case that a declarative methodology applied to distributed systems building makes certain analysis tasks, such as state monitoring and forensic discovery, more tractable [40]. Observing that in a distributed environment, errors typically arise from emergent misbehavior, network malfunction, or attack from malicious adversaries, they concluded that effectively identifying and recovering from distributed failures requires substantial correlation of information from many nodes, and frequently at high levels of functional abstraction. In later work, the authors demonstrated the advantages of building distributed systems and workloads by expressing the application functionality in terms of a set of continuous declarative queries over host and network-level state [30]. The authors extended this system with an introspection model and set of utilities for monitoring the behavior of various system components. Using queries over the introspection model, users of the system can maintain awareness of many operational and security-critical aspects of the distributed system as it executes. The authors do not discuss the issue of post-mortem analysis in any detail, focusing primarily on on-line analysis and situational awareness.

Cuppens and Miège developed a system called CRIM to correlate alerts across multiple IDSes, thus achieving a cooperative framework where IDS alerts reinforce or contradict each other [12]. An attack is defined as a combination of events that satisfy logical conditions (pre-conditions and post-conditions). The system then correlated events to eliminate duplicates, grouped events that were logically related to the same attack, and connected events that were related to each other through a data dependency. CRIM used an underlying language called LAMBDA to describe attacks. LAMBDA used predicates to describe pre-conditions and post-conditions and special predicates to capture relationships among events (e.g., alert_correlation).

Our present work considers the applicability of a declarative language to post-mortem security analysis of intrusions and introduces several security-specific features. In contrast to previous work, we focus on both formalizing the event language and on making it highly expressive for any security analysis.

9.3 Overview and Case Study

Intrusions pose several challenges for those faced with their onslaught. Three important high-level challenges are preventing intrusions, detecting the occurrence of an intrusion, and recovering from successful intrusions. The third challenge includes the subproblems of identifying all system entities affected by the intrusion and identifying weaknesses in the system components that allowed the intrusion to occur in the first place.

We are concerned here with the third challenge. In a typical network setting, an administrator may have numerous sources of relevant information available, including application logs, intrusion detection logs at both the host and network level, and the entire state of the persistent store. Each of these sources can potentially contain an overwhelming amount of information. In an enterprise setting, it is not unreasonable to expect log files with gigabytes of data. Culling the relevant information from these sources is a difficult problem.

While these sources may contain all of the information that is required to identify, understand, and recover from an intrusion, that information is obscured by the high volume of operational noise generated by everyday, legitimate use of the system. To further complicate analysis, the information often comes from numerous distinct sources. A security administrator's attack analysis tasks would be simplified if there were a way for him to automatically filter out the irrelevant information that corresponds to legitimate activity and to focus instead on the relevant details from each source as a coherent whole. We address this problem.

This paper describes a tool that filters out the irrelevant portions of an event history, leaving only those that provide information that may be valuable when trying to understand and recover from an intrusion. The tool does this by reasoning about the system in terms of the events in recorded activity logs as well as the causal dependencies among the events. The tool additionally provides facilities for reasoning about the intrusion at different levels of granularity to allow an administrator to see attack events at varying complexities.

To provide concrete motivation for the technical developments discussed throughout the remainder of the paper, we performed an intrusion on a Linux system and collected event information corresponding to the intrusion. The information that we collected includes basic audit information such as process creation and file activity. Our goal was to collect the appropriate information to allow us to simulate a typical scenario encountered by a system administrator immediately after an intrusion has taken place. We found answers to several questions, including:

- Which system users were involved in the intrusion, either as victims or perpetrators?
- Which process, service, or module did the attacker use to initially compromise the system?
- Did the attacker leave any artifacts on the system, perhaps in the form of a rootkit or modified authentication data?
- Which files or processes on the system may have been affected indirectly as a result of the attack?

Previous research has indicated that finding answers to such questions manually can be an expensive and time-consuming process [44]. Typically, the process involves sifting through multiple sources of information and building a coherent timeline of logged events and the causal relationships between them. Using our Linux intrusion case study as a motivating example, we will demonstrate that many of these questions can be answered using automated tools that embody the principles discussed in our survey of related work described in Section 2.

9.3.1 Intrusion Scenario

We performed an intrusion with characteristics similar to that used for the Honeynet Project Forensic Challenge [44]. We configured an instance of VMware [46] to run a specific installation of Linux with known vulnerabilities, and we then exploited the vulnerabilities to gain access to the system. The virtual machine (VM) ran a default installation of Redhat Linux 6.2, an older distribution of Linux with publicly disclosed vulnerabilities. This installation runs a version of the rpc.statd service with a buffer overflow vulnerability. From a machine on a separate virtual network, we connected to the rpc.statd service and transmitted a malformed request constructed to exploit the vulnerability. Our exploit subsequently diverts the control flow of rpc.statd to malicious code that forks a command shell with input and output diverted to a network connection, allowing us (the attacker) to connect at a later time and perform arbitrary tasks on the victim machine. As our remote shell was spawned by rpc.statd, it runs with root privileges. To conclude our attack simulation, we connected to the shell and created a file in the root directory named /hacked. We then closed the remote shell and restarted the rpc.statd process to hide immediate evidence of the intrusion.

While this simulated intrusion scenario does not demonstrate any ostensibly malicious behavior, such as theft or modification of data on the system, it will serve our needs from a technical standpoint just as well as a scenario with real malicious activity.

9.3.2 System Auditing

To collect audit information for further analysis of the intrusion, we used the strace utility included with many Linux distributions. This utility makes use of the ptrace system call to monitor system call invocations along with the argument information associated with each invocation. Our use of strace for audit information corresponds to the common practice of using system call information for intrusion detection [15, 47].

As the ptrace system call provides information for a single process at a time, the functionality of strace is limited by this restriction. We are concerned with global system audit information, so we ran a service in the background that continually polled the running processes on the system and attached an instance of `strace` to any that were not being traced at the time of the poll. While not ideal for production environments, we found that this technique provided adequate information for experimental purposes.

To maintain the realism of our scenario, we do not record invocations of all system calls made on the system. Most intrusion detection and auditing mechanisms monitor only the system events that may be involved in an intrusion or security incident [17]. In keeping with this, we monitor system calls related to file, network, process, inter-process communication, and administrative operations. The following system calls are monitored and recorded, along with full listings of the arguments passed to them: *creat, unlink, open, socket, dup, dup2, fcntl, link, symlink, read, readv, recv, recvfrom, recvmsg, write, writev, sendfile, send, sendto, sendmsg, close, execve, fork, vfork, clone, mmap2, kill, pipe.*

9.4 Intrusion Analysis Framework

We are developing a tool called SLog that provides a simplified view of the events and objects on a system and the ways in which they may be related to a detected intrusion. We rely on three key observations and principles.

1. *Recovery will occur more quickly if the user is able to easily distinguish the events and objects that are related to an intrusion from those that are not.* We would like our tool to allow the user to create a compact summary of all the intrusion-relevant events that have occurred, while excluding all events corresponding to everyday legitimate behavior.
2. *Users should be able to use our tool to recover information about an intrusion that occurred before they installed the tool.* We do not want to assume that the user was aware of our tool before the intrusion occurred; this rules out the use of specialized event information provided by a system monitoring facility of our own construction. However, the system or network may contain several different sources of information, each relevant to the intrusion in some way. Therefore, we would like our tool to be able to use any and all event information that the user may be able to provide. Finally, we would like our system to incorporate these disparate information sources with very little effort to the user.
3. *Events from system and application logs are often complex and numerous.* For example, logging system call invocations made by Firefox over a one-minute time period resulted in over 340,000 events. To make matters worse, each such event is associated with a fair amount of data in the form of argument information that requires significant knowledge about the workings of the operating system. Even if our tool is capable reducing the logs to only those events related to the intrusion, the user is left with a great deal of analysis work if he is forced to think in terms of these events. We would like our system to offer facilities for further reducing the amount of information about intrusion-relevant events that is ultimately presented to the user.

When simplifying this information, we will follow one principle that is rooted in the adversarial nature of the problem setting. Any removal of potentially relevant information for the purpose of simplification leaves the attacker with opportunities for evasion. Therefore, any simplification applied by our tool should consist of lossless summaries of aggregate event information.

We developed a general SLog workflow that will help realize our desired goals. In this workflow, the output of one step feeds into the next as input.

1. *Information Extraction and Normalization.* We extract the information from disparate sources and organize it in a normalized format, preferably in a way that allows information from distinct sources to be correlated and analyzed together.
2. *Event Correlation and Dependence Analysis.* We analyze the extracted information and establish the dependencies among various system elements and events. With this additional information, the event history can be partitioned into parts that are relevant to the intrusion and those that are not.

3. *Simplification and Refinement.* Once the information sources have been analyzed, we present a view of the results to the user. The user may wish to look at the information at a coarse granularity with little exposed complexity, or at a fine granularity with significant complexity revealed.

We incorporate each functional aspect of the above workflow into a declarative programming language, giving the SLog user sophisticated programmatic capabilities.

9.4.1 Information Extraction and Normalization

One of the most important features of an intrusion analysis system is an extraction technique that scales well to very large data sources. As we would like to allow the user to reason about arbitrary events, it may often be the case that the events of interest occur frequently and are information-rich. We would also like the extraction technique to be relatively straightforward and intuitive for the user to work with.

We selected the declarative information extraction techniques developed by Shen *et al.* [39]. Shen *et al.* modified the Datalog language to accommodate *embedded procedural predicates* for the purpose of extracting information from loosely-structured data. Rather than corresponding to facts or rules, procedural predicates correspond to external programs that can take arguments from the Datalog program as it is evaluated, and return information in a similar fashion. Shen *et al.* showed how each procedural predicate can correspond to a single information extraction routine, such as *getLine* to return the set of lines from a file. When used in conjunction in a traditional Datalog rule statement, these procedural predicates can provide a powerful mechanism for extracting complex information from unstructured sources.

```
creat(?time,?pid,?file,?flags,?ret) :- docs(?d), lines(?d,?line),
    time(?line,?time), syscall(?line,'creat'), arg(?line,'1',?file),
    arg(?line,'2',?flags), retval(?line,?ret),pid(?line,?pid).
unlink(?time,?pid,?file) :- docs(?d), lines(?d,?line),
    time(?line,?time), pid(?line,?pid), syscall(?line,'unlink'),
    arg(?line,'1',?file).
open(?time,?pid,?file,?perms,?ret) :- docs(?d), lines(?d,?line),
    time(?line,?time), syscall(?line,'open'),
```

Fig. 9.1 Example extraction program for `strace` logs using procedural predicates.

An example set of Datalog rules to extract information from system call logs is presented in Figure 9.1. In this example that extracts information about `creat`, `unlink`, and `open` system calls, all of the predicates except `docs` are procedural. To understand how the extraction works, consider that `lines` returns a relation consisting of all of the lines in *d*, `time` returns the timestamp on each line, `syscall` extracts the system call name on a line from an `strace` log, and `arg` extracts the given argument number from the line. When the rule is satisfiable over the files specified in `docs` and the data returned from the procedural predicates according to one of these rules, the corresponding relation is added to the context of the Datalog program. Shen *et al.* showed that as long as each procedural predicate operates in a *finite, deterministic* fashion, then the semantics of a Datalog program that uses the predicate can be understood in terms of the typical least-model semantics [39].

We selected this technique as it directly and fully addresses our requirements for an extraction technique. First, in their exposition of the technique, the authors demonstrate its ability to scale to sizable datasets. This is accomplished through aggressive workflow optimizations of an extraction program based on the underlying statistics of the dataset. Beyond the optimizations presented by Shen et al., the ability to optimize declarative programs in data intensive settings is a commonly cited reason for their use [3]. Second, the declarative extraction specifications are simple to construct and understand. Although this claim is based on subjective opinion, in our personal experience it is a frequently held sentiment. Finally, the ability of this technique to return precise, complete results follows from the well-defined semantics of Datalog.

9.4.2 Event Correlation and Dependence Analysis

Presenting only the events that are relevant to the intrusion requires some notion of the relationships between events. We will focus this work on the data dependence relation between events.

To reliably and accurately compute dependencies between the events we are given, we require some additional semantic information from the user. Rather than relying only on value equivalence when inferring dependencies, we use three additional pieces of information:

1. *Type Information*: We only reason about the equality between two pieces of data if they are of the same type.
2. *Kill Events*: We say that certain events kill certain pieces of data when they reference them. For example, the `close` system call kills the file descriptor that is passed to it.
3. *Definition and Use Information*: We incorporate definition and use information into the calculations. In order for A to be dependent on B, A must *use* a data location that B *defined*.

The use of this additional information greatly increases the precision of our dependence calculations, as well as the user's control over which data elements are used in inferring dependencies. The type and kill information reduce the number of spurious dependencies calculated by SLog, while the definition and use information allow the user to precisely specify that only a subset of the available event data is actually relevant in the dependence calculations.

Let $data(A)$ be the set of all data elements associated with event A, $use(A)$ be the set of all data elements used by A, $def(A)$ be the set of all data elements defined by A, and $kill(A)$ be the set of all data elements killed by A. Furthermore, as we are reasoning about events that presumably occur on a continuous timeline, we attach a time value to each event, $time(A)$. We say that event A is data-dependent on event B ($depends(A,B) = True$) if

1. $\exists\, d_A \in Data(A),\ d_B \in data(B)$ such that $d_A = d_B$
2. $type(d_A) = type(d_B)$
3. $d_A \in use(A)$ and $d_B \in def(B)$
4. $time(A) > time(B)$
5. $\nexists$ event C such that $d_C \in data(C)$, $d_C \equiv d_A$, $d_C \in kill(C)$, and $time(B) < time(C) < time(A)$

Intuitively, these rules require that for one event to be dependent on another, the two events must contain a piece of data of the same type and value, and that the dependence-inducing piece of data is not killed between the occurrence of the two events. This notion is similar to the *def-use* dependencies calculated by various program analyses for the purpose of static and dynamic slicing over program code [52].

After inferring dependencies between the events available to our analysis, the task of selecting only the events that are relevant to the intrusion at hand is fairly straightforward and borrows from the concept of a *backwards slice* in program analysis. For our purposes, a backwards slice simply corresponds to the transitive closure of the *depends* relation specified above, starting at a specified event. More precisely, we say that event B is in the backwards slice of event A if

1. $depends(A,B)$ is true, *or*
2. $\exists\ B_1,\ldots,B_n$ such that $depends(A,B_1) = true \land depends(B_1,B_2) = true \land \cdots \land depends(B_n,B) = true$

Given some event E that is clearly and unquestionably a symptom of an intrusion, we can constrain our view of the events to only those that may have caused this suspicious event by performing a backwards slice on E.

9.4.3 Simplification and Refinement

Any simplifications performed by the system should not result in the loss of relevant information. Rather, the simplifications take the form of aggregate summaries that present an abstracted view of the low-level event data in the logs. The most useful abstractions for the purpose of simplification are those that correspond to everyday system entities that people are familiar with. For instance, we might consider abstracting sequences of file-related system call events into file objects and dependencies between the processes that invoke the system calls. Specifically, given the following portion of a system call log:

```
fork(void) = 1985
execve("/bin/cat", ["cat", "/tmp/strace.log"], ...) = 0
...
open("/tmp/strace.log", O_RDONLY|O_LARGEFILE) = 3
open("/dev/null'', O_RDWR|O_LARGEFILE) = 4
read(3, "1985 10:58:00.804012 execve(\"/s/"..., 4096) = 4096
write(4, "1985 10:58:00.804012 execve(\"/s/"..., 4096) = 4096
close(4) = 0
close(3) = 0
```

It may be useful to abstract away from specific system call instances, viewing the read and write operations as single dependencies between abstract *file* and *process* objects:

```
file("/bin/cat").
file("/tmp/strace.log").
file("/dev/null").
process(1985).
depends(process(1985), file("/bin/cat")).
depends(file("/dev/null"), process(1985)).
...
```

Our system will enable such abstractions, as defined by the user.

9.5 The SLog Declarative Programming Language

SLog uses a declarative language in the spirit of other popular declarative languages such as Prolog and Datalog. Here, we describe its syntax and semantics.

9.5.1 Language Constructs and Syntax

The SLog language syntax is derived from Datalog and has three first-class entities:

- *Events/Objects:* Events can correspond either to concrete event instances extracted from data sources or to abstracted events defined in terms of previously inferred events and objects.

```
1    open(time_t, file_t, string_t, handle_t).
2    read(time_t, handle_t, string_t, int_t, int_t).
3    close(time_t, handle_t, int_t).
4
5    def(open,'handleType','4').
6    use(read,'handleType','2').
7    kill(close, handle_t).
8    level(open,'1').
9
10   open(?time,?file,?perms,?ret)  :- docs(?d),
11     lines(?d, ?line), time(?line, ?time),
12     syscall(?line, 'open'), arg(?line, '1', ?file),
13     arg(?line, '2', ?perms), retval(?line, ?ret).
14   read(?time,?file,?data,?len,?ret)  :- docs(?d),
15     lines(?d, ?line), time(?line, ?time),
16     syscall(?line, 'read'), arg(?line, '1', ?file),
17     arg(?line, '2', ?data), arg(?line, '3', ?len),
18     retval(?line, ?ret).
19   close(?time,?file,?ret)  :- docs(?d), lines(?d, ?line),
20     time(?line, ?time), syscall(?line, 'close'),
21     arg(?line, '1', ?file), retval(?line, ?ret).
22
23   ?-slice('close,'11:05:35.466110').
```

Fig. 9.2 Example program for file-related activities.

- *Data:* All events are associated with a finite amount of data. Data instances are instantiated with event and type specifications.
- *Dependence Relations:* Besides the default dependence relation induced by data instances, custom dependence relations may be instantiated at runtime in terms of previously inferred events, data, or dependence relations.

There are seven distinct types of statements recognized by the language.

- *Event Abstraction Specifiers:* These statements are used to specify the fact that *event* belongs to a set of events corresponding to a particular *level* of abstraction. By convention, concrete log entries correspond to $level = 1$.
  $level(event, level)$.
- *Type Specifiers:* Given an event named *event*, we specify the type information of its associated data with a type specifier statement in the following manner:
  $eventT(type_1, type_2, \ldots, type_n)$.
- *Kill Statements:* We specify that *event* kills it's nth parameter, which is of type *type*, in the following way:
  $kill(event, type, n)$.
- *Def and Use Statements:* We specify that *event* uses its nth argument, which is of type *type*, in the following way:
  $use(event, type, n)$.
  And similarly, for data defined by *event*:
  $def(event, type, n)$.
- *Custom Dependence Relations:* Custom dependence relations can be specified with a fair amount of freedom. They correspond to a typical Datalog rule statement where the head must be of the form $depends(event_1, id_1, event_2, id_2)$. Here, $event_1$, $event_2$ correspond to valid event instances as specified by an event specification statement. id_1, id_2 correspond to unique identifiers for the events. In the case of concrete log events, this identifier is usually a time.

- *Event Descriptors:* Event descriptors are at the core of the language. They are used to extract event information, including associated data, from logs and to define abstracted events in terms of previously inferred events and data. They are of the form:
  $event(data_1,\ldots,data_n) :\text{-} ext_1(data_1),\ldots,ext_m(data_{n-1},data_n)$.
  Here, ext_1, ... ,ext_m correspond to external procedural predicates that are invoked as the statement is evaluated. These procedural predicates extract a portion of data from the information sources and are the primary innovation presented in the work of Shen et al. [39]. The body of event descriptors is not restricted to any particular form as long as extraction predicates are used.
- *Query Statements:* Currently, we only allow query statements corresponding to backwards slices from a particular event. A query statement is of the form:
  $?\text{-} slice(event,id,?eventN,?idN)$.

We present an example program in Figure 9.2. This program extracts strace log events corresponding to common file-related activities and queries for a backwards slice on a specific instance of the `close` system call.

9.5.2 Semantics

The semantics of a program can be understood in terms of transformations that are performed on each of the inferred events, and applications of the dependence relations to these transformed event instances. Evaluation proceeds as follows:

1. Event instances are instantiated by executing all of the event description statements. This is done using standard Datalog program evaluation algorithms [1], except external programs must be invoked for each extractor used in an event description statement.
2. Event instance tuples are transformed into vertical tuples, one for each event instance and associated data instance. Specifically, a new set of tuples is created with attributes corresponding only to events and event identifiers. Furthermore, a new set of tuples is created for each data instance attached to an inferred event. A template for the transformation semantics is presented in Figure 9.3. Structuring the data in this way allows dependencies between events to be inferred using a small number of very general rules.
3. Query statements are executed over the transformed vertical tuples. Executing a query implies inferring all of the relevant event dependencies to compute the requested backward slice. This is performed using Datalog fact inference over the transformed, vertically-partitioned tuples computed in Step 2. For visualization purposes, we output the results of the query in a graph description language such as Graphviz DOT.

We present a short example of how the first two evaluation steps would operate over the following line from an `strace` log when given the program from Figure 9.2:

```
11:05:36.464761 open("/etc/ld.so.cache", O_RDONLY) = 3
```

First, the extraction statement on line 10 would produce the following tuple:

```
open('11:05:36', '/etc/ld.so', 'O_RDONLY', '3').
```

Next, the transformation step would produce the following tuples:

```
eventinstance('open', '11:05:36')
data('open', '11:05:36', '1', 'timeType', '11:05:36')
data('open', '11:05:36', '2', 'fileType', '"/etc/ld.so"')
data('open', '11:05:36', '3', 'stringType', 'O_RDONLY')
data('open', '11:05:36', '4', 'handleType', '3')
```

$$eventT(\tau_1, \tau_2, \ldots, \tau_n), event(\alpha_1, \alpha_2, \ldots, \alpha_n) \rightarrow eventinstance(event, \alpha_1),$$
$$data(event, \alpha_1, \tau_1, \alpha_1),$$
$$data(event, \alpha_1, \tau_2, \alpha_2),$$
$$\ldots,$$
$$data(event, \alpha_1, \tau_n, \alpha_n)$$

Fig. 9.3 Transformation semantics. To enable easy dependence inference, event instance tuples are transformed into a new set of tuples, one for each data element associated with the event.

9.6 Functional Evaluation

We return to our case study (discussed in Section 9.3) to evaluate the SLog language's efficacy with regards to our stated questions.

9.6.1 Collected Data

The event log sources that we use in our case study were collected using strace. Strace records each instance of a specified set of system calls together with their corresponding argument information. We wrote extraction specifications for a number of important system call events, and a set of event abstractions that allow us to view these events in terms of files and processes. The abstraction that we selected corresponds to the desired output of the BackTracker tool designed by King et al. [26]. Dependencies are calculated between file and process events in an intuitive manner using observed system call invocations. For instance, we say that a process is dependent on another process if one forks the other,

```
depends('process',?pid1,'process',?pid2) :- fork(?t3,?pid2,?pid1).
```

The data collected by strace for this case study corresponds to the operation of our victim machine from the moment the first user logs in until the system is shut down. As we are only concerned with the security-critical subset of the system calls executed in this time period, this corresponds to 2885 system call events executed by 50 processes that may be relevant, as well as their associated argument information. As our goal with this case study is to demonstrate the utility of the tool in a realistic scenario rather than to demonstrate the full range of its functionality, we wish only to use it to replicate the output of a tool of *well known* utility, such as BackTracker. For this reason, we only used information from strace logs rather than from multiple sources, as has been discussed throughout the paper.

9.6.2 Usage and Results

In our scenario, the "attacker" left a file in the root directory named "/hacked". Using this as our initial evidence, we can use the language to discover the system entities that were involved in the creation of /hacked with the query:

```
?-slice('file', '/hacked', ?e, ?i).
```

The final output of the tool as applied to this case study is presented in graphical format in Figure 9.4. Five nodes corresponding to configuration files have been removed to allow the image to fit on the page. This analysis was produced by telling the tool to perform a backwards slice on the file

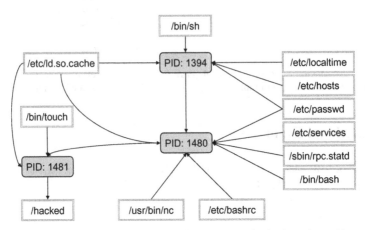

Fig. 9.4 Final output of the case study. The file /hacked is the intrusion evidence left behind by the imaginary attacker. Performing a backwards slice on this evidence implicates /sbin/rpc.statd, among a very few other potential sources.

named /hacked. This is realistic given the scenario, as this file is an object on the system that is clearly and indisputably a symptom of the intrusion and a likely point of discovery by a system administrator. The graph in Figure 9.4 shows us that the tool is capable of returning a small subset of the events and objects relevant to an intrusion; the node representing the vulnerable process that allowed the intrusion, rpc.statd, is only three hops away from the node representing /hacked. Furthermore, we see that the output does not contain a large volume of irrelevant information that the user must sort through to obtain an understanding of the intrusion.

As previously stated, the language interpreter currently only supports backwards slices on the event data. This enables users of the language to identify events and system components that were involved in the *creation* or *influenced* a given entity in the log. This functionality is useful for performing tasks such as finding system components to remove or patch after an intrusion, or implicating certain users for involvement in an intrusion. It does not allow language users to find system entities that have been affected or otherwise *tainted* by an intrusion. For example, it may be desirable to know whether or not an intruder left certain files on a system as part of a rootkit or modified the system authentication files to give himself a seemingly legitimate means of access to the system in the future. For this, a *forward slice* must be performed to identify all of the events and entities that are in some way dependent on a given event. Incorporating this functionality into our tool is not difficult, as it amounts to reversing the order of arguments in the *depends* relation and computing the transitive closure, as with backward slices. If Datalog evaluation techniques that utilize dynamic programming [36] are used to evaluate SLog programs that calculate forward slices, then the functionality comes at no additional runtime cost.

9.7 Conclusion

In this paper, we discussed the problems of intrusion analysis and understanding. We began with a survey of much of the related work in this area, including topics in digital forensic analysis of intrusions, intrusion detection and recovery, security analysis, and event collection and processing.

Analyzing the contributions from these somewhat disparate areas of research, we postulated that many of the techniques surveyed share a common operational theme that is based on inferring relationships between events in logs, and we later used the relationships to query for information relevant to the intrusion. However, as most of the solutions were developed in a top-down manner, often as a response to a particular family of attacks or for use on a particular type of system, there did not exist a unified, coherent framework for performing this type of analysis on a wide range of systems.

To address the need for such a framework, we developed a logic and corresponding language for performing this type of analysis in generalized settings. We took an event-oriented approach, where the system and information relevant to the intrusion are thought of in terms of events on and between objects on the system that are recorded on one or more log files. Furthermore, we defined a notion of dependence between events and objects on the system as a way to refine our view of the events and focus on only the information that is explicitly relevant to an intrusion. We designed and implemented a tool, SLog, based on these principles and observations that allows a user to specify syntactic and semantic information about the events found in an arbitrary set of log sources and perform detailed analysis of the events. SLog provides facilities for performing semantic abstraction over sequences of events inferred from log sources, allowing the user to simplify his view of the events. We evaluated the effectiveness of our language and tool by performing a case study of an intrusion in a realistic simulated environment. We found that we were able to use the raw event information recorded in logs to automatically pinpoint the small subset of entities on a system that were responsible for the intrusion, without the need for extensive manual analysis. In the future, we will extend our tool to support different types of analyses, and study its application in larger, more challenging settings.

Acknowledgments

This work was supported by National Science Foundation grants CNS-0627501, CCF-0524051, 0311808, 0433540, 0448452, CNS-0448476, CNS-0627551. We would also like to thank Remzi Arpaci-Dusseau, Drew Davidson, and Lorenzo Martignoni for their helpful comments and advice throughout the course of this work.

References

1. Bancilhon, F., Ramakrishnan, R.: An amateur's introduction to recursive query processing strategies. In: Proceedings of the 1986 ACM SIGMOD international conference on Management of data, pp. 16–52. ACM, New York, NY, USA (1986)
2. Bhatkar, S., Chaturvedi, A., Sekar, R.: Dataflow anomaly detection. In: Proceedings of the 2006 IEEE Symposium on Security and Privacy, pp. 48–62. IEEE Computer Society, Washington, DC, USA (2006)
3. Brewer, E.A.: Combining Systems and Databases: A Search Engine Retrospective, pp. 711–724. MIT Press (2005)
4. Buchholz, F.P., Shields, C.: Providing process origin information to aid in computer forensic investigations. Journal of Computer Security 12(5), 753–776 (2004)
5. Burtscher, M.: VPC3: a fast and effective trace-compression algorithm. In: Proceedings of the joint international conference on Measurement and modeling of computer systems, pp. 167–176. ACM, New York, NY, USA (2004)
6. CERT Coordination Center: Overview of attack trends. http://www.cert.org/archive/pdf/attack_trends.pdf. Retrieved February 16, 2009

7. Chen, P.M., Noble, B.D.: When virtual is better than real. In: Proceedings of the Eighth Workshop on Hot Topics in Operating Systems, p. 133. IEEE Computer Society, Washington, DC, USA (2001)
8. Chow, J., Pfaff, B., Garfinkel, T., Christopher, K., Rosenblum, M.: Understanding data lifetime via whole system simulation. In: 13th USENIX Security Symposium. San Diego, California (2004)
9. Christodorescu, M., Jha, S., Kruegel, C.: Mining specifications of malicious behavior. In: Proceedings of the the the 6th joint meeting of the European software engineering conference and the ACM SIGSOFT symposium on The foundations of software engineering, pp. 5–14. ACM, New York, NY, USA (2007)
10. Conradie, L., Mountzia, M.A.: A relational model for distributed systems monitoring using flexible agents. In: Proceedings of the 3rd Workshop on Services in Distributed and Networked Environments, p. 10. IEEE Computer Society, Washington, DC, USA (1996)
11. Cretu-Ciocarlie, G.F., Budiu, M., Goldszmidt, M.: Hunting for problems with Artemis. In: G. Bronevetsky (ed.) First USENIX Workshop on the Analysis of System Logs. USENIX Association (2008)
12. Cuppens, F., Miège, A.: Alert correlation in a cooperative intrusion detection framework. In: Proceedings of the 2002 IEEE Symposium on Security and Privacy, p. 202. IEEE Computer Society, Washington, DC, USA (2002)
13. Debar, H., Wespi, A.: Aggregation and correlation of intrusion-detection alerts. In: Proceedings of the 4th International Symposium on Recent Advances in Intrusion Detection, pp. 85–103. Springer-Verlag, London, UK (2001)
14. Dunlap, G., King, S., Cinar, S., Basrai, M., Chen, P.: ReVirt: Enabling intrusion analysis through virtual-machine logging and replay. In: 5th Symposium on Operating System Design and Implementation. Boston, Massachusetts (2002)
15. Forrest, S., Hofmeyr, S.A., Somayaji, A., Longstaff, T.A.: A sense of self for unix processes. In: Proceedings of the 1996 IEEE Symposium on Security and Privacy, p. 120. IEEE Computer Society, Washington, DC, USA (1996)
16. Giffin, J.T., Dagon, D., Jha, S., Lee, W., Miller, B.P.: Environment-sensitive intrusion detection. In: 8th International Symposium on Recent Advances in Intrusion Detection, *Lecture Notes in Computer Science*, vol. 3858, pp. 185–206. Springer (2005)
17. Giffin, J.T., Jha, S., Miller, B.P.: Automated discovery of mimicry attacks. In: Proceedings of the 9th International Symposium on Recent Advanced in Intrusion Detection, pp. 41–60 (2006)
18. Goel, A., Farhadi, K., Po, K., Feng, W.c.: Reconstructing system state for intrusion analysis. ACM SIGOPS Operating System Review **42**(3), 21–28 (2008)
19. Goel, A., Feng, W.c., Maier, D., Feng, W.c., Walpole, J.: Forensix: A robust, high-performance reconstruction system. In: Proceedings of the Second International Workshop on Security in Distributed Computing Systems, pp. 155–162. IEEE Computer Society, Washington, DC, USA (2005)
20. Goel, A., Po, K., Farhadi, K., Li, Z., de Lara, E.: The Taser intrusion recovery system. In: 20th ACM Symposium on Operating System Principles. Brighton, United Kingdom (2005)
21. Gu, G., Porras, P., Yegneswaran, V., Fong, M., Lee, W.: BotHunter: Detecting malware infection through IDS-driven dialog correlation. In: Proceedings of the 16th USENIX Security Symposium (2007)
22. Jain, S., Shafique, F., Djeric, V., Goel, A.: Application-level isolation and recovery with solitude. In: Proceedings of the 3rd ACM SIGOPS/EuroSys European Conference on Computer Systems 2008, pp. 95–107. ACM, New York, NY, USA (2008)
23. Jiang, X., Buchholz, F., Walters, A., Xu, D., Wang, Y., Spafford, E.H.: Tracing worm break-in and contaminations via process coloring: A provenance-preserving approach. IEEE Transactions on Parallel and Distributed Systems **19**(7) (2008)
24. Jiang, X., Walters, A., Buchholz, F., Xu, D., Wang, Y., Spafford, E.: Provenance-aware tracing of worm break-in and contaminations: A process coloring approach. In: 26th IEEE International Conference on Distributed Computing Systems. Lisboa, Portugal (2006)

25. Khanna, G., Yu Cheng, M., Varadharajan, P., Bagchi, S., Correia, M.P., Veríssimo, P.J.: Automated rule-based diagnosis through a distributed monitor system. IEEE Transactions on Dependable and Secure Computing **4**(4), 266–279 (2007)
26. King, S.T., Chen, P.M.: Backtracking intrusions. In: Proceedings of the nineteenth ACM symposium on Operating systems principles. ACM, New York, NY, USA (2003)
27. Kruger, L., Wang, H., Jha, S., McDaniel, P., Lee, W.: Towards discovering and containing privacy violations in software. Tech. rep., University of Wisconsin – Madison (2005)
28. Lakkaraju, K., Yurcik, W., Lee, A.J.: NVisionIP: netflow visualizations of system state for security situational awareness. In: Proceedings of the 2004 ACM workshop on Visualization and data mining for computer security, pp. 65–72. ACM, New York, NY, USA (2004)
29. Liu, P., Jajodia, S., McCollum, C.D.: Intrusion confinement by isolation in information systems. In: Proceedings of the IFIP WG 11.3 Thirteenth International Conference on Database Security, pp. 3–18. Kluwer, B.V., Deventer, The Netherlands, The Netherlands (2000)
30. Loo, B.T., Condie, T., Hellerstein, J.M., Maniatis, P., Roscoe, T., Stoica, I.: Implementing declarative overlays. SIGOPS Operating System Review **39**(5), 75–90 (2005)
31. Marzullo, K., Peisert, S., Bishop, M., Kevin, S.: Analysis of computer intrusions using sequences of function calls. IEEE Transactions on Dependable and Secure Computing **4**(2), 137–150 (2007)
32. Muniswamy-Reddy, K.K., Wright, C.P., Himmer, A., Zadok, E.: A versatile and user-oriented versioning file system. In: Proceedings of the 3rd USENIX Conference on File and Storage Technologies, pp. 115–128. USENIX Association, Berkeley, CA, USA (2004)
33. Mysore, S., Mazloom, B., Agrawal, B., Sherwood, T.: Understanding and visualizing full systems with data flow tomography. SIGARCH Computer Architecture News **36**(1), 211–221 (2008)
34. Newsome, J., Song, D.: Dynamic taint analysis for automatic detection, analysis, and signature generation of exploits on commodity software. In: Proceedings of the Network and Distributed System Security Symposium (2005)
35. Reynolds, P., Killian, C., Wiener, J.L., Mogul, J.C., Shah, M.A., Vahdat, A.: Pip: detecting the unexpected in distributed systems. In: Proceedings of the 3rd conference on Networked Systems Design & Implementation, pp. 9–9. USENIX Association, Berkeley, CA, USA (2006)
36. Sagonas, K., Swift, T., Warren, D.S.: XSB as an efficient deductive database engine. SIGMOD Rec. **23**(2), 442–453 (1994)
37. Santry, D.J., Feeley, M.J., Hutchinson, N.C., Veitch, A.C.: Elephant: The file system that never forgets. Workshop on Hot Topics in Operating Systems **0**, 2 (1999)
38. Schneier, B., Kelsey, J.: Secure audit logs to support computer forensics. ACM Transactions on Information System Security **2**(2), 159–176 (1999)
39. Shen, W., Doan, A., Naughton, J.F., Ramakrishnan, R.: Declarative information extraction using datalog with embedded extraction predicates. In: Proceedings of the 33rd international conference on Very large data bases, pp. 1033–1044. VLDB Endowment (2007)
40. Singh, A., Maniatis, P., Roscoe, T., Druschel, P.: Using queries for distributed monitoring and forensics. Proceedings of the 1st ACM SIGOPS/EuroSys European Conference on Computer Systems 2006 pp. 389–402 (2006)
41. Sitaraman, S., Venkatesan, S.: Forensic analysis of file system intrusions using improved backtracking. In: Proceedings of the Third IEEE International Workshop on Information Assurance, pp. 154–163. IEEE Computer Society, Washington, DC, USA (2005)
42. Stinson, E., Mitchell, J.C.: Characterizing bots' remote control behavior. In: 4th International Conference on Detection of Intrusions & Malware, and Vulnerability Assessment. Lucerne, Switzerland (2007)
43. Sun, W., Liang, Z., Sekar, R., Venkatakrishnan, V.N.: One-way isolation: An effective approach for realizing safe execution environments. In: Proceedings of the Network and Distributed System Security Symposium, pp. 265–278 (2005)
44. The Honeynet Project: Forensic challenge. www.honeynet.org/challenge/index.html. Retrieved February 16, 2009

45. Verbowski, C., Kiciman, E., Kumar, A., Daniels, B., Lu, S., Lee, J., Wang, Y.M., Roussev, R.: Flight data recorder: monitoring persistent-state interactions to improve systems management. In: Proceedings of the 7th symposium on Operating systems design and implementation, pp. 117–130. USENIX Association, Berkeley, CA, USA (2006)
46. VMware, Inc.: VMware Server [Computer Software]. Available from http://www.vmware.com. Retrieved February 16, 2009
47. Wagner, D., Soto, P.: Mimicry attacks on host-based intrusion detection systems. In: Proceedings of the 9th ACM conference on Computer and communications security, pp. 255–264. ACM, New York, NY, USA (2002)
48. Whitaker, A., Cox, R.S., Gribble, S.D.: Using time travel to diagnose computer problems. In: Proceedings of the 11th workshop on ACM SIGOPS European workshop, p. 16. ACM, New York, NY, USA (2004)
49. Whitaker, A., Shaw, M., Gribble, S.D.: Denali: Lightweight virtual machines for distributed and networked applications. In: Proceedings of the USENIX Annual Technical Conference (2002)
50. Yin, H., Liang, Z., Song, D.: HookFinder: Identifying and understanding malware hooking behaviors. In: Proceedings of the 15th Annual Network and Distributed System Security Symposium (2008)
51. Yin, H., Song, D., Egele, M., Kruegel, C., Kirda, E.: Panorama: Capturing system-wide information flow for malware detection and analysis. In: ACM Symposium on Computer and Communications Security. Alexandria, Virginia (2007)
52. Zhang, X., Gupta, R., Zhang, Y.: Efficient forward computation of dynamic slices using reduced ordered binary decision diagrams. In: Proceedings of the 26th International Conference on Software Engineering, pp. 502–511. IEEE Computer Society, Washington, DC, USA (2004)

Chapter 10
Automated Software Vulnerability Analysis

Emre C. Sezer, Chongkyung Kil, and Peng Ning

Abstract Despite decades of research, software continues to have vulnerabilities. Successful exploitations of these vulnerabilities by attackers cost millions of dollars to businesses and individuals. Unfortunately, most effective defensive measures, such as patching and intrusion prevention systems, require an intimate knowledge of the vulnerabilities. Many systems for detecting attacks have been proposed. However, the analysis of the exploited vulnerabilities is left to security experts and programmers. Both the human effort involved and the slow analysis process are unfavorable for timely defensive measure to be deployed. The problem is exacerbated by zero-day attacks.

This chapter presents two recent research efforts, named MemSherlock and CBones, for automatically aiding experts in identifying and analyzing unknown vulnerabilities. Both methods rely on monitoring user applications during their runtime and checking for inconsistencies in their memory or memory access patterns. MemSherlock is a post-mortem analysis tool that monitors an application's memory operations to determine malicious ones, indicative of an ongoing attack. It produces valuable information regarding the vulnerability and the attack vector. CBones takes snapshots of the memory and looks for inconsistencies by identifying invariants for an application's memory and verifying them at runtime. Experimental evaluation shows that both methods are capable of providing critical information about vulnerabilities and attack vectors.

10.1 Introduction

Despite decades of research, software continues to have vulnerabilities – software bugs that can be manipulated by an attacker to gain favorable results such as starting a shell or escalating privileges. Vulnerabilities exploited successfully by attackers cause a wide range of difficulties from stolen identities to disruption of services and cost millions of dollars to businesses and individuals. The causes of such vulnerabilities are many and varied. The most significant reason is shown to be memory corruption; CERT advisories demonstrate that memory corruption attacks constitute approximately half of all reported attacks. Some common memory corruption attacks include stack and heap overflows along with format string attacks.

The main cause of memory corruption vulnerabilities is the use of weakly typed languages such as C. One such example is character strings which are simply denoted by a pointer to the beginning character. Therefore, the compiler usually does not know the length of a string and the

Department of Computer Science, NC State University, Raleigh, NC, 27695
{ecsezer, ckil, pning}@ncsu.edu

S. Jajodia et al., (eds.), *Cyber Situational Awareness*,
Advances in Information Security 46, DOI 10.1007/978-1-4419-0140-8_10,
© Springer Science+Business Media, LLC 2010

programmer is expected to perform necessary bounds checking. This is a design philosophy where the language is kept flexible but requires more of the programmer. The benefit of this flexibility is that programmers can write highly optimized code which is essential for performance critical applications. Despite the repercussions of using a weakly typed language, both the number of legacy software and the desire for performance makes C the language of choice even today. There have been proposals to use dialects of C which provide safer mechanisms for dealing with arrays and pointers [15, 23]. However, the performance overhead has prevented these schemes from being widely deployed.

Many security countermeasures have been proposed to remove software vulnerabilities once they are identified. Patching has been adopted by almost all mainstream operating systems and applications, such as Microsoft Windows, Linux, Mac OS, and Microsoft Office, to remove newly discovered vulnerabilities. Moreover, researchers have developed methods for providing protection from attacks that exploit a specific vulnerability even when the attacker is trying to obfuscate the attack. For example, Shield [32] was developed to provide temporary protection of vulnerable systems after the vulnerabilities are identified but before patches are applied properly. As another example, a filtering technique was developed to defend against (polymorphic) exploits of known vulnerabilities [14], and automatic generation of vulnerability-based signatures (for known vulnerabilities) was also investigated [2]. Although providing varying levels of protection, all these approaches require specific vulnerability information in order to function correctly.

A research avenue uses static analysis of source code to find vulnerabilities at compile time (e.g., (e.g., [6, 7, 13, 19]). Static analysis techniques can be applied to source code or the compiled binary. In the former case, the analysis has access to semantic information such as types, initial values, etc., but also introduces the requirement of having access to the source code, which is not always available. The main drawback of static analysis approaches is the number of false positives reported. Real-world evaluations have shown that static analysis based detection tools tend to generate a large number of false positives without guaranteeing the detection of all vulnerabilities. A major difficulty in static analysis stems from pointers. At a given program point, determining to which object a pointer refers is difficult, and in some cases impossible, limiting the benefits of static analysis when trying to determine software bugs and vulnerabilities.

Besides static analysis techniques, dynamic approaches have also been investigated to detect exploits and signal the presence of a vulnerability. Address space randomization [16, 28] relocates program sections and variables within the virtual address space to thwart attacks. The attacks usually result in crashing the application instead of succeeding normally. TaintCheck [25] and Minos [11] track the progress of user specified data. In the event that they detect an attack, they can trace back to the program point from which the data originated to provide some information about the attack vector (i.e., the inputs used by the attacker to exploit the vulnerability, generally derived from the content of a network packet). Others try to obtain a signature (a bit string that uniquely identifies the vector) for the attack vector automatically (e.g., DACODA [12], COVERS [21]). However, despite the detection of potentially unknown attacks, many such approaches cannot give precise information about the exploited vulnerabilities.

Once a vulnerability is detected, a security expert generally tries to reproduce the attack, find the corruption point and analyze the conditions that must be met and finally provide a patch or publish a security advisory. This process is very time consuming, often giving the attacker days in which to cause damage. We have already seen zero-day worms that spread around the world in a matter of hours such as Code Red [3] and Slammer [4], which mandates faster methods of analysis.

In the following, we present two systems built to automatically aid experts in identifying and analyzing unknown vulnerabilities. Both methods rely on monitoring user applications during their runtime and checking for inconsistencies in their memory or memory access patterns. MemSherlock [30] is a post-mortem analysis tool that monitors an application's memory operations to determine malicious ones, indicative of an ongoing attack. It then produces valuable information regarding the vulnerability and the attack vector. CBones [17] is another tool used in security debugging. Instead of checking memory operations, it takes snapshots of the memory and looks for inconsistencies. Namely, it first identifies some invariants for an application's memory and then verifies them during runtime.

10.2 Common Ground

MemSherlock and CBones rely on different methods to determine the corruption point in a vulnerability, as explained in the following two sections. The two systems, however, share some common ground. They are both application level debuggers. They first gather necessary information from the target application by a combination of static analysis of source and binary code. Armed with this information, they monitor the application at runtime and perform their checks.

Both systems require runtime information that current off-the-shelf hardware cannot provide. For example, MemSherlock relies on capturing memory operations to determine the instruction pointer (IP) and the destination memory address. CBones relies on capturing function calls and returns. To facilitate these requirements, we use Valgrind [24], an open-source CPU emulator for x86 architectures, which uses dynamic binary instrumentation. It allows programmers to modify, rewrite or instrument a code block that is about to be executed. Using this method, a programmer can insert his own functions at various program points. We use this functionality to capture and instrument memory operations in MemSherlock, and function call and return instructions in CBones.

In order to diagnose a vulnerability, we first need to detect the existence of the vulnerability. Generally, the vulnerability analysis is laden with execution monitoring and extensive logging or checking mechanisms, making the analysis too slow to be used in production environments. We assume that a light-weight intrusion detection system (IDS) is employed along with an attack replay mechanism to initially detect the existence of a vulnerability. The application is then run under the security debugging tools and the attacks are replayed. Another important observation is that, for successful debugging, the system needs to determine the point of corruption. The point of detection and the point of corruption are usually not the same and can often be quite a bit apart both in the sense of time and instructions in the program binary. Therefore, a big portion of the two systems' contribution lies in the ability to accurately determine the point of corruption.

We present how each system can be used to improve the analysis of software vulnerabilities. To further evaluate the effectiveness of the methods, we use a test suite of freely available software known to have vulnerabilities. The test suite consists of 12 real world applications and attack programs that exploit their vulnerabilities. Section 10.5 compares the relative effectiveness of the two methods and further discusses their capabilities.

10.3 MemSherlock: An Automated Debugger for Unknown Memory Corruption Vulnerabilities

The goal of MemSherlock is to assist programmers in understanding and patching unknown memory corruption vulnerabilities by automatically detecting and providing information about such vulnerabilities. MemSherlock is a debugging tool and is deployed after an attack has been observed and recorded. For example, an application can be run using address space randomization and an attack would most likely crash the system. Then the input is replayed while the application is run under MemSherlock to debug the vulnerability.

To identify memory corruption, we take advantage of an observation made in [33]. That is, in most programs, a given variable typically is accessed by only a few instructions (or the corresponding statements in the source code). This observation can be extended further in the context of memory corruption attacks: in order for a memory corruption attack to succeed, an attacker needs to use an instruction (in the victim program) to modify a memory region into which the instruction should not write. To exploit this observation, we track memory operations during the debugging process, and verify that the current instruction can indeed write to that memory address. Specifically, we determine the memory regions and associate with each of them a set of instructions that can modify it. For a given memory region m, the set of instructions that can modify m is called the *write set* of m, denoted WS(m).

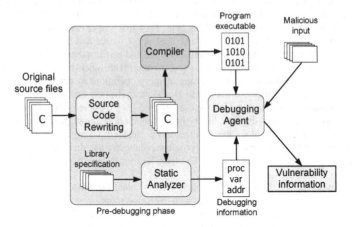

Fig. 10.1 Overview of MemSherlock

Figure 10.1 illustrates the procedure for using MemSherlock. MemSherlock requires a pre-debugging phase to collect the information needed for security debugging. In particular, it needs to collect the write set of each critical memory region. It is non-trivial to obtain such write sets and track the write operations during debugging, particularly due to the complications caused by pointers and complex program constructs. As illustrated in Figure 10.1, during the pre-debugging phase, MemSherlock first performs source code rewriting to handle pointers and complex program constructs, then uses static analysis of source code to collect information necessary for debugging (e.g., write set information), and finally invokes static analysis of binary code to associate the collected information with memory locations.

Once invoked for debugging, MemSherlock takes as input the instrumented version of the program, the auxiliary debugging information (e.g., the variables in the program along with their sizes and their write sets) generated during the pre-debugging phase, and malicious network payloads. During the debugging process MemSherlock verifies the modifications to memory regions with the write set information, and identifies an illegal write when the updating instruction is not in the write set. Thus, MemSherlock can capture memory corruption at the time of the modification, pinpointing the exact instruction or statement in source code that is responsible for the corruption.

In addition to the above verification, MemSherlock keeps track of the propagation of input data as well as the program instructions involved in the propagation. As a result, upon the detection of memory corruption, MemSherlock can identify precisely parts of the program involved in the propagation of the malicious input and determine how that malicious input leads to memory corruption. By integrating further the auxiliary information collected during the pre-debugging phase, MemSherlock presents all the vulnerability information at source code level to facilitate the understanding and patching of the vulnerabilities.

10.3.1 Generating Write Sets

The primary objective of the pre-debugging phase is to generate the write sets of memory regions used by applications. In this phase, we need to determine all program variables and extract their write sets. Moreover, we need to provide information for the debugging agent so that during the debugging phase, it can link memory regions to program variables and their write sets. A particular challenge in this phase is handling pointers and certain dereferences (e.g., chained dereferences and `struct`).

10.3.1.1 Extracting Write Sets from Source Code

We perform source code analysis to determine all the program variables and extract their write sets. The write set of a variable v includes statements that assign v or library function calls where v is passed as a modifiable argument (e.g., `memcpy(v, src)`). To facilitate this process, we provide the static analyzer with not only the source code, but also a specification file for every shared library linked to the program. The specification file includes the names of library functions that modify their arguments and identifies the modified arguments. An entry in the write set is a pair consisting of a file name and a line number. The static analyzer also determines the size of the variables, and for local variables, the function in which they appear. Such information will be used by MemSherlock during the debugging phase.

Handling Pointers

Pointers require some special attention since given a pointer variable, the statements that modify the pointer variable and those that modify the pointer's referent object modify two different memory regions. To address this issue, we keep two separate write sets for every pointer variable p: One for the pointer variable itself (WS(p)), and the other for the referent object ref(p) (WS(ref(p))). Note that a pointer may point to different objects during the course of execution. During the debugging process, when the referent object `ref(p)` is determined, the debugging agent adds WS(ref(p)) to the referent object's write set.

Note that WS(ref(p)) represents the write set of p's referent object, possibly updated through pointer p. Thus, when p is updated, for example, to point to a different object, WS(ref(p)) should be removed from the write set of the referent object to which p previously pointed, since it is no longer possible to update this object through pointer p.

1 int i = 0;	WS(i) ={1}
2 int *p = &i;	WS(p) ={2,4}
3 *p = 1;	WS(ref(p)) ={3}
4 p = NULL;	

Line	ref(p)	WS(i)
1	N/A	{1}
2	i	{1,3}
3	i	{1,3}
4	NULL	{1}

(a) Code example   (b) Write sets after static analysis   (c) ref(p) and WS(i) during monitoring

Fig. 10.2 Example illustrating model of pointers during static analysis and security debugging

Figure 10.2 shows an example of the write sets of pointers and their referent objects. We can see that after static analysis, WS(i) contains the instruction on line 1 and WS(ref(p)) contains only line 3. Note that ref(p) remains unresolved during static analysis. During security debugging however, p's value is updated on lines 2 and 4. At these points, we can see that ref(p) is resolved to i and NULL, respectively. During the execution of lines 2 and 3, while p points to i, WS(i)

changes to include the instructions in WS(ref(p)). However, once p's referent object changes to
NULL on line 4, WS(i) goes back to its original value.

Since we use the debugging agent to determine dynamically when a pointer variable is updated
and find the corresponding memory region, we can avoid pointer alias analysis during static analysis. Indeed, general pointer alias analysis is known to be an undecidable problem [18, 29]. Our
approach allows us to bypass it without sacrificing the analysis accuracy.

Handling Chained Dereferences

Chained dereferences make it difficult for the debugging agent to track the memory writes and verify the write set constraint. Examples of chained dereferences include **p, array[1][2] and
*(p+q). We use source code rewriting to transform chained dereferences to simple ones so that
the techniques discussed in Section 10.3.1.1 can be applied. We perform this transformation only
if the expression potentially is updated. For example, x = var.arr[5]->name need not be
transformed since the modified variable x is already in a simple form and var.arr[5]->name
is not updated at all.

```1 int z;` `2 int *y = &z;` `3 int **x = &y;` `4 **x = 10;```	```1 int z;` `2 int *y = &z;` `3 int **x = &y;` `4 int *temp = *x;` `5 *temp = 10;```

Fig. 10.3 Example of chained dereference

Figure 10.3 shows an example of chained dereferencing on the left. The static analyzer models
the chained dereference on line 4 as a simple dereference, and adds line 4 to WS(ref(x)). This is
because we model variable updates as low-level write instructions, which do not have any access
to type information. However, we cannot determine the number of dereferences that have occurred
in calculating the final target address of a write instruction. Thus, at line 4, the agent is unable to
determine the relationship between x and z. When it detects a write to z, it first checks if line 4 is
in WS(z) and then WS(y). Both checks fail, since line 4 is only in WS(ref(x)) and z is not the
referent of x.

To handle such chained dereferences, we use automatic source code rewriting. Any chained
dereference can be translated into simple dereferences by introducing one or a few temporary
variables. For a chained dereference of the form *X, we declare a temporary variable t whose type
is that of X and assign the value of X to t. In the above example, we can replace line 4 with lines 4
and 5 on the right in Figure 10.3.

After the transformation, upon executing line 4, the debugging agent sets temp's referent to
z and adds temp to z's list of references. When line 6 attempts to write to z, the debugging
agent determines it as a legitimate write, because temp is one of z's references and line 6 is in
WS(ref(temp)).

As we have shown, extracting write sets in a meaningful manner is a non-trivial task. There
are other corner cases that need to be handled (such as struct fields, arrays and unions), but for
the sake of brevity we omit these discussions. The interested reader can find a thorough analysis
in [30].

10.3.1.2 Mapping Variables to Memory Regions

The aforementioned static analysis at the source code level allows us to extract write sets of variables. To facilitate the debugging process, we have to provide additional information to the debugging agent so that it can associate the variables with memory regions and identify the write sets of those memory regions during debugging time.

We perform binary analysis to determine the location of memory regions corresponding to variables. This is trivial for global variables, since global variables are assigned static addresses after compilation. Local variables, however, have dynamic addresses depending on when the functions containing the local variables are called. To address this issue, we use the addresses of functions that contain the local variables and their frame pointer offset values to identify local variables. The debugging agent can use these values and the actual function calls to calculate the real memory addresses during debugging. The binary analysis also provides information about segment sizes and locations as well as the addresses of functions.

10.3.2 Debugging Vulnerabilities

During the debugging phase, MemSherlock monitors the program execution to detect memory corruption and infer vulnerability information. As discussed earlier, MemSherlock verifies the modifications to memory regions with the write set information, and identifies an illegal write when the updating instruction is not in the write set. To accomplish automated vulnerability analysis, the MemSherlock debugging agent needs to perform three primary tasks:

1. *State Maintenance:* Keep track of the memory regions along with their write sets as the program executes. This is necessary, because the active memory regions and their write sets change as the program executes.
2. *Memory Checking:* Track and verify memory update operations to detect memory corruption.
3. *Vulnerability Extraction:* Generate vulnerability information once a memory corruption is detected.

In the following, we present a few key data structures, which will be used in the later discussion, and then explain the three primary tasks in detail.

10.3.2.1 Key Data Structures

The MemSherlock debugging agent uses several key data structures. For each monitored memory region r, the agent creates a MemoryRegion object m, which stores r's address, size and write set. Additionally, the MemoryRegion object for each pointer p stores WS(ref(p)) and a pointer to its referent object's MemoryRegion. At any time during debugging, MemSherlock maintains all the active memory regions. We collectively refer to these memory regions as ActiveMemoryRegions. For each user-defined function in the executable, a Procedure object is created to store the function's name, its address in the code segment, and a list of MemoryRegions corresponding to its local variables. For local variables, their addresses are stored as frame pointer offsets.

Certain memory regions, such as a function's return address or saved registers, never should be written by source-level instructions*. These memory regions, along with meta data adjacent to dynamically allocated memory regions and segments in the virtual memory that do not have write permissions (e.g., code segment, kernel space), are stored in NonWritableRegions.

---

* MemSherlock begins monitoring these regions after the frame pointer is set. Therefore, they should not be updated until the function returns

Since functions may be called recursively, MemSherlock maintains a data structure `ProcedureStack`, a stack of `Procedures` whose elements correspond to the user-level functions currently on the execution stack. Maintaining this stack is necessary to ensure that MemSherlock can monitor local variables correctly when there are several instances of the same function on the execution stack.

These key data structures facilitate the MemSherlock debugging process. In particular, state maintenance actions update the data structures so that the current state of execution is reflected accurately, while memory checking actions ensure that only legitimate write instructions are executed.

10.3.2.2 State Maintenance

It is necessary to maintain the list of active memory regions and their current write sets at any time of program execution. MemSherlock updates its internal data structures at certain runtime events. For example, when a function call is made, the local variables of the function are added to the list of monitored memory regions and their write sets are generated accordingly.

We discuss the critical events and the corresponding state maintenance in detail below:

Pointer Value Updates and Pointer-Type Function Arguments: When an update to a pointer variable p with the address of a `MemoryRegion` m is detected, the MemSherlock debugging agent first determines the new referent object by searching through `ActiveMemoryRegions`. The referent pointer of m is set accordingly if m is found. If the new referent cannot be matched to a monitored memory region, this implies that there could be a potential dangling pointer or misuse of a pointer.

Function Calls and Returns: When a user-defined function is called, MemSherlock pushes a `Procedure` record associated with it onto `ProcedureStack`. MemSherlock then calculates the real addresses of its local variables by adding their offsets to the current frame pointer. The function's return address, the saved frame pointer, and any padded regions between local variables are then added to `NonWritableRegions`, enabling MemSherlock to capture illegal writes to these regions. (Note that the static analysis performed in the pre-debugging phase does not provide sufficient information about these memory regions.) This is especially useful in detecting stack buffer overruns. When the function returns, MemSherlock pops the corresponding `Procedure` record off `ProcedureStack`, and removes its return address, the saved frame pointer, and the padded regions from `NonWritableRegions`.

Heap Memory Management: When a heap memory region is allocated using the `malloc` family of functions, MemSherlock creates a new `MemoryRegion` object and adds it to `ActiveMemoryRegions`. In addition, any memory manager meta data adjacent to the block is added to `NonWritableRegions`. This not only ensures that the meta data is protected, but also facilitates the detection of heap buffer overruns.

When `free` is invoked on a memory region, MemSherlock first checks that the region is in `ActiveMemoryRegions`. If so, MemSherlock frees the region, and removes the corresponding `MemoryRegion` record from `ActiveMemoryRegions`. Otherwise, MemSherlock generates an error message, indicating that the program has tried to free a non-heap allocated region, which might indicate a double free error.

10.3.2.3 Memory Checking

When a memory write to an address `addr` occurs, MemSherlock searches through `ActiveMemoryRegions` to look for a `MemoryRegion` that *covers* addr (i.e., addr falls in this `MemoryRegion`). Moreover, MemSherlock also searches for pointer-type `MemoryRegions` pointing to such a `MemoryRegion`. Once found, MemSherlock verifies that the write instruction's address is in the WS of this `MemoryRegion`, or in one of the memory regions whose pointers point to it. Note that this implies that the memory region m for a pointer-type variable p can be verified in two ways. If the destination address is in m then the membership is checked for WS(p). If the destination address is in the referent object's memory region then the membership is checked for WS(ref(p)).

If MemSherlock cannot find a `MemoryRegion` corresponding to the write destination address `addr`, it will perform the same search in `NonWritableRegions`. If a match is found, this means the write instruction is trying to corrupt a non-writable region, and MemSherlock emits an error message.

10.3.2.4 Generating Vulnerability Information

Unlike most other memory level monitoring tools, MemSherlock detects memory corruption at the time of memory write. This enables MemSherlock to pinpoint the exact statement in the source code responsible for the corruption. In many cases, just knowing the point of corruption is sufficient to determine the vulnerability. For example, most programmers look for a buffer overflow when the problem statement is a `strcpy`. However, to provide more vulnerability information, MemSherlock incorporates the taint analysis from TaintCheck [25] to check if the value written to the destination address during the corruption is tainted. If so, MemSherlock performs additional analysis to report the source of the tainted data (e.g., network packet) and a dynamic slice of the source code that propagated the tainted data. The programmer can see how the tainted data is introduced and causes the vulnerability to be exploited.

As described earlier, MemSherlock keeps a close watch on memory regions and operations performed on them. In return, MemSherlock can determine the memory region being modified and the program variable to which the memory region corresponds. It also determines if the memory region was updated through the use of the variable or dereferencing of a pointer variable. This greatly simplifies the analysis of the vulnerability, since the programmer does not have to iterate through the call stack and pointer aliasing to determine the original memory region being modified.

When generating the output of the analysis, we can highlight the statements in the source code (through the translation from instructions to file name and line number pairs), and associate these statements with the memory regions involved in the exploit. Figure 10.5 in Section 10.3.3 shows an example of the output, using one of our test cases.

10.3.3 Automated Debugging Using MemSherlock

MemSherlock can provide crucial information about exploited vulnerabilities to aid programmers in debugging, signature generation, patching, etc. To demonstrate the depth of information MemSherlock can provide, we use the vulnerability output from Null HTTP as an example.

Figure 10.4 shows the error message displayed by MemSherlock when NullHTTP's heap is overflowed. The first paragraph displays the location of the error; both the instruction number and the source file location which states that line 108 was responsible for this memory corruption. The error message then provides the destination memory address and the memory region to which it corresponds. In this particular example, since the destination address is the meta data of the heap memory region, the heap memory region that was allocated is shown rather than the meta data's.

Knowing the corruption point, a programmer easily can guess that the `recv` function call is responsible for the overflow. What is not apparent from this information alone is that the reason the buffer is overflowed is not due to an oversize packet alone. The size of the overflowed buffer

```
--20361--
--20361-- Error type: Heap Buffer Overflow
--20361-- Dest Addr: 3AB3E360
--20361-- IP: 0x804E5C7: ReadPOSTData (http.c:108)
--20361-- Dest address resolved to:
--20361-- Global variable "heap var"
          @ 3AB3E280 (size: 224)
--20361--
--20361-- Memory allocated by 0x804E531:
          ReadPOSTData (http.c:100)
--20361--
--20361-- TAINTED destination 3AB3E360
--20361-- Fully tainted from:
--20361--      0x804E5C7: ReadPOSTData (http.c:108)
--20361--
--20361-- TAINTED size used during allocation
--20361-- Tainted from:
--20361--      0x804E456: ReadPOSTData (http.c:100)
--20361--      0x804FBB5: read_header (http.c:153)
--20361--      0x805121B: sgets (server.c:211)
--20361--
```

Fig. 10.4 A typical error message from the debugger

is calculated from user data, and a negative value provided by the user can cause the buffer to be smaller than expected. The error message states that the buffer was allocated from line 100 in http.c and also performs taint analysis on both the array and the size value that was used during allocation.

MemSherlock produces enough information to detail this vulnerability. A more intuitive display of the vulnerability can be generated by extracting a dynamic slice of the program and presenting it as a graph. Figure 10.5 shows the fragments from the source code, highlighting the statements involved in the propagation of the tainted data. It includes the critical program steps from the time when the malicious input is introduced to the time of memory corruption.

As highlighted in Figure 10.5, the function read_header calls sgets, passing its local variable line as an argument. The sgets function taints the memory region belonging to line through the recv library function call. Note that the argument used while calling recv is buffer. This assignment is captured during the function call to sgets and the connection is shown clearly in Figure 10.5. Once sgets returns, the value in line is converted into a decimal number at line 153 in read_header. This statement propagates the taint into another heap memory region belonging to conn[sid].dat->in_ContentLength. The dotted line between the two memory regions shows the taint propagation. Later, the tainted heap memory region is used as the size argument in ReadPOSTData at line 100, where the calloc function call at line 100 creates a new memory region. (Note that TaintCheck itself cannot capture the connection between the tainted size argument and the newly created memory region. MemSherlock uses a Valgrind client call inserted by *SrcRewrite* to capture it.) Finally, with the call to recv at line 108, ReadPOSTData taints the newly created memory region and also overflows it at the same time, for which the debugger issues the error message.

As illustrated in Figure 10.5, MemSherlock can simplify the security debugging process greatly by providing the information on how a memory corruption vulnerability is exploited, and thus significantly reduce the time and effort required in understanding and fixing unknown memory corruption vulnerabilities.

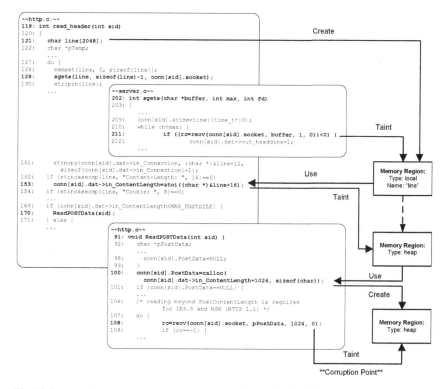

Fig. 10.5 A graphical representation of the vulnerability in Null HTTP

10.4 CBones: Security Debugging Using Program Structural Constraints

A vulnerability debugger first needs to determine the point of memory corruption. Where MemSherlock relied on observing memory operations, CBones relies on verifiable invariants during runtime. A process's virtual address space is divided and used according to the operating system and the compiler with which the program was compiled. Furthermore, usually each segment of memory is logically divided into smaller chunks that represent memory objects in the program or metadata used by the compiler to determine the program state. CBones uses the structural properties that these memory objects or metadata always satisfy to derive program structural constraints for each program. These constraints can be verified at runtime to ensure that the program complies with the assumptions made by the operating system and/or the compiler. Violations of these constraints thus indicate the existence of a security vulnerability.

CBones uses a combination of static analysis and dynamic monitoring to accomplish its goal. Static analysis is used to determine structural constraints for a given program automatically. These constraints are then passed to the dynamic monitoring component which verifies whether the constraints are satisfied during execution. Any violation of these constraints signals a misbehavior, which indicates an attack or a bug.

As a proof-of-concept implementation we focus our attention on Linux operating systems running applications written in C and compiled with the GCC compiler. Our set of constraints include those generated for the operating system and compiler, and some others generated for the standard

Fig. 10.6 Security debugging process with CBones

C library. It is worth mentioning that similar structural constraints can be generated for different platforms, compilers, etc. Indeed, the proposed method is applicable to a broad range of operating systems and compilers despite our choice in this study.

Figure 10.6 shows the security debugging process used by CBones. First, the binary executable is analyzed by the Constraint Extractor to determine the structural constraints. Then the set of constraints are passed to the Monitoring Agent along with the program executable. The Monitoring Agent executes the program and checks for any constraint violations, replaying previously captured attacks exploiting one or more security vulnerabilities of the target program. If a structural constraint is violated, the execution is halted and an error message is generated. The error message states the violated constraint, outputs the program state, and indicates the instruction responsible for the violation.

In the following we first present structural constraints used by CBones, and then show how these structural constraints can be used in security debugging.

10.4.1 Program Structural Constraints

The Linux executable file format ELF (Executable and Linkable Format) [10] has a typical virtual memory layout as shown in Figure 10.7. Although some of the addresses can be user-specified, by default, the program code, data, stack and other memory segments are located as depicted in the figure and the ordering of these segments are fixed. For example, the stack segment is always at a higher address than the heap and the code segments, and the heap is always higher than the code and the data segments. Therefore, we present the program structural constraints with respect to these segments, namely the stack, the heap and the data segments. In the following we present a subset of the constraints used by CBones. The interested reader can find the full list and implementation details in [17].

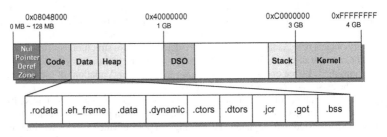

Fig. 10.7 An example of an ELF program runtime process memory layout

10.4.1.1 Stack Constraints

The stack is perhaps the most commonly attacked segment of the virtual memory. For each procedure called, an activation record of an appropriate size is pushed onto the stack. Figure 10.8 illustrates a simple program and a simplified stack layout after function main calls cal_Sum, which in turn calls get_Num. The figure also shows the various logical subdivisions in the activation record. For x86 architectures, the special register $ebp points to the return address in the activation record of the last function called. *Arguments* hold the values of the arguments that the caller passes to the callee when making the function call. *Return Address* is where the execution will return once the function completes execution. *Previous Frame Pointer* is the saved $ebp register value. When the function returns, the $ebp value is restored to point back to the previous activation record of the caller function. Sometimes additional registers can be pushed onto the stack to free up more registers for the current function. These registers are saved in the *Saved Registers* area and are restored upon function return. The rest of the activation record holds the local variables of the function.

The return address has been the most frequent target for attackers, however, a recent attack trend study [22] shows that other elements in the stack (e.g., frame pointer, saved registers) also have been exploited [8, 9, 27]. Such stack-based exploits require illegal modification of the stack structure. So, security bugs in a program can be detected by monitoring the structural changes of the stack during program execution. Next, we present the program structural constraints for the stack region.

Caller-callee relationship constraint: When a function A (caller) calls another function B (callee), we say that A and B have a caller-callee relationship. A given function generally calls a small number of other functions. We can find out all possible caller-callee relationship between functions, and represent such relationships in a *call-graph*, in which all functions are represented as nodes, and a possible caller-callee relationship is represented as a directed edge from the caller to the callee. The constraint here is that, at runtime, every function call should represent an edge in this call-graph.

Return address constraint: Return address is a critical element in an activation record, since it changes a program's control flow. A valid return address should always point to an executable region such as the code section or the executable section of the dynamically loaded libraries.

Frame pointer constraint: The frame pointer ($ebp register) is a reference point for the stack frame and is used as a base address to access memory objects in the stack that are defined as offsets from this pointer. The invariant is that the value of the frame pointer should not be changed during a function's execution once it has been set in the function's prologue. The frame pointer is changed at a function's epilogue (leave instruction) according to the IA-32 instruction set manual.

Saved registers constraint: Saved registers generally hold function pointers or values that refer to memory objects in a program's runtime process. Although saved registers are not critical to the program's control flow, they can be used as a bridge to a successful exploit. For example, one of the data attacks in [8] uses an address register ($esi) to execute an attacker-provided command. The saved registers constraint is that their values should not be changed during a function execution once they are set at the function's prologue.

Saved frame pointer constraint: Upon a function call, the caller's frame pointer is saved in the callee's activation record. Since the frame pointer is held in the $ebp register, the constraint for saved registers applies directly. However, due to its special use, we found more constraints for the saved frame pointer. First, it should point to a higher memory address than where it is stored. Second, since a frame pointer actually points to the saved frame pointer in the activation record, one should be able to walk the stack (following the saved registers as a linked list), and traverse every activation record. Finally, at the top of the stack, the saved frame pointer for function main (or the alternate entry function) should be NULL.

10.4.1.2 Heap Constraints

A powerful feature of the C language is its dynamic memory management. Generally, dynamic memory is manipulated via the `malloc` family of library functions. There are various dynamic memory management schemes, Lea [20], Hoard [1], and OpenBsd [26] to name a few. In this paper, we follow Lea's scheme which is used in Linux systems to derive our heap based program structural constraints. Lea's scheme uses boundary tags to manage allocated and freed memory chunks. Each memory block is preceded by a small bookkeeping region that stores the information about the block in use or in the case of available blocks, the next available block. Figure 10.9 shows an example heap structure. A boundary tag of allocated chunk (e.g., `DATA(A)`) includes information about its size and indicates whether the chunk is in-use with the last bit of the size field (`PINUSE_BIT`). If a chunk is free, the tag includes pointers to the previous and the next free chunks.

Memory allocation/deallocation requests constraint: Since the structure of heap is changed dynamically by `malloc` related function calls, the first thing we need to check is whether such memory allocation/deallocation requests are made from valid locations. The idea is similar to the caller-callee relationship constraint in the stack, since we verify valid structural changes in a heap using caller-callee relationships for `malloc` family of function calls.

Boundary tag (metadata) constraint: Boundary tags, or hereafter referred to as metadata, are used and manipulated by the library that implements the memory management scheme. In our case, the metadata should only be modified through legitimate calls to `malloc` family of functions.

Allocated memory chunks link constraint: The metadata allows the memory manager to traverse the list of allocated or available memory blocks as a linked list. Therefore, a verification program should be able to traverse the same list using the metadata. A broken link between allocated memory chunks indicates the corruption of the heap structure.

10.4.1.3 Data Constraints

Although there are not many structural changes in the data section, we have found that some of the structural characteristics can help detect security bugs.

Shared library function pointers constraint: The global offset table (GOT) is a table of library function pointers. These function pointers initially point to the dynamic library loader and are updated via the loader when a library is loaded at runtime. Various attacks have tried to exploit these function pointers (e.g., [5]). The structural constraint is very simple: the library function pointers should point to library functions.

10.4.2 Security Debugging through Constraints Verification

As discussed earlier, CBones performs security debugging by verifying whether program structural constraints are violated at run time. To do so successfully, we have to answer two important questions related to the verification of these constraints: "what to verify", and "when to verify". We have described the program structural constraints in the previous subsection, which answered the first question. In this subsection, we answer the second question, i.e., when to verify.

We first introduce some terms to facilitate our explanation. Most structural constraints state that a memory region should be constant. Obviously, we need to clarify the time frame during which such a constraint is valid. We define the *lifetime* of a memory region to be the duration from the time when the memory region is set for the current context, to the time when the memory region is discarded or released. Take for example an activation record in the stack. We described that the return address and the saved registers are structural invariants and should be constant throughout the execution of the function. The lifetime of the memory region holding a saved register does not start at function call time, but rather after the function prologue has pushed the register value onto the stack and ends when the function call returns. A metadata's lifetime starts with the dynamic memory allocation and ends with the deallocation of the same memory region. For a data constraint, the lifetime of the .ctors and .dtors segments starts with program execution and ends at program termination.

Our second term describes the program state. A program is said to be in a *transient state w.r.t. a structural constraint* if the memory region related to the structural constraint is being modified. For example, consider a heap memory region allocated in a program. The program is in a transient state w.r.t. the memory region from the time when a malloc family of functions is called to its return. In general, for a heap related structural constraint, this transient time frame is the period from the call to a malloc family of functions to the function return. For a stack related structural constraint, this time frame includes the period from the time a function call occurs to the time the function prologue sets up the activation record.

Most of the constraints are based on memory segments that are dynamic. The stack changes with every function call/return, and the heap is modified with every memory allocation/deallocation. In theory, we can verify all the structural constraints continuously at every instruction. Indeed, any structural constraint that relies on a specific memory region can be checked at any given time, provided the program is not in a transient state w.r.t. that constraint. Such an approach will introduce substantial overhead, which is prohibitive in practice. On the other hand, the structural constraints related to a memory region must be checked at least before the memory region becomes inaccessible, so that potential violation of structural constraints will not be missed.

A simple solution is to perform *coarse-grained* constraint verification. That is, to verify the structural constraints before function returns and memory deallocations, since both the activation record for the returning function and the metadata of the dynamic memory region will become inaccessible after these actions. This allows us to capture violations of program structural constraints (as long as the exploit does not "fix" such violations). However, we will not be able to pinpoint the instruction that causes the constraint violation. Certainly, this is highly undesirable in security debugging.

In order to address the dilemma between unacceptable performance overhead and inaccuracy in identifying the constraint violations, CBones uses a two-stage approach. In the first stage, CBones narrows the location of a constraint violation point down to a single function call, and then in the second stage, it determines precisely the constraint violation point.

Specifically, in the first stage, CBones is executed in the coarse-grained debugging mode, where the CBones monitoring agent verifies the structural constraints before function returns and memory deallocations. CBones then identifies the function call after which a constraint violation is detected. CBones is then re-executed with the same target program and input for the second time to start the second stage. In order to obtain more information and provide the instruction responsible for the corruption, in the second stage CBones switches to a fine-grained debugging mode when it reaches the function call identified in the first stage. CBones then monitors all the memory writes during the function call. If a memory write instruction causes the constraints to be violated, CBones raises a flag and outputs the instruction attempting to corrupt the memory. As discussed earlier, the fine-grained debugging mode incurs high performance overheads. CBones works around this problem by only performing fine-grained monitoring during the function call identified in the first stage.

10.4.3 Extracting Constraints

Stack constraints rely on the organization of the activation records of the call stack. For each function, the function's name and address are extracted from the debugging information. A function's activation record size depends on its local variables and the number of registers saved on the stack. The list and size of local variables are extracted from debugging information as well. In order to find the number of saved registers, the application binary is disassembled, and each function's prologue is checked to see if it is followed by register pushes onto the stack. Static analysis of binary code is used also in determining caller-callee relationships.

Data constraints rely on the heap metadata. The size of the metadata is fixed and its location is determined at runtime when memory is allocated and deallocated. Data Constraints rely on fixed sections, whose location and size are available in the compiled binary.

10.4.4 Runtime Monitoring

The CBones *Monitoring Agent* is responsible for verifying the program structural constraints and reporting any violations. Once again we use Valgrind to implement our tool. The Monitoring Agent uses some internal data structures to store the procedure information provided by the Constraint Extractor and to keep program state during debugging. A Procedure data structure is created for every entry in the input file and a CallStack stores activation records during the runtime. The Monitoring Agent also keeps another data structure ChunkList to track the dynamically allocated memory regions.

The Monitoring Agent uses a procedure called cb_check_all_constraints to verify all program structural constraints that are available. As discussed earlier, we cannot verify whether a structural constraint is violated when the program is in transient state w.r.t. this constraint. Since the only times when such cases may happen is when the target program makes a function call or a call to a malloc family of functions, in coarse-grained debugging mode the Monitoring Agent captures function calls to validate the structural constraints. Once the program leaves its *transient* state, the Monitoring Agent calls cb_check_all_constraints to verify all the remaining structural constraints. Moreover, the Monitoring Agent marks a "safe point" if no constraint violation is detected. The last "safe point" before the constraint violation will be used in stage 2 as the indication to switch to the fine-grained debugging mode.

In the following we list the events of interest and the actions taken by the Monitoring Agent.

Function calls: The Monitoring Agent handles function calls in several stages. Initially, when a jump due to a call instruction is captured, the Monitoring Agent determines the caller and the callee and verifies the caller-callee relationship constraint. This constraint is checked only for client program functions and not the library functions. The second stage occurs when the callee sets its frame pointer. The Monitoring Agent creates a new activation record for the callee and adds it to the current thread's CallStack. The alignment of the frame pointer is checked also. The third stage only applies to procedures that save registers in their activation record. Once all the registers are pushed onto the stack, a snapshot of the invariant region in the activation record is taken and stored in the activation record. Since no further changes to the invariant region is expected, the program is no longer in its transient state. The Monitoring Agent calls cb_check_all_constraints to verify the other structural constraints, and marks a "safe point" if there is no constraint violation.

Function returns: When a procedure is returning, the Monitoring Agent captures the jump due to a ret instruction and verifies that the return address is a valid return address for the returning procedure. A function epilogue contains, at the very least, a leave and a ret instruction. The leave instruction, which precedes the ret, restores all the saved registers. Therefore when the Monitoring Agent captures a function return, the registers, including the frame pointer, already are restored to the caller's values. Nevertheless, the activation record of the callee still is intact and can be examined. The Monitoring Agent verifies that the invariant region of the activation record is intact and removes the activation record of the returning function from the current thread's CallStack. It then calls cb_check_all_constraints and marks the return address as a "safe point".

malloc/free calls: The Monitoring Agent intercepts malloc family of function calls via wrapper functions. These functions allow the Monitoring Agent to perform bookkeeping on dynamically allocated memory regions. For each newly allocated memory, the Monitoring Agent first calls malloc to allocate the memory, and then creates a new chunk and add it to ChunkList. Two additional checks verify that the heap boundary constraint and the alignment constraint are satisfied. When a free call is intercepted, the Monitoring Agent first verifies that the metadata is intact. It then calls free and finally removes the chunk corresponding to the memory from ChunkList. During deallocation, the Monitoring Agent simply calls cb_check_all_constraints to verify that the metadata is intact. This is possible since the Monitoring Agent actually determines when to deallocate the memory, and hence the program is not in a transient state until it does.

Memory writes: When running in the fine-grained debugging mode in the second stage, the Monitoring Agent captures all memory writes by instrumenting the binary code. If the destination address belongs to any of the invariant regions in stack or heap, a flag is raised to mark the instruction attempting to violate the corresponding structural constraint. Capturing memory writes is not trivial, since memory can be updated through system calls and kernel functions. The Monitoring Agent's current implementation captures system calls and performs the necessary checks before the memory is updated. In one of the test cases, a large memory copy operation is performed by manipulating the page table through the use of kernel functions. Since Valgrind cannot trace into kernel space, such a memory modification would go unnoticed. This means that the current implementation of CBones would not be able to determine the instruction responsible for the corruption. It should be noted that this does not mean that the attack is unnoticed.

10.4.5 Security Debugging Using CBones

Sumus [31] is a game server with a stack overflow vulnerability. Figure 10.10(a) shows the snippet of the source code responsible for this vulnerability. The boldface line copies the contents of p1 into the local array tmdCad. p1 points to the string after GET in the HTTP request. The programmer assumes that this input string has a small size. An attacker may exploit this assumption by sending a message longer than the size of tmpCad. At first glance, this looks like a trivial stack overflow; the overflow should corrupt the local variables and then the return address. However, as the buffer is overflowed, the instruction first overwrites faltan and then kk, which is actually used to index tmpCad. With a carefully designed input, the overwrite skips to the formal arguments' memory region, not overwriting the return address. This behavior of the attack makes it much more difficult and time-consuming to debug manually. Another important note is that this attack cannot be captured by systems looking for control-hijacking attacks alone, since the return address remains intact.

For comparison purposes, we first ran Sumus under *gdb*. However, *gdb* was able to capture the program's crash only after RespondeHTTPPendiente calls the send function (not shown in figure). Therefore, it is non-trivial to locate the corrupting instruction using gdb, if not entirely impossible.

We then ran Sumus under CBones which was able to detect the exploit and determine the corrupting instruction fully automatically. Although this attack does not corrupt the invariant region of RespondeHTTPPendiente, it does corrupt the invariant region of the caller function main. Therefore, CBones was able to detect a violation of the caller-callee relationship constraint in the

| Application | Vuln. | Description | Captured? | |
Name	Type		MemSherlock	CBones
Streamripper	S	Winamp plugin for recording	N/A	Yes
GHTTP	S	A small HTTP server	Yes	Yes
Icecast	S	A mp3 broadcast server	Yes	Yes
Sumus	S	A game server for 'mus'	Yes	Yes
Monit	S	Multi-purpose anomaly detector	Yes	Yes
Newspost	S	Automatic news posting	Yes	Yes
Prozilla	S	A download accelerator for Linux	No	Yes
NullHTTP	H	Null HTTP, HTTP server	Yes	Yes
Xtelnet	H	A telnet server	Yes	Yes
Wsmp3	H	Web server with mp3 broadcasting	Yes	Yes
Power	F	UPS monitoring utility	Yes	Yes
OpenVMPS	F	Open source VLan management policy server	Yes	Yes

Table 10.1 List of test applications. Type abbreviations: (S)tack overflow, (H)eap overflow and (F)ormat string.

first stage. In the second stage, CBones started the fine-grained debugging mode from the last "safe point" (0x8050136), detected the (illegal) memory write into the return address in the stack frame of the `main` function and raised a flag accordingly. Figure 10.10(b) shows the output of CBones. The error message clearly states that a memory write to an invariant region has occurred and displays the instruction number responsible for the memory write.

10.5 Comparison

In the previous two sections we have shown how MemSherlock and CBones can aid in debugging vulnerabilities. To show the effectiveness of the two methodologies used by the two systems, we used 12 real-world applications with a variety of vulnerabilities, along with the attack programs that exploit these vulnerable applications. Table 10.1 lists the applications, the kind of vulnerability they have and whether or not they were detected and analyzed by our systems successfully. Seven of the test cases have stack buffer overflow vulnerabilities, three have heap overflow vulnerabilities, and the other two have format string vulnerabilities. It is worth noting that other types of memory corruption attacks rely on these three vulnerabilities. For example, return-to-library attacks are a variation of stack overflows, whereas the malloc-free attack relies on overflowing a heap buffer and corrupting the meta data used by the memory manager.

Table 10.1 shows that both MemSherlock and CBones are capable of detecting memory corruption attacks but more importantly they do so at the point of memory corruption. This information is very useful and it is sufficient in most cases. It should be noted that the reason for MemSherlock failing to detect the Prozilla attack is because the memory write operation was not observed. Instead of using memory operations, a large copy of a page is performed by manipulating page tables. This is simply a shortcoming of the implementation, therefore, we can claim that all the attacks in our test cases were detected and the vulnerabilities were analyzed successfully.

Despite having similar results, these two systems have very different characteristics. MemSherlock is capable of producing very detailed vulnerability information and is able to track even tainted data to its origin. However, it is a complex system and needs to consider a number of corner cases. This leads to a number of false positives and negatives and it is unclear whether they can be eliminated completely. CBones on the other hand uses a set of constraints that need to be satisfied for successful execution. Therefore, theoretically it is possible to eliminate all false positives. However, the structural constraints are not complete in the sense that there are certain types of attacks that still can go unnoticed. In order to improve CBones, one could try to find more constraints that potentially could detect other attacks. Care must be taken when choosing the constraints as they may not be verifiable easily.

10.6 Conclusion

We have demonstrated the feasibility of automatic vulnerability analysis tools and shown how they can assist a security expert in analyzing the vulnerability. Not only do these systems alleviate the burden from the security analyst, but they can be used also as foundations towards building fully automated patch generators or vulnerability based signature generators. These tools bridge the important gap between tools that rely on vulnerability information and tools that detect attacks and thereby detect the presence of a vulnerability.

The two systems we have introduced work towards the same end using different methodologies. They each have their strengths and weaknesses. MemSherlock provides critical information for unknown memory corruption vulnerabilities, including: (1) the corruption point in the source code, (2) the slice of source code that helps the malicious input to reach the corruption point and (3) the description of how the malicious input exploits the unknown vulnerability. Its shortcomings are the performance overhead and complexity. The flexibility of the C programming language requires many corner cases to be handled. It may be impossible to find elegant solutions for each case which may result in possible false positives or negatives.

CBones automatically extracts program structural constraints from program binaries and analyzes security bugs in vulnerable programs. Compared with the previous approaches, CBones provides several benefits: (1) full automation (neither training nor manual specification is required), (2) no need for source code analysis or instrumentation, (3) no requirement of additional hardware support and (4) no false alarms. Using program structural constraints provides an analysis free from false positives. CBones is also an order of magnitude faster than MemSherlock. Despite those advantages, it cannot match the capabilities of MemSherlock and is limited in the types of vulnerabilities it can analyze.

As of this writing, both tools are in their prototype stage. Future work includes revising the implementation to improve performance and the possibility of applying Structural Constraints in the context of detecting unknown exploits.

References

1. E.D. Berger, K.S. McKinley, R.D. Blumofe, and P.R. Wilson. Hoard: A scalable memory allocator for multithreaded applications. In *Ninth International Conference on Architectural Support for Programming Languages and Operating Systems (ASPLOS-IX)*, November 2000.
2. David Brumley, James Newsome, Dawn Song, Hao Wang, and Somesh Jha. Towards automatic generation of vulnerability-based signatures. In *Proceedings of the IEEE Symposium on Security and Privacy*, May 2006.
3. CERT. http://www.cert.org/advisories/CA-2001-19.html.
4. CERT. http://www.cert.org/advisories/CA-2003-04.html.
5. S. Cesare.   Shared library call redirection using elf plt infection, April 2007. http://vx.netlux.org/lib/vsc06.html.
6. H. Chen, D. Dean, and D. Wagner. Model checking one million lines of c code. In *Proceedings of the 11th Annual Network and Distributed System Security Symposium (NDSS)*, February 2004.

7. H. Chen and D. Wagner. MOPS: an infrastructure for examining security properties of software. In *Proceedings of the 9th ACM Conference on Computer and Communications Security (CCS'02)*, November 2002.
8. Shou Chen, Jun Xu, and Emre C. Sezer. Non-control-data attacks are realistic threats. In *Proceedings of 14th USENIX Security Symposium*, 2005.
9. E. Chien and P. Szor. Blended attacks exploits, vulnerabilities and buffer-overflow techniques. In *Techniques in Computer Viruses, Virus Bulletin Conference*, 2002.
10. Tool Interface Standard (TIS) Committee. Executable and linking format (elf) specification, 1995.
11. J. R. Crandall and F. T. Chong. Minos: Control data attack prevention orthogonal to memory model. In *Proceedings of the 37th Annual IEEE/ACM International Symposium on Microarchitecture*, pages 221–232, December 2004.
12. J. R. Crandall, Z. Su, S. F. Wu, and F. T. Chong. On deriving unknown vulnerabilities from zero-day polymorphic and metamorphic worm exploits. In *Proceedings of the 13th ACM Conference on Computer and Communications Security*, pages 235–248, 2005.
13. H. Feng, J. Giffin, Y. Huang, S. Jha, W. Lee, and B. Miller. Formalizingsensitivity in static analysis for intrusion detection. In *Proceedings of the 2004 IEEE Symposium on Security and Privacy*, May 2004.
14. Dawn Song James Newsome, David Brumley. Vulnerability-specific execution filtering for exploit prevention on commodity software. In *Proceedings of the 13th Annual Network and Distributed System Security Symposium (NDSS '06)*, Feb 2006.
15. T. Jim, G. Morrisett, D. Grossman, M. Hicks, J. Cheney, and Y. Wang. Cyclone: A safe dialect of C. In *USENIX Annual Technical Conference*, June 2002.
16. Chongkyung Kil, Jinsuk Jun, Christopher Bookholt, Jun Xu, and Peng Ning. Address space layout permutation (aslp): Towards fine-grained randomization of commodity software. In *Computer Security Applications Conference, 2006. ACSAC '06. 22nd Annual*, pages 339–348, Dec. 2006.
17. Chongkyung Kil, E.C. Sezer, Peng Ning, and Xiaolan Zhang. Automated security debugging using program structural constraints. In *Computer Security Applications Conference, 2007. ACSAC 2007. Twenty-Third Annual*, pages 453–462, Dec. 2007.
18. W. Landi. Undecidability of static analysis. *ACM Letters on Programming Languages and Systems*, 1(4):323–337, December 1992.
19. D. Larochelle and D. Evans. Statically detecting likely buffer overflow vulnerabilities. In *Proceedings of the 10th USENIX Security Symposium*, August 2001.
20. D. Lea. A memory allocator. http://gee.cs.oswego.edu/dl/html/malloc.html.
21. Z. Liang and R. Sekar. Fast and automated generation of attack signatures: a basis for building self-protecting servers. In *Proceedings of the 13th ACM Conference on Computer and Communications Security*, pages 213–222, 2005.
22. NIST national vulerability database. http://nvd.nist.gov/.
23. G. Necula, S. McPeak, and W. Weimer. CCured: Type-safe retrofitting of legacy software. In *Proceedings of the 29th ACM SIGPLAN-SIGACT symposium on Principles of Programming Languages*, pages 128–139, 2002.
24. Nicholas Nethercote. Dynamic binary analysis and instrumentation, 2004. valgrind.org/docs/phd2004.pdf.
25. J. Newsome and D. Song. Dynamic taint analysis for automatic detection, analysis, and signature generation of exploits on commodity software. In *Proceedings of The 12th Annual Network and Distributed System Security Symposium (NDSS '05)*, February 2005.
26. Open group base specifications issue 6, ieee std 1003.1, 2004 edition.
27. The Frame Pointer Overwrite. http://doc.bughunter.net/buffer-overflow/frame-pointer.html.
28. PaX Team. http://pax.grsecurity.net/docs/aslr.txt.
29. G. Ramalingam. The undecidability of aliasing. *ACM Transactions on Programming Languages and Systems*, 16(5):1467–1471, September 1994.
30. Emre C. Sezer, Peng Ning, Chongkyung Kil, and Jun Xu. Memsherlock: An automated debugger for unknown memory corruption vulnerabilities. In *CCS '07: Proceedings of the 14th ACM conference on Computer and communications security*, pages 562–572, New York, NY, USA, 2007. ACM.

31. Sumus vulnerability. Common vulnerabilities and exposures (cve) 2005-1110, April 2005. http://cve.mitre.org/cgi-bin/cvename.cgi?name=CVE-2005-1110.
32. H. Wang, C. Guo, D. Simon, and A. Zugenmaier. Shield: Vulnerability-driven network filters for preventing known vulnerability exploits. In *Proceedings of ACM SIGCOMM*, August 2004.
33. Pin Zhou, Wei Liu, Long Fei, Shan Lu, Feng Qin, Yuanyuan Zhou, Samuel Midkiff, and Josep Torrellas. Accmon: Automatically detecting memory-related bugs via program counter-based invariants. In *MICRO 37: Proceedings of the 37th annual International Symposium on Microarchitecture*, pages 269–280, Washington, DC, USA, 2004. IEEE Computer Society.

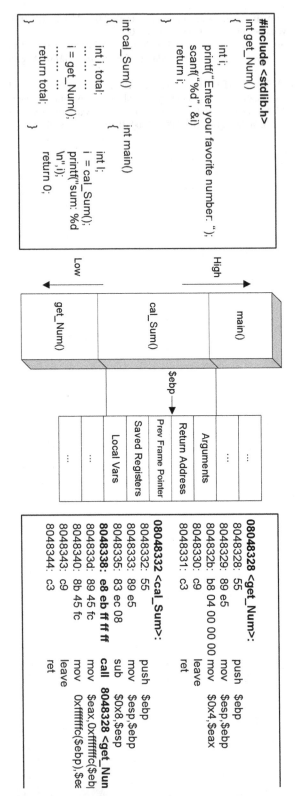

Fig. 10.8 An example of stack structure and caller-callee relationship

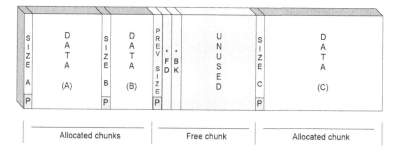

Fig. 10.9 An example of heap structure

```
void RespondeHTTPPendiente( int Pos )
{
int j ,kk ,faltan ;
char tmpCad[100], *p1, *p2 ;

 ...
Buffer[400] = 0 ;
p1 = strstr( Buffer, "GET" ) ;
if( p1 == NULL ) p1 = strstr( Buffer, "Get" ) ;
if( p1 == NULL ) p1 = strstr( Buffer, "get" ) ;
if( p1 != NULL ) {
  j = 5 ;
  kk = 0 ;
  if( j < strlen(p1) )
    while ( p1[j] != ' ' && p1[j] )
      tmpCad[kk++] = p1[j++] ; ← Security bug
    tmpCad[kk] = 0 ;
  }
  ...
}
```

```
(1) --4169-- Checking call from 805180B to function RespondeHTTPPendiente(8050136)
(1) --4169-- Checking constraints at 805180B
(1) --4169-- Call: Last safe point is 8050136
 ...         ...         ...
(1) --4169-- Checking memory write to AFEFE8B8 of size 4
(1) --4169-- $ebp setting for RespondeHTTPPendiente - ebp: AFEFE8B8
 ...         ...         ...
 ...         ...         ...
(1) --4169-- Error: Writing to stack frame of main from instruction 805020A
(1) ==4169==    at 0x805020A: RespondeHTTPPendiente (sumus.c:1308)
(1) ==4169==    by 0x805180F: main (sumus.c:1666)
```

```
80501f0:    75 02             jne   80501f4 <RespondeHTTPPendiente+0xbe>
80501f2:    eb 24             jmp   8050218 <RespondeHTTPPendiente+0xe2>
  tmpCad[kk++] = p1[j++] ;
80501f4:    8b 45 f0          mov   0xfffffff0($ebp),$eax
 ...
8050208:    8a 00             mov   ($eax),$al
805020a:    88 02             mov   %al,($edx)
805020c:    8d 45 f4          lea   0xfffffff4($ebp),$eax
 ...
8050216:    eb be             jmp   80501d6 <RespondeHTTPPendiente+0xa0>
  tmpCad[kk] = 0 ;
8050218:    8d 85 78 ff ff ff lea   0xffffff78($ebp),$eax
```

(a) Source code   (b) Security bug report

Fig. 10.10 An example of automated bug diagnosis using CBones

Part VI
The Machine Learning Aspect

Part VI
The Vigilant Learning Aspect

Chapter 11
Machine Learning Methods for High Level Cyber Situation Awareness

Thomas G. Dietterich, Xinlong Bao, Victoria Keiser, and Jianqiang Shen

11.1 Introduction

Cyber situation awareness needs to operate at many levels of abstraction. In this chapter, we discuss situation awareness at a very high level—the behavior of desktop computer users. Our goal is to develop an awareness of what desktop users are doing as they work. Such awareness has many potential applications including

- providing assistance to the users themselves,
- providing additional contextual knowledge to lower-level awareness components such as intrusion detection systems, and
- detecting insider attacks.

The work described here grew out of the TaskTracer system, which is a Microsoft Windows add-in that extends the Windows desktop user interface to become a "project-oriented" user interface. The basic hypothesis is that the user's time at the desktop can be viewed as multi-tasking among a set of active projects. TaskTracer attempts to associate project "tags" with each file, folder, web page, email message, and email address that the user accesses. It then exploits these tags to provide project-oriented assistance to the user.

To do this, TaskTracer inserts instrumentation into many Windows programs including Microsoft Outlook, Word, Excel, Powerpoint, Internet Explorer, and Windows Explorer (the file browser). This instrumentation captures events at a semantically-meaningful level (e.g., open excel file, navigate to web page, reply to email message) rather than at the level of system calls or

Thomas G. Dietterich
Oregon State University, 1148 Kelley Engineering Center, Corvallis, OR, 97331 USA, e-mail:
tgd@cs.orst.edu

Xinlong Bao
Oregon State University, 1148 Kelley Engineering Center, Corvallis, OR, 97331 USA, e-mail:
bao@eecs.oregonstate.edu

Victoria Keiser
Oregon State University, 1148 Kelley Engineering Center, Corvallis, OR, 97331 USA, e-mail:
baileyvi@eecs.oregonstate.edu

Jianqiang Shen
Oregon State University, 1148 Kelley Engineering Center, Corvallis, OR, 97331 USA, e-mail:
shenj@eecs.oregonstate.edu

S. Jajodia et al., (eds.), *Cyber Situational Awareness*,
Advances in Information Security 46, DOI 10.1007/978-1-4419-0140-8_11,
© Springer Science+Business Media, LLC 2010

keystrokes. This instrumentation also allows TaskTracer to capture so-called "provenance events" that record information flow between one object and another, such as copy-paste, attach file to email message, download file from web page, copy file from flash drive, and so on. These provenance events allow us to automatically discover and track user workflows.

This chapter begins with a description of the TaskTracer system, the instrumented events that it collects, and the benefits it provides to the user. We then discuss two forms of situation awareness that this enables. The first is to track the current project of the user. TaskTracer applies a combination of user interface elements and machine learning methods to do this. The second is to discover and track the workflows of the user. We apply graph mining methods to discover workflows and a form of hidden Markov model to track those workflows. The chapter concludes with a discussion of future directions for high level cyber situation awareness.

11.2 The TaskTracer System

The goal of the TaskTracer system is to support multi-tasking and interruption recovery for desktop users. Several studies (e.g., [7]) have documented that desktop knowledge workers engage in continual multi-tasking. In one study that we performed [3], we found that the median time to an interruption is around 20 minutes and the median time to return back to the interrupted project is around 15 minutes. Often, many hours or days can pass between periods when the user works on a particular project. After these longer interruptions, the user requires even more assistance to find the relevant documents, web pages, and email messages.

To provide assistance to knowledge workers, the TaskTracer attempts to associate all files, folders, email messages, email contacts, and web pages with user-declared projects. We will refer to these various data objects as "resources". To use TaskTracer, the user begins by defining an initial hierarchy of projects. To be most effective, a project should be an ongoing activity such as teaching a class ("CS534"), working on a grant proposal ("CALO"), or performing an ongoing job responsibility ("Annual performance reviews"). Projects at this level of abstraction will last long enough to provide payoff to the user for the work of defining the project and helping with the resource-to-project associations.

11.2.1 Tracking the User's Current Project

Once the projects are defined, TaskTracer attempts to infer the user's current project as the user works. Three methods are employed to do this. First, the user can directly declare to the system his or her current project. Two user interface components support this. One is a drop-down combo-box in the Windows TaskBar that allows the user to type a project name (with auto-completion) or select a project (with arrow keys or the mouse) to declare as the current project (see Figure 11.1). Another user interface component is a pop-up menu (accessed using the keystroke Control + Backquote) of the 14 most recently used projects (see Figure 11.2). This supports rapid switching between the set of current projects.

The second way that TaskTracer tracks the current project of the user is to apply machine learning methods to detect project switches based on desktop events. This will be discussed below.

The third method for tracking the user's current project is based on applying machine learning methods to tag incoming email messages by project. When the user opens an email message, TaskTracer automatically switches the current project to be the project of the email message. Furthermore, if the user opens or saves an email attachment, the associated file is also associated with that project. The user can, of course, correct tags if they are incorrect, and this provides feedback to the email tagger. We will discuss the email tagger in more detail in the next section.

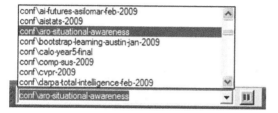

Fig. 11.1 The Windows TaskBar component for declaring the user's current project.

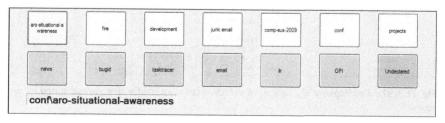

Fig. 11.2 The pop-up menu that shows the 14 most recently-used projects. The mouse and arrow keys can be used to select the project to switch to.

TaskTracer exploits its awareness of the current project to associate each new resource with the user's current project. For example, if the user creates a new Word file or visits a new web page, that file or web page is associated with the current project. This concept of automatically associating resources with a current project (or activity) was pioneered in the UMEA system [9].

11.2.2 Assisting the User

How does all of this project association and tagging support multi-tasking and interruption recovery? TaskTracer provides several user interface components to do this. The most important one is the TaskExplorer (see Figure 11.3). The left panel of TaskExplorer shows the hierarchy of projects defined by the user. The right panel shows all of the resources associated with the selected project (sorted, by default, according to recency). The user can double click on any of these items to open them. Hence, the most natural way for the user to recover from an interruption is to go to TaskExplorer, select a project to resume (in the left panel), and then double-click on the relevant resources (in the right panel) to open them. A major advantage of TaskExplorer is that it pulls together all of the resources relevant to a project. In current desktop software such as Windows, the relevant resources are scattered across a variety of user interfaces including (a) email folders, (b) email contacts, (c) file system folders, (d) browser history and favorites, (e) global recent documents (in the Start menu), and (f) recent documents in each Office application. Pulling all of these resources into a single place provides a unified view of the project.

The second way that TaskTracer supports multi-tasking and interruption recovery is by making Outlook project-centered. TaskTracer implements email tagging by using the Categories feature of Outlook. This (normally hidden) feature of Outlook allows the user to define tags and associate them with email messages. The TaskTracer email tagger utlizes this mechanism by defining one category tag for each project. TaskTracer also defines a "search folder" for each tag. A search folder is another Outlook feature that is normally hidden. It allows the user to define a "view" (in the database sense) over his or her email. This view looks like a folder containing email messages

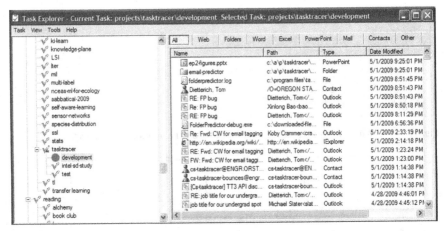

Fig. 11.3 The TaskExplorer displays all of the resources associated with a project, sorted by recency.

(see Figure 11.4). In the case of TaskTracer, the view contains all email messages associated with each project. This makes it easy for the user to find relevant email messages.

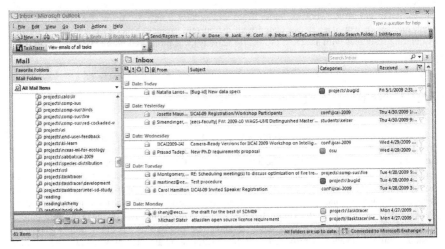

Fig. 11.4 TaskTracer tags each email message with the project to which it is associated. This tag is assigned as a "category" for the email message. At left are search folders for each of the TaskTracer projects.

A third method of assisting the user is the Folder Predictor. TaskTracer keeps track of which folders are associated with each project. Based on the current project, it can predict which folders the user is likely to want to visit when performing an Open or Save. Before each Open/Save, Task-Tracer computes a set of three folders that it believes will jointly minimize the expected number of mouse clicks to get to the target folder. It then initializes the File Open/Save dialogue box in the most likely of these three folders and places shortcuts to all three folders in the so-called "Places

Bar" on the left (see Figure 11.5). Shortcuts to these three folders are also provided as toolbar buttons in Windows Explorer so that the user can jump directly to these folders by clicking on the buttons (see Figure 11.6). Our user studies have shown that these folder predictions reduce the average number of clicks by around 50% for most users as compared to the Windows default File Open/Save dialogue box.

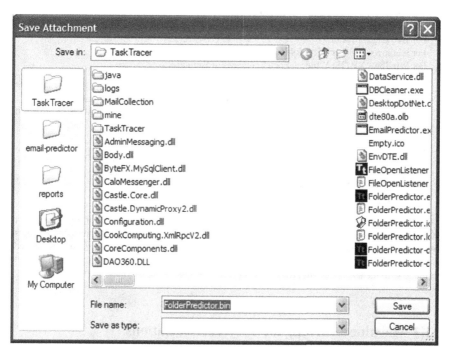

Fig. 11.5 The Folder Predictor places three shortcuts in the "Places Bar" on the left of the File Open/Save dialogue box. In this case, these are "Task Tracer", "email-predictor", and "reports".

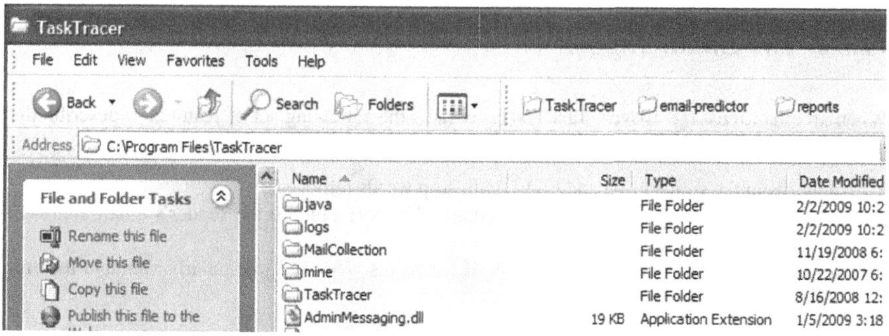

Fig. 11.6 The Folder Predictor adds a toolbar to the windows file browser (Windows Explorer) with the folder predictions; see top right.

11.2.3 Instrumentation

TaskTracer employs Microsoft's addin architecture to instrument Microsoft Word, Excel, Power-point, Outlook, Internet Explorer, Windows Explorer, Visual Studio, and certain OS events. This instrumentation captures a wide variety of application events including the following:

- For documents: New, Open, Save, Close,
- For email messages: Open, Read, Close, Send, Open Attachment, New Email Message Arrived,
- For web pages: Open,
- For windows explorer: New folder, and
- For Windows XP OS: Window Focus, Suspend/Resume/Idle.

TaskTracer also instruments its own components to create an event whenever the user declares a change in the current project or changes the project tag(s) associated with a resource.

TaskTracer also instruments a set of provenance events that capture the flow of information *between* resources. These include the following:

- For documents: SaveAs,
- For email messages: Reply, Forward, Attach File, Save Attachment, Click on Web Hyperlink,
- For web pages: Navigate (click on hyperlink), Upload file, Download file,
- For windows explorer: Rename file, Copy file, Rename folder, and
- For Windows XP OS: Copy/Paste, Cut/Paste.

All of these events are packaged up as TaskTracer events and transmitted on the TaskTracer publish/subscribe event bus. A component called the Association Engine subscribes to these events and creates associations between resources and projects. Specifically, when a resource is opened and has window focus for at least 10 seconds, then the Association Engine automatically tags that resource with the user's current project.

11.3 Machine Learning for Project Associations

There are three machine learning components in TaskTracer: (a) the email tagger, (b) the project switch detector, and (c) the folder predictor. We now describe the algorithms that are employed in each of these.

11.3.1 The Email Tagger

When an email message arrives, TaskTracer extracts the following set of features to describe the message:

- All words in the subject line and body (with stop words removed),
- One boolean feature for each recipient email address (including the sender's email address), and
- One boolean feature for each unique *set* of recipients. This is a particularly valuable feature, because it captures the "project team".

These features are then processed by an online supervised learning algorithm to predict which project is the most appropriate to assign to this email message. Our team recently completed a comparison study of several online multiclass learning algorithms to determine which one worked best on our email data set. The data set consists of 21,000 messages received by Tom Dietterich, dating from 2004 to 2008. There are 380 classes (projects), ranging in size from a single message to 2500 messages. Spam has already been removed.

Six different machine learning algorithms were examined: Bernoulli Naive Bayes [6], Multinomial Naive Bayes [11], Transformed Weight-Normalized Complement Naive Bayes [13], Term Frequency-Inverse Document Frequency Counts [14], Online Passive Aggressive [5], and Confidence Weighted [5].

Bernoulli Naive Bayes (BNB) is the standard Naive Bayes classification algorithm which is frequently employed for simple text classification [6]. BNB estimates for each project j and each feature x, $P(x|j)$ and $P(j)$, where x is 1 if the feature (i.e., word, email address, etc.) appears in the message and 0 otherwise. A message is predicted to belong to the project j that maximizes $P(j)\prod_x P(x|j)$, where the product is taken over all possible features. (This can be implemented in time proportional to the length of the email message.)

Multinomial Naive Bayes (MNB) [11] is a variation on Bernoulli Naive Bayes in which x is a multinomial random variable that indexes the possible features, so $P(x|j)$ is a multinomial distribution. We can conceive of this as a die with one "face" for each feature. An email message is generated by first choosing the project according to $P(j)$ and then rolling the die for project j once to generate each feature in the message. A message is predicted to belong to the project j that maximizes $P(j)\prod_x P(x|j)$, but now the product x is over all appearances of a feature in the email message. Hence, multiple occurrences of the same word are captured.

Rennie et al. [13] introduced the Transformed Weight-Normalized Complement Naive Bayes (TWCNB) algorithm. This improves MNB through several small adaptations. It transforms the feature count to pull down higher counts while maintaining an identity transform on 0 and 1 counts. It uses inverse document frequency to give less weight to words common among several different projects. It normalizes word counts so that long documents do not receive too much additional weight for repeated occurrences. Instead of looking for a good match of the target email to a project, TWCNB looks for a poor match to the project's complement. It also normalizes the weights.

Term Frequency-Inverse Document Frequency (TFIDF) is a set of simple counts that reflect how closely a target email message matches a project by dividing the frequency of a feature within a project by the log of the number of times the feature appears in messages belonging to all other projects. A document is predicted to belong to the project that gives the highest sum of TFIDF counts [14].

Crammer et al. [5] introduced the Online Passive Aggressive Classifier (PA), the multiclass version of which uses TFIDF counts along with a shared set of learned weights. When an email message is correctly predicted by a large enough confidence, the weights are not changed ("passive"). When a message is incorrectly predicted, the weights are aggressively updated so that the correct project would have been predicted with a high level of confidence.

Confidence Weighted Linear Classification (CW) is an online algorithm introduced by Dredze et al. [5]. It maintains a probability distribution over the learned weights of the classifier. Similar in spirit to PA, when a prediction mistake is made, CW updates this probability distribution so that with probability greater than 0.9, the mistake would not have been made. The effect of this is to more aggressively update weights in which the classifier has less confidence and less aggressively for weights in which it has more confidence.

It should be emphasized that all of these algorithms only require time linear in the size of the input and in the number of projects. Hence, these algorithms should be considered for other cyber situation awareness settings that require high speed for learning and for making predictions.

Figure 11.7 shows a precision-coverage plot comparing the online performance of these algorithms. Online performance is measured by processing each email message in the order that the messages were received. First, the current classifier is applied to predict the project of the message. If the classifier predicts the wrong project, then this is counted as an error. Second, the classifier is told the correct project, and it can then learn from that information. Each curve in the graph corresponds to varying a confidence threshold θ. All of these classifiers produce a predicted score (usually a probability) for each possible project. The confidence score is the difference between the score of the top prediction and the score of the second-best prediction. If this confidence is greater than θ, then the classifier makes a prediction. Otherwise, the classifier "abstains". By varying θ,

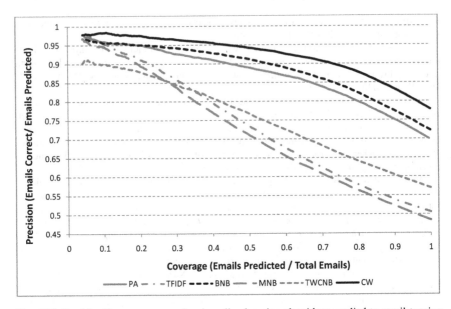

Fig. 11.7 Precision/Coverage curves for six online learning algorithms applied to email tagging by project.

we obtain a tradeoff between coverage (shown on the horizontal axis)—which is the percentage of email messages for which the classifier made a prediction—and precision (on the vertical axis)—which is the probability that the prediction is correct. For email, a typical user would probably want to adjust θ so that coverage is 100% and then manually correct all of the mislabeled email.

We can see that the best learning algorithm overall is the Confidence Weighted (CW) classifier. It achieves about 78% precision at 100% coverage, so the user would need to correct 22% of the email tags. In contrast, without the email tagger, the user would need to assign tags (or sort email into folders) 100% of the time, so this represents a 78% reduction in the amount of time spent tagging or sorting email messages.

One surprise is that the venerable Bernoulli Naive Bayes algorithm performed the second-best, and many classifiers that were claimed to be improvements over BNB performed substantially worse. This probably reflects the fact that email messages are quite different from ordinary textual documents.

11.3.2 Project Switch Detector

As we discussed above, TaskTracer monitors various desktop events (Open, Close, Save, SaveAs, Change Window Focus, and so on). In addition, once every minute (or when the user declares a project switch), TaskTracer computes an information vector $\mathbf{X}_t$ describing the time interval t since the last information vector was computed. This information vector is then mapped into feature vectors by two functions: $\mathbf{F}_P:(\mathbf{X}_t, y_j) \to \mathbb{R}^k$ and $\mathbf{F}_S : (\mathbf{X}_t) \to \mathbb{R}^m$. The first function $\mathbf{F}_P$ computes *project-specific* features for a specified project y_j; the second function $\mathbf{F}_S$ computes *switch-specific* features. The project-specific features include

- Strength of association of the active resource with project y_j: if the user has explicitly declared that the active resource belongs to y_j (e.g., by drag-and-drop in TaskExplorer), the current project is likely to be y_j. If the active resource was implicitly associated with y_j for some duration (which happens when y_j is the declared project and then the resource is visited), this is a weaker indication that the current project is y_j.
- Percentage of open resources associated with project y_j: if most open resources are associated with y_j, it is likely that y_j is the current project.
- Importance of window title word x to project y_j. Given the bag of words Ω, we compute a variant of TF-IDF [8] for each word x and project y_j: $\mathrm{TF}(x,\Omega) \cdot \log \frac{|\overline{S}|}{\mathrm{DF}(x,\overline{S})}$. Here, $\overline{S}$ is the set of all feature vectors not labeled as y_j, $\mathrm{TF}(x,\Omega)$ is the number of times x appears in Ω and $\mathrm{DF}(x,\overline{S})$ is the number of feature vectors containing x that are not labeled y_j.

These project-specific features are intended to predict whether y_j is the current project.

The switch-specific features predict the likelihood of a switch regardless of which projects are involved. They include

- Number of resources closed in the last 60 seconds: if the user is switching projects, many open resources will often be closed.
- Percentage of open resources that have been accessed in the last 60 seconds: if the user is still actively accessing open resources, it is unlikely there is a project switch.
- The time since the user's last explicit project switch: immediately after an explicit switch, it is unlikely the user will switch again. But as time passes, the likelihood of an undeclared switch increases.

To detect a project switch, we adopt a sliding window approach: at time t, we use two information vectors ($\mathbf{X}_{t-1}$ and $\mathbf{X}_t$) to score every pair of projects for time intervals $t-1$ and t. Given a project pair $\langle y_{t-1}, y_t \rangle$, the scoring function g is defined as

$$g(\langle y_{t-1}, y_t \rangle) = \Lambda_1 \cdot \mathbf{F}_P(\mathbf{X}_{t-1}, y_{t-1}) + \Lambda_1 \cdot \mathbf{F}_P(\mathbf{X}_t, y_t)$$
$$+ \phi(y_{t-1} \neq y_t)(\Lambda_2 \cdot \mathbf{F}_S(\mathbf{X}_{t-1}) + \Lambda_3 \cdot \mathbf{F}_S(\mathbf{X}_t)),$$

where $\Lambda = \langle \Lambda_1, \Lambda_2, \Lambda_3 \rangle \in \mathbb{R}^n$ is a set of weights to be learned by the system, $\phi(p) = -1$ if p is true and 0 otherwise, and the dot ($\cdot$) means inner product. The first two terms of g measure the likelihood that y_{t-1} and y_t are the projects at time $t-1$ and t (respectively). The third term measures the likelihood that there is no project switch from time $t-1$ to t. Thus, the third component of g serves as a "switch penalty" when $y_{t-1} \neq y_t$.

The project switch detector searches for the pair $\langle \hat{y}_1, \hat{y}_2 \rangle$ that maximizes the score function g. If $\hat{y}_2$ is different from the current declared project and the score is larger than a confidence threshold, then a switch is predicted. At first glance, this search over all pairs of projects would appear to require time quadratic in the number of projects. However, the following algorithm computes the best score in linear time:

$$y_{t-1}^* := \underset{y}{\operatorname{argmax}} \Lambda_1 \cdot \mathbf{F}_P(\mathbf{X}_{t-1}, y)$$
$$A(y_{t-1}^*) := \Lambda_1 \cdot \mathbf{F}_P(\mathbf{X}_{t-1}, y_{t-1}^*)$$
$$y_t^* = \underset{y}{\operatorname{argmax}} \Lambda_1 \cdot \mathbf{F}_P(\mathbf{X}_t, y)$$
$$A(y_t^*) = \Lambda_1 \cdot \mathbf{F}_P(\mathbf{X}_t, y_t^*)$$
$$S = \Lambda_2 \cdot \mathbf{F}_S(\mathbf{X}_{t-1}) + \Lambda_3 \cdot \mathbf{F}_S(\mathbf{X}_t)$$
$$y^* = \underset{y}{\operatorname{argmax}} \Lambda_1 \cdot \mathbf{F}_P(\mathbf{X}_{t-1}, y) + \Lambda_1 \cdot \mathbf{F}_P(\mathbf{X}_t, y)$$
$$AA(y^*) = \Lambda_1 \cdot \mathbf{F}_P(\mathbf{X}_{t-1}, y^*) + \Lambda_1 \cdot \mathbf{F}_P(\mathbf{X}_t, y^*)$$

Each pair of lines can be computed in time linear in the number of projects. We assume $y_{t-1}^* \neq y_t^*$. To compute the best score $g(\langle \hat{y}_1, \hat{y}_2 \rangle)$, we compare two cases: $g(y^*, y^*) = AA(y^*)$ is the best score for the case where there is no change in the project from $t-1$ to t, and $g(y_{t-1}^*, y_t^*) = A(y_{t-1}^*) + A(y_t^*) + S$ if there is a switch. When $y_{t-1}^* = y_t^*$, we can compute the best score for the "no switch" case by tracking the top two scored projects at time $t-1$ and t.

A desirable aspect of this formulation is that the classifier is still linear in the weights Λ. Hence, we can apply any learning algorithm for linear classification to this problem. We chose to apply a modified version of the Passive-Aggressive (PA) algorithm discussed above. The standard Passive-Aggressive algorithm works as follows: Let the real projects be y_1 at time $t-1$ and y_2 at time t, and $\langle \hat{y}_1, \hat{y}_2 \rangle$ be the highest scoring incorrect project pair. When the system makes an error, PA updates Λ by solving the following constrained optimization problem:

$$\Lambda_{t+1} = \operatorname*{argmin}_{\Lambda \in \mathbb{R}^n} \frac{1}{2} \|\Lambda - \Lambda_t\|_2^2 + C\xi^2$$
$$\text{subject to } g(\langle y_1, y_2 \rangle) - g(\langle \hat{y}_1, \hat{y}_2 \rangle) \geq 1 - \xi.$$

The first term of the objective function, $\frac{1}{2} \|\Lambda - \Lambda_t\|_2^2$, says that Λ should change as little as possible (in Euclidean distance) from its current value Λ_t. The constraint, $g(\langle y_1, y_2 \rangle) - g(\langle \hat{y}_1, \hat{y}_2 \rangle) \geq 1 - \xi$, says that the score of the correct project pair should be larger than the score of the incorrect project pair by at least $1 - \xi$. Ideally, $\xi = 0$, so that this enforces the condition that the margin (between correct and incorrect scores) should be 1.

The purpose of ξ is to introduce some robustness to noise. We know that inevitably, the user will occasionally make a mistake in providing feedback. This could happen because of a slip in the UI or because the user is actually inconsistent about how resources are associated with projects. In any case, the second term in the objective function, $C\xi^2$, serves to encourage ξ to be small. The constant parameter C controls the tradeoff between taking small steps (the first term) and fitting the data (driving ξ to zero). Crammer et al. [2] show that this optimization problem has a closed-form solution, so it can be computed in time linear in the number of features and the number of classes.

The Passive-Aggressive algorithm is very attractive. However, one risk is that Λ can still become large if the algorithm runs for a long time, and this could lead to overfitting. Hence, we modified the algorithm to include an additional regularization penalty on the size of Λ. The modified weight-update optimization problem is the following:

$$\Lambda_{t+1} = \operatorname*{argmin}_{\Lambda \in \mathbb{R}^n} \frac{1}{2} \|\Lambda - \Lambda_t\|_2^2 + C\xi^2 + \frac{\alpha}{2} \|\Lambda\|_2^2$$
$$\text{subject to } g(\langle y_1, y_2 \rangle) - g(\langle \hat{y}_1, \hat{y}_2 \rangle) \geq 1 - \xi.$$

The third term in the objective function, $\frac{\alpha}{2} \|\Lambda\|_2^2$, encourages Λ to remain small. The amount of the penalty is controlled by another constant parameter, α.

As with Passive-Aggressive, this optimization problem has a closed-form solution. Define $\mathbf{Z}_t = \langle \mathbf{Z}_t^1, \mathbf{Z}_t^2, \mathbf{Z}_t^3 \rangle$ where

$$\mathbf{Z}_t^1 = \mathbf{F}_P(\mathbf{X}_{t-1}, y_1) + \mathbf{F}_P(\mathbf{X}_t, y_2) - \mathbf{F}_P(\mathbf{X}_{t-1}, \hat{y}_1) - \mathbf{F}_P(\mathbf{X}_t, \hat{y}_2)$$
$$\mathbf{Z}_t^2 = (\phi(y_1 \neq y_2) - \phi(\hat{y}_1 \neq \hat{y}_2)) \mathbf{F}_S(\mathbf{X}_{t-1})$$
$$\mathbf{Z}_t^3 = (\phi(y_1 \neq y_2) - \phi(\hat{y}_1 \neq \hat{y}_2)) \mathbf{F}_S(\mathbf{X}_t).$$

Then the updated weight vector can be computed as

$$\Lambda_{t+1} := \frac{1}{1+\alpha} (\Lambda_t + \tau_t \mathbf{Z}_t),$$

where

$$\tau_t = \frac{1 - \Lambda_t \cdot \mathbf{Z}_t + \alpha}{\|\mathbf{Z}_t\|_2^2 + \frac{1+\alpha}{2C}}.$$

The time to compute this update is linear in the number of features. Furthermore, the cost does not increase with the number of classes, because the update involves comparing only the predicted and correct classes.

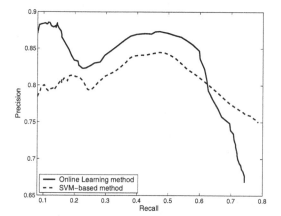

Fig. 11.8 User 1: Precision of different learning methods as a function of the recall, created by varying the confidence threshold.

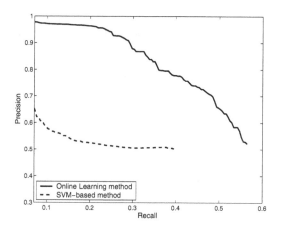

Fig. 11.9 User 2: Precision of different learning methods as a function of the recall, created by varying the confidence threshold.

To evaluate the Project Switch Detector, we deployed TaskTracer on Windows machines in our research group and collected data from two regular users, both of whom were fairly careful about declaring switches. In addition, an earlier version of the Switch Detector that employed a simpler set of features and a support vector machine (SVM) classifier was running throughout this time, and the users tried to provide feedback to the system throughout.

The first user (User 1) is a "power user", and this dataset records 4 months of daily work, which involved 299 distinct projects, 65,049 instances (i.e., information vectors), and 3,657 project switches. The second user (User 2) ran the system for 6 days, which involved 5 projects, 3,641 instances, and 359 projects switches.

To evaluate the online learning algorithm, we make the assumption that project switches observed in the users' data are all correct. We then perform the following simulation. Suppose the user forgets to declare every fourth switch. We feed the information vectors to the online algorithm and ask it to make predictions. A switch prediction is treated as correct if the predicted project is correct and if the predicted time of the switch is within 5 minutes of the real switch point. When a prediction is made, our simulation provides the correct time and project as feedback.

The algorithm parameters were set based on experiments with non-TaskTracer benchmark sets. We set $C = 10$ (which is a value widely-used in the literature) and $\alpha = 0.001$ (which gave good results on separate benchmark data sets).

Performance is measured by *precision* and *recall*. Precision is the number of switches correctly predicted divided by the total number of switch predictions, and recall is the number of switches correctly predicted divided by the total number of undeclared switches. We obtain different precision and recall values by varying the score confidence threshold required to make a prediction.

The results comparing our online learning approach with the SVM approach are plotted in Figures 11.8 and 11.9. The SVM method only uses the bag of words from the window titles and pathname/URL to predict project switches. As we described above, the online passive-aggressive approach incorporates much richer contextual information. This makes our new approach more accurate. For Figure 11.8, we see that for levels of recall below 60%, the passive-aggressive approach has higher precision. If we tune the confidence threshold to achieve 50% recall (so half of all project switches are missed), the precision is greater than 85%, so there are only 15% false predictions. Qualitatively, the user reports that these false predictions are typically very sensible. For example, suppose the user is working on a new project P_{new} and needs to access a document from a previous project P_{old}. When the document is opened, the project switch detector will predict that the user is switching to P_{old}, but in fact, the user wants the document to now become associated with P_{new}. It is hard to see how the project switch detector can avoid this kind of error. For the second user, the online passive-aggressive approach is hugely superior to the SVM method.

It should be noted that the new method is also much more efficient than the SVM method. On an ordinary PC, the passive-aggressive algorithm only took 4 minutes to compute predictions for User 1's 65,049 instances while the SVM approach needed more than 12 hours!

11.3.3 The Folder Predictor

The Folder Predictor is much simpler than either of the other two learning methods. Folder Predictor maintains a count $N(j, f)$ for each project j and folder f. $N(j, f)$ is the discounted number of opens or saves of files stored in folder f while the current project is j. Each time the user opens or saves a file in folder f when the current project is j, this count is updated as

$$N(j, f) := \rho N(j, f) + 1,$$

where ρ is a discount factor, which we typically set at 0.85. At the same time, for all other folders, $f' \neq f$, the counts are updated as

$$N(j, f') := \rho N(j, f').$$

Given these statistics, when the user initiates a new Open or Save, Folder Predictor estimates the probability that the user will want to use folder f as

$$P(f|j) = \frac{N(j, f)}{\sum_f N(j, f)},$$

where j is the user's current project.

As we described in Section 11.2, the Folder Predictor modifies the "Places Bar" of the File Open/Save dialogue box to include shortcuts to three folders, which we will refer to as f_1 (the top-most), f_2, and f_3. In addition, where Windows permits, TaskTracer initializes the dialogue box to start in f_1. Given the probability distribution $P(f|j)$, the Folder Predictor chooses these three folders in order to minimize the expected number of clicks that the user will need to perform in order to reach the user's desired folder. Specifically, Folder Predictor computes (f_1, f_2, f_3) as follows:

$$(f_1, f_2, f_3) = \underset{(f_1, f_2, f_3)}{\operatorname{argmin}} \sum_f P(f|j) \min\{clicks(f_1, f), 1 + clicks(f_2, f), 1 + clicks(f_3, f)\}. \quad (11.1)$$

In this formula, $clicks(i, j)$ is the number of clicks (or double clicks) it takes to navigate from folder i to folder j in the folder hierarchy. We performed a user study that found, among other things, that the most common way that users find and open files is by clicking up and down in the folder hierarchy using the File Open/Save dialogue box. Hence, the number of click operations (where a single click or a double click are both counted as one operation) is just the tree distance between folders i and j. The min in Equation 11.1 assumes that the user remembers enough about the layout of the folder hierarchy to know which of the three folders f_1, f_2, or f_3 would be the best starting point for navigating to the target folder. The second and third items inside this minimization include an extra click operation, because the user must click on the Places Bar shortcut before navigating through the hierarchy.

Users can have thousands of folders, so we do not want to consider every possible folder as a candidate for f_1, f_2, and f_3. Instead, we consider only folders for which $P(f|j) > 0$ and the ancestors of those folders in the hierarchy.

Table 11.1 Folder Predictor Data Sets

ID	User Type	Data Collection Time	Set Size
1	Professor	12 months	1748
2	Professor	4 months	506
3	Graduate Student	7 months	577
4	Graduate Student	6 months	397

To evaluate the Folder Predictor, we collected Open/Save data from four TaskTracer users. Table 11.1 summarizes the data. One beautiful aspect of folder prediction is that after making a prediction, TaskTracer will always observe the user's true target folder, so there is no need for the user to provide any special feedback to the Folder Predictor. We added a small amount of instrumentation to collect the folder that Windows would have used if Folder Predictor had not been running.

Figure 11.10 compares the average number of clicks for these four users using Folder Predictor with the average number of clicks that would have been required by the Windows defaults. Folder Predictor has reduced the number of clicks by 49.9%. The reduction is statistically significant ($p < 10^{-28}$). Figure 11.11 shows a histogram of the number of clicks required to reach the target folder under the windows default and with the folder predictor. Here we see that the Windows default starts in the target folder more than 50% of the time, whereas Folder Predictor only does this 42% of the time. But if the Windows default is wrong, then the target folder is rarely less than 2 clicks away, and often 7, 8, or even 12 clicks away. In contrast, the Folder Predictor is often one click away, and the histogram falls smoothly and rapidly. The reason Folder Predictor is often one click away is that if $P(f|j)$ is positive for two or more sibling folders, the folder that minimizes the expected number of clicks is often the parent of those folders. The parent is only 1 click away, whereas if we predict the wrong sibling, then the other sibling is 2 clicks away.

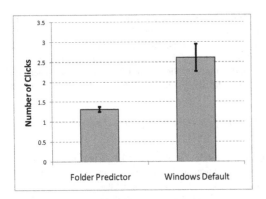

Fig. 11.10 Mean number of clicks to reach the target folder

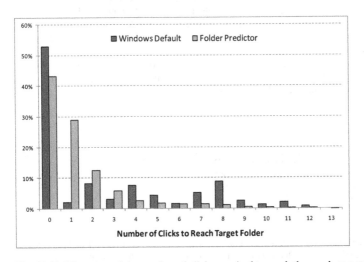

Fig. 11.11 Histogram of the number of clicks required to reach the user's target folder.

Figure 11.12 shows a learning curve for Folder Predictor. We see that as it observes more Opens and Saves, it becomes more accurate. After 30 Opens/Saves, the expected number of clicks is less than 1.

Qualitatively, Folder Predictor tends to predict folders that are widely spaced in the folder hierarchy. Users of TaskTracer report that it is their favorite feature of the system.

11.4 Discovering User Workflows

For many knowledge workers, a substantial fraction of their time at the computer desktop is occupied with routine workflows such as writing reports, performance reviews, filling out travel reimbursements, and so on. It is easy for knowledge workers to lose their situation awareness and forget

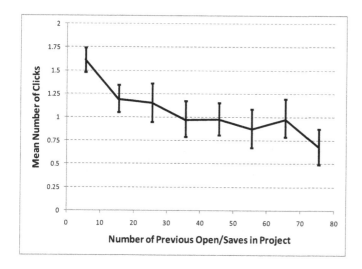

Fig. 11.12 Learning curve for the Folder Predictor showing the number of clicks as a function of the amount of training data (opens and saves) within the project.

to complete a workflow. This is true even when people maintain "to-do" lists (paper or electronic). Indeed, electronic to-do managers have generally failed to help users maintain situation awareness. One potential reason is that these tools introduce substantial additional work, because the user must not only execute the workflows but also maintain the to-do list [1].

An interesting challenge for high level situation awareness is to create a to-do manager that can maintain itself. Such a to-do manager would need to detect when a new to-do item should be created and when the to-do item is completed. More generally, an intelligent to-do manager should track the status of each to-do item (due date, percentage complete, etc.). Often, a to-do item requires making requests for other people to perform certain steps, so it would be important for a to-do manager to keep track of items that are blocked waiting for other people (and offer to send reminder emails as appropriate).

A prerequisite for creating such an intelligent to-do manager is developing a system that can discover and track the workflows of desktop knowledge workers. The central technical challenge is that because of multi-tasking, desktop workflows are interleaved with vast amounts of irrelevant activity. For example, a workflow for assembling a quarterly report might require two weeks from start to finish. During those two weeks, a busy manager might receive 1000 email messages, visit several hundred web pages, work on 50-100 documents, and make progress on dozens of other workflows. How can we discover workflows and then track them when they are embedded in unrelated multi-tasking activity?

Our solution to this conundrum is to assume that a workflow will be a connected subgraph within an *information flow graph* that captures flows of information among resources. For example, a travel authorization workflow might involve first exchanging email messages with a travel agent and then pasting the travel details into a Word form and emailing it to the travel office. Finally, the travel office replies with an authorization code. Figure 11.13 shows a schematic representation of this workflow as a directed graph. The advantage of this connected-subgraph approach is that it allows us to completely ignore all other desktop activity and focus only on those events that are connected to one another via information flows. Of course the risk of this approach is that in order for it to succeed, we must have *complete* coverage of all possible information flows. If an information flow link is missed, then the workflow is no longer a connected graph, and we will not be able to discover or track it.

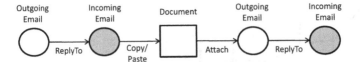

Fig. 11.13 Information flow graph for the travel authorization workflow. Circular nodes denote email messages, and squares denote documents. Shaded nodes denote incoming email messages. Each node is labeled with the type of resource, and each edge is labeled with an information flow action. Multiple edges can connect the same two nodes (e.g., SaveAs and Copy/Paste).

Our current instrumentation in TaskTracer captures many, but not all, important information flows. Cases that we do not capture include pasting into web forms, printing a document as a pdf file, exchanging files via USB drives, and utilities that zip and unzip collections of files. We are also not able to track information flows that occur through "cloud" computing tools such as Gmail, GoogleDocs, SharePoint, and wiki tools. Finally, sometimes the user copies information visually (by looking at one window and typing in another), and we do not detect this information flow. Nonetheless, our provenance instrumentation does capture enough information flows to allow us to test the feasibility of the information-graph approach.

The remainder of this section describes our initial efforts in this direction. These consist of three main steps: (a) building the information flow graph, (b) mining the information flow graph to discover workflows, and (c) applying an existing system, WARP, to track these workflows.

11.4.1 Building the Information Flow Graph

The basic information flow graph is constructed from the provenance events captured by Task-Tracer. In addition, for this work, we manually added two other information flow events that are not currently captured by our instrumentation: (a) converting from Word files to PDF files and (b) referring to a document from an email message (e.g., by mentioning the document title or matching keywords).

As we will see below, our graph mining algorithm cannot discover loops. Nonetheless, we can handle certain kinds of simple loops by pre-processing the graph. Specifically, if the graph contains a sequence of SaveAs links (e.g., because the user created a sequence of versions of a document), this sequence is collapsed to a single **SaveAs*** relationship. Similarly, if the graph contains a sequence of email messages to and from a single email address, this is collapsed to a single **ReplyTo*** relationship.

11.4.2 Mining the Information Flow Graph

The goal of our graph mining algorithm is to find all frequent subgraphs of the information flow graph. These correspond to recurring workflows. Two subgraphs match if the types of the resources match and if they have the same set of edges with the same event labels. A subgraph is frequent if it occurs more than s times; s is called the minimum support threshold.

To find frequent subgraphs, we apply a two-step process. The first step is to find frequent subgraphs while ignoring the labels on the edges. We apply the GASTON algorithm of Nijssen and Kok [12] to find maximal subgraphs that appear at least s times in the information flow graph. The second step is then to add edge labels to these frequent subgraphs to find all frequent labeled subgraphs. We developed a dynamic programming algorithm that can efficiently find these most frequent labeled subgraphs [15].

11.4.3 Recognizing Workflows

The labeled subgraphs can be converted to a formalism called the Logical Hidden Markov Model or LHMM [10]. An LHMM is like a standard HMM except that the states are logical atoms such as ATTACH(MSG1, FILE1), which denotes the action of attaching a file (FILE1) to an email message (MSG1). This formalism allows us to represent the parameters of a workflow, such as the sender and recipients of an email message, the name of a file, and so on.

Each frequent labeled subgraph is converted to a LHMM as follows. First, each edge in the subgraph becomes a state in the LHMM. This state generates the corresponding observation (the TaskTracer event) with probability 1. An initial "Begin" state and a final "End" state are appended to the start and end of the LHMM. Second, state transitions are added to the LHMM for each observed transition in the matching subgraphs from the information flow graph. If an edge was one of the "loop" edges (ReplyTo* or SaveAs*), then a self-loop transition is added to the LHMM. Transition probabilities are estimated based on the observed number of transitions in the information flow graph. The "Begin" state is given a self-loop with probability α. Finally, each state transition in the LHMM is replaced by a transition to a unique "Background" state. The Background state generates *any* observable event. It also has a self-loop with probability β. This state is intended to represent all of the user actions that are not part of the workflow.

Hung Bui (personal communication) has developed a system called WARP that implements a recognizer for logical hidden Markov networks. It does this by performing a "lifted" version of the usual probabilistic reasoning algorithms designed for standard HMMs. WARP handles multiple interleaved workflows by using a Rao-Blackwellized Particle Filter [4], which is an efficient approximate inference algorithm.

11.4.4 Experimental Evaluation

To evaluate our discovery method, we collected desktop data from four participants at SRI International as part of the DARPA-sponsored CALO project. The participants performed a variety of workflows involving preparing, submitting, and reviewing conference papers, preparing and submitting quarterly reports, and submitting travel reimbursements. These were interleaved with other routine activities (reading online newspapers, handling email correspondence). Events were captured via TaskTracer instrumentation and augmented with the two additional event types discussed above to create information flow graphs. Figure 11.14 shows one of the four flow graphs. There were 26 instances of known workflows in the four resulting information flow graphs.

Figure 11.15 shows an example of one discovered workflow. This workflow arose as part of two scenarios: (a) preparing a quarterly report and (b) preparing a conference paper. In both cases, an email message is received with an attached file. For the quarterly report, this file is a report template. For the conference paper, the file as a draft paper from a coauthor. The user saves the attachment and then edits the file through one or more SaveAs events. Finally, the user attaches the edited file to an email that is a reply to the original email message.

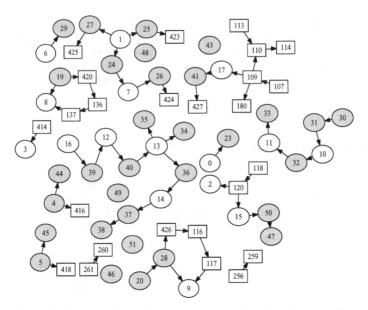

Fig. 11.14 Example of an information flow graph. Round nodes are email messages and rectangles are documents. Shaded nodes are incoming email messages. Each node is numbered with its resource id number.

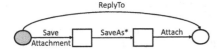

Fig. 11.15 Example of a discovered workflow.

Another workflow that we discovered was the counterpart to this in which the user starts with a document, attaches it to an outgoing email message, and sends it to another person (e.g., to have them edit the document and return it). There is a series of exchanged emails leading to an email reply with an attached file from which the user saves the attachment. Our current system is not able to fuse these two workflows into a multi-user workflow, although that is an important direction for future research.

Three other workflows or workflow sub-procedures were discovered from the four participants' information graphs.

To evaluate the method, we performed two experiments. First, we conducted a leave-one-user-out cross-validation by computing how well the workflows discovered using the three remaining users matched the information flow graph of the held-out user. For each information graph, we first manually identified all instances of known workflows. Then for each case where a discovered workflow matched a subgraph of the information graph, we scored the match by whether it overlapped a known workflow. We computed the precision, recall, and F1 score of the matched nodes and arcs for the true workflows. The precision is the fraction of the matched nodes and arcs in the information graph that are part of known workflows. The recall is the fraction of all nodes and arcs in known workflows that are matched by some discovered workflow subgraph. The F1 score is computed as

$$F1 = \frac{2(\text{precision} \times \text{recall})}{\text{precision} + \text{recall}}.$$

With a minimum support of 3, we achieved an F1 score of 91%, which is nearly perfect.

The second experiment was to test the ability of the WARP engine to recognize these workflows in real time. Each discovered workflow was converted to a Logical HMM. Then the events recorded from the four participants were replayed in time order and processed by WARP. For each event, WARP must decide whether it is the next event of an active workflow instance, the beginning of a new workflow instance, or a background event. After each event, we scored whether WARP had correctly interpreted the event. If it had not, we then corrected WARP and continued the processing. We computed WARP's precision and recall as follows. Precision is the ratio of the number of workflow states correctly recognized divided by the total number recognized. Recall is the ratio of the number of workflow states correctly recognized divided by the total number of true workflow states in the event sequence. WARP obtained a precision of 91.3%, a recall of 66.7%, and an F1 score of 77.1%. As these statistics show, WARP is failing to detect many states. Most of these were the initial states of workflows. An analysis of these cases shows that most initial states involve an email message. There are many email messages, but only a small fraction of them initiate new workflows. We believe that distinguishing these "workflow initiation" emails requires analyzing the body of the email to detect information such as a request for comments, a call for papers, a response to a previous request, and so on. Neither TaskTracer nor WARP currently has any ability to do this kind of analysis.

11.5 Discussion

This chapter has presented the TaskTracer system and its machine learning components as well as a workflow discovery system and its workflow tracking capabilities. These operate at two different levels of abstraction. TaskTracer is tracking high level projects. These projects are unstructured tags associated with a set of resources (files, folders, email messages, web pages, and email addresses). TaskTracer does a very good job of tracking these high level projects, and it is able to use this project information to organize the user's information and support interruption recovery and information re-finding.

The workflow discovery work is looking for more detailed patterns of information flow. The most important idea in this work is to capture a large set of information flow actions, represent those as an information flow graph, and then formulate the workflow discovery problem as one of finding frequently-occurring subgraphs within the information flow graph. The workflow discovery algorithm was able to find the key subgraphs corresponding to known workflows. However, it often did not discover the complete workflows but only the "kernels". For example, a complete workflow for quarterly reporting involved a combination of two workflow fragments discovered by our system: one fragment for receiving the report template and filling it out and another fragment for sending the report template to multiple team members, collecting their responses, and then editing them into the original report template. Hence, the workflows discovered by the system do not necessarily correspond directly to the user's notion of a workflow. Nonetheless, these discovered workflows could be very useful for providing a kind of "auto-completion" capability, where the system could offer to perform certain steps in a workflow (e.g., saving a file attachment or initiating an email reply with the relevant file attached).

Another shortcoming of our workflow discovery approach is that it cannot discover workflows involving conditional (or unconditional) branching. Unconditional branching occurs when there are multiple ways of achieving the same goals. For example, when submitting a letter of reference, a web page may support either pasting text into a text box or uploading a text file to a web site. Conditional branching could occur when a workflow involves different steps under certain conditions. For example, a travel requisition may require different steps for international travel versus domestic travel. Extending our workflow discovery methods to handle such cases is an important area for future research.

The focus of this chapter has been on high level situation awareness to support the knowledge worker. But it is also interesting to consider ways in which high level situation awareness could help with cyber defense. One possibility is that this high level situation awareness could provide greater contextual understanding of lower-level actions. For example, if a user is visiting a novel web page or sending email to a novel recipient, this could be the start of an insider attack or it could be a new instance of a known workflow. In the latter case, it is unlikely to be an attack.

A second possibility is that this higher level situation awareness could help distinguish those actions (e.g., sending email messages, accessing web pages) that were intentionally initiated by the user from actions initiated by malware. The user-initiated actions should involve known workflows and known projects, whereas the malware actions would be more likely to involve files and web sites unrelated to the user's current project.

11.6 Concluding Remarks

The difficulty of maintaining cyber situation awareness varies depending on the level of abstraction that is required. This chapter has described two of the highest levels: projects and workflows. An important challenge for future research is to integrate situation awareness at all levels to provide systems that are able to exploit a broad range of instrumentation and context to achieve high accuracy, rapid response, and very low false alarm rates. Research is still quite far from this goal, but the work reported in this chapter suggests that this goal is ultimately achievable.

Acknowledgements

This material is based upon work supported by the Defense Advanced Research Projects Agency (DARPA) under Contract No. FA8750-07-D-0185/0004. Any opinions, findings and conclusions or recommendations expressed in this material are those of the authors and do not necessarily reflect the views of the DARPA or the Air Force Research Laboratory (AFRL).

References

1. Bellotti, V., Dalal, B., Good, N., Bobrow, D.G., Ducheneaut, N.: What a to-do: studies of task management towards the design of a personal task list manager. In: ACM Conference on Human Factors in Computing Systems (CHI2004), pp. 735–742. ACM, NY (2004)
2. Crammer, K., Dekel, O., Keshet, J., Shalev-Shwartz, S., Singer, Y.: Online passive-aggressive algorithms. Journal of Machine Learning Research 7, 551–585 (2006)
3. Dietterich, T.G., Slater, M., Bao, X., Cao, J., Lonsdale, H., Spence, C., Hadley, G., Wynn, E.: Quantifying and supporting multitasking for intel knowledge workers. Tech. rep., Oregon State University, School of EECS (2009)
4. Doucet, A., de Freitas, N., Murphy, K.P., Russell, S.J.: Rao-Blackwellised particle filtering for dynamic Bayesian networks. In: UAI'00: Proceedings of the 16th Conference in Uncertainty in Artificial Intelligence, pp. 176–183. Morgan Kaufmann (2000)

5. Dredze, M., Crammer, K., Pereira, F.: Confidence-weighted linear classification. In: A. Mc-Callum, S. Roweis (eds.) Proceedings of the 25th Annual International Conference on Machine Learning (ICML 2008), pp. 264–271. Omnipress (2008)

6. Duda, R.O., Hart, P.E., Stork, D.G.: Pattern Classification, Second Edition. John Wiley and Sons, Inc. (2000)

7. Gonzalez, V.M., Mark, G.: "constant, constant, multi-tasking craziness": Managing multiple working spheres. In: Proceedings of the SIGCHI conference on Human factors in computing systems, pp. 113–120. ACM Press (2004)

8. Joachims, T.: Transductive inference for text classification using support vector machines. In: Proceedings of the 16th International Conference on Machine Learning (ICML), pp. 200–209. Morgan Kaufmann, Bled, Slovenia (1999)

9. Kaptelinin, V.: UMEA: Translating interaction histories into project contexts. In: Proceedings of the SIGCHI conference on Human Factors in Computing Systems, pp. 353–360. ACM Press (2003)

10. Kersting, K., De Raedt, L., Raiko, T.: Logial hidden Markov models. Journal of Artificial Intelligence Research (JAIR) **25**, 425–456 (2006)

11. McCallum, A., Nigam, K.: A comparison of event models for naive Bayes text classification. In: AAAI-98 Workshop on Learning for Text Categorization (1998)

12. Nijssen, S., Kok, J.N.: A quickstart in frequent structure mining can make a difference. In: Proceedings of KDD-2004, pp. 647–652 (2004)

13. Rennie, J.D.M., Shih, L., Teevan, J., R., K.D.: Tackling the poor assumptions of naive Bayes text classifiers. In: Proceedings of the International Conference on Machine Learning (ICML2003), pp. 616–623 (2003)

14. Salton, G., Buckley, C.: Term-weighting approaches in automatic text retrieval. In: Information Processing and Management, pp. 513–523 (1988)

15. Shen, J., Fitzhenry, E., Dietterich, T.: Discovering frequent work procedures from resource connections. In: Proceedings of the International Conference on Intelligent User Interfaces (IUI-2009), pp. 277–286. ACM, New York, NY (2009)

Author Index

S. Jajodia et al., (eds.), *Cyber Situational Awareness*,
Advances in Information Security 46, DOI 10.1007/978-1-4419-0140-8,
© Springer Science+Business Media, LLC 2010